50 Top Tools for Employee Wellbeing

50 Top Tools for Employee Wellbeing

A complete toolkit for developing happy, healthy, productive and engaged employees

Debbie Mitchell

KoganPage

Publisher's note
Every possible effort has been made to ensure that the information contained in this book is accurate at the time of going to press, and the publishers and author cannot accept responsibility for any errors or omissions, however caused. No responsibility for loss or damage occasioned to any person acting, or refraining from action, as a result of the material in this publication can be accepted by the editor, the publishers or the author.

First published in Great Britain and the United States in 2018 by Kogan Page Limited

2nd Floor, 45 Gee Street	c/o Martin P Hill Consulting	4737/23 Ansari Road
London	122 W 27th Street	Daryaganj
EC1V 3RS	New York, NY 10001	New Delhi 110002
United Kingdom	USA	India

The right of Debbie Mitchell to be identified as the author of this work has been asserted by her in accordance with the Copyright, Designs and Patents Act 1988.

ISBN   978 0 7494 8218 3
E-ISBN   978 0 7494 8219 0

British Library Cataloguing-in-Publication Data

A CIP record for this book is available from the British Library.

Library of Congress Cataloging-in-Publication Control Number

2016046146

Typeset by Integra Software Services Pvt. Ltd., Pondicherry
Print production managed by Jellyfish
Printed and bound in Great Britain by CPI Group (UK) Ltd, Croydon CR0 4YY

For my husband, Paul, whose inclusion in my life
ensures my continued wellbeing

CONTENTS

FIGURES AND TABLES

Figures

Tables

PREFACE

I've worked as a human resources (HR) professional for many years. I've worked in a variety of industries and sectors as an in-house personnel manager, HR manager, HR business partner and, latterly, as a specialist in organizational development (OD), change management and engagement. Since 2011 I've been working as an independent consultant, facilitator, coach and occasional interim HR business partner (HRBP) or OD specialist. My experience has taken me across public sector, retail, the space business, small manufacturing, fast-moving consumer goods (FMCG), in the United Kingdom and internationally, working with small family businesses through to large multinationals, in tech start-ups and traditional businesses, in offices with trees and beanbags as well as those with traditional 1970s office or cubicle set-ups. I've worked with progressive and disruptive organizations, traditional ones, and those that don't really know what they want to be yet.

My work has led me to draw one common conclusion about how we approach people management – there is a tendency to over-complicate it when we really don't need to. In the context of wellbeing, there can also be a tendency to be afraid of it. People managers worry about causing offence, about stepping over the boundaries of reasonableness in what they can ask people about or about breaking employment law rules and regulations.

My take on this – and many other people management issues – is that it does not have to be so complicated. Much of people management is about demonstrating trust, empathy and caring, and managing people with positive intent, working from the assumption that they come to work to do their very best. So when it comes to wellbeing, my view is the same. There is a huge amount of medicine, psychology and science behind some aspects of it, and that is important. And it is important that those aspects are led and managed by the experts in the field. But that doesn't mean that people managers can ignore, or wash their hands of, issues that could or have presented themselves, in the hope that a specialist can sort it out. It is a fundamental responsibility to show a duty of care to those who work for you. People managers need to understand some of the potential issues, triggers and avoidance or management strategies. This book aims to help them do that, with a simple approach to a number of tools or initiatives that could proactively avoid or reactively manage wellbeing at work, both simply and effectively.

ACKNOWLEDGEMENTS

My thanks go to all those I have had the privilege of working with over the years, during my employed career and as a consultant, developing knowledge and experience of how to make workplaces inspiring, healthy and enjoyable.

To the amazing Vivienne Palmer, who has helped to pull this book together, rewarded only with copious cups of tea and many, many biscuits (and occasionally fruit – for her wellbeing).

To my husband Paul, for tolerating late nights and weekend working, poor housekeeping and a loss of humour as I wrote the book. Normal service will be resumed!

Thanks also to those who have offered their insights and practical experiences for inclusion in this book. I think their expertise add to the practicality and relevance of the tools they have contributed to, and I thank them very much for taking the time and effort to participate. I urge those of you interested in finding out more to look them up (see 'Further support', page 235), and see what they have to offer – they are very clever people, with lots to offer, and I'm sure they would love to hear from you.

It is not the intention to claim ownership of any of the individual ideas in this book. They are a collection of tools experienced, created, developed and adapted over my career, and I thank all those who have inspired, contributed and participated. I will be pleased to acknowledge the copyright or origination of any unacknowledged material if necessary.

ABOUT THIS BOOK

Who should use this book?

With around 14.7 per cent of people facing some form of mental health challenge in the workplace, and a suggestion that 12.7 per cent of absences in the United Kingdom are connected to mental health (according to the Mental Health Foundation, 2017), employers need to be more proactive.

Employees experiencing high levels of stress and low levels of physical activity are losing up to 27 days of productive working time each year (Vitality Britain's Healthiest Workplace, 2016), and that impacts the bottom line.

If these statistics surprise or worry you, or if you are not surprised, but feel a need to do something about it where you work, in your team or for yourself, then you need this book.

It is intended for people managers and human resources professionals alike. It is written to provide guidance and support to those who might need it, with useful information to help employees to maintain a sense of wellbeing, without it costing huge amounts of money, and without the need to involve or buy in significant expertise.

It doesn't matter what size or type of organization you work in – the tools are industry-agnostic, and whether you run a small business of five or six people, or work within a multinational corporation, you should find tools and tips in this book that are useful to you. The principle is that as the reader of this toolkit, and as a manager or supervisor in any function, you could implement some of these tools to help to prevent, recognize and address employee wellbeing issues or opportunities among your team, function or entire workforce.

The philosophy behind the book

Throughout my career, both in house and as an external consultant, I have facilitated workshops where I have been told that managers just don't have time or the required level of skill specialist knowledge to do these things.

This book of tools, like my previous book *50 Top Tools for Employee Engagement*, is intended to break down some of those barriers and to remove the excuses.

Whilst I recognize that managers cannot become experts in mental or physical wellbeing, there is information they can utilize and action they can take to promote wellbeing at work. Much of it starts with them. So whilst this book, and the tools that are described, are absolutely not intended to replace specialist and expert help as and when that is needed, it does provide some useful pointers to things that can positively promote or reactively address wellbeing from a layperson's perspective. At times, that specialist might be needed, and the tools where this is important point to sources of help or expertise, or highlight the need for it in given situations.

The tools in this book are not entirely focused on obvious wellbeing topics – whilst there is mention of stress, or balance, there are other tools that are perhaps more indirectly connected, but if promoted can demonstrate not only that you are paying attention to such issues when they arise, but that you are a caring employer who seeks to prevent rather than cure.

Managers may be concerned that they don't have the required level of skill or specialist knowledge required to manage wellbeing. The risk is that this unfamiliarity and a reluctance to address issues could lead to them becoming bigger. A tendency to ignore them, or consider them not the managers' business or responsibility, can mean a lack of attention to the issues that is sorely needed.

Managers raise concerns with me that they don't know how to address wellbeing issues. Understanding how they might promote wellbeing, and some of the small things that they can do to positively impact employee wellbeing, will no doubt send positive messages.

Managers raise concerns that they 'don't have the TIME' to get involved in employee wellbeing issues, and that they are concerned about delving into the personal emotions and domestic issues that may affect an employee's work. Most of the tools included here are not lengthy activities, and are certainly not time wasted. The investment of time to ensure that any employee can and will work at their very best for you has to be valuable – it will positive impact your bottom line in the end.

And finally, managers will struggle with the financials, securing or spending their budget on 'nice to do' activities that don't appear to bring immediate benefits. Budgets are constrained to some degree in most businesses, and unless there is a clear return on investment, the extra that managers think they need will not be forthcoming. Most of the tools included in this book are low cost or no cost. However even when there is a need to allocate budget, the investment has to be considered against the alternative – to have a healthy budget and an unhealthy workforce won't make sense. Ultimately you will pay because of time lost through absence, loss of productivity, reduced levels of customer service and poor employer reputation.

Like *50 Top Tools for Employee Engagement*, the concept of the book is to provide a simple guide or toolkit that enables managers in any size organization, and regardless of seniority or specialist knowledge, to connect to tools that can help them to promote, identify and address wellbeing issues without immediate recourse to specialists, significant budgets or endless days away.

Employee wellness is an individual thing – there are big differences in our individual tolerances for illness, stress, challenge, etc. We have lifestyle preferences that may impact our wellness – those who get regular exercise and those who don't, or those that practise mindfulness, and those that carry on regardless. And different people will have different things going on in their lives that impact their tolerance or aptitude for making changes, being healthy or being present. As a result, there can be no single-fix answer for how to improve employee wellbeing, other than to pay attention to it as an overall way of running your business, as a leadership principle, with a strategy and intent to support it. The tools in this book can help you to segment where you need to, pay attention to specific issues if they arise, and to implement a strategy within your business.

By bringing these various tools and activities together in one place, by making them accessible to all, and by providing some suggestions on methods for evaluation, I hope to enable and inspire people managers throughout a variety of organizations to take responsibility to actively promote the wellbeing of their employees – simply, cheaply but effectively.

How the tools are categorized

The book is organized in sections for engaging employees at each stage of the employment lifecycle, and also to support certain key activities on the business agenda. However, this is a guideline – and you should look to use the range of tools as you see fit for your business.

The tools part of this book is divided into five main parts. The categorization of the tools has been based on the research into defining what enables employee wellbeing, which will be described in more detail in the following chapters. The categories are as follows:

- **Leadership and advocacy:** In this section we consider what your leaders need to know, and how you might set out your strategy for wellbeing.

- **Career:** In the career section, we consider wellbeing tools that enable personal and professional growth and development, address the need for feedback and recognition (non-financial) and the value employees get from being involved in initiatives, programmes and decisions.

- **Physical and mental:** Here we consider physical wellness issues, how you manage absence and illness, and actions you can take to encourage employees to stay physically healthy. We take a look at some ideas and initiatives you can introduce and advocate to encourage mental wellbeing in individuals, both proactively and reactively. We also consider the physical working environment, and touch on the balance needed between work and home.

- **Social and community:** This section reflects the fact that many employees want to get more out of work than just work, and presents tools to enable great relationships, inclusion and social responsibility.

- **Financial:** Finally, we touch on financial wellbeing – very much a specialist subject, so here we take a brief look at some things that employers can do to encourage it.

The structure of each tool

Introduction

The introduction aims to give an overview of the tool, and make a broad connection to wellbeing. This is a broad overview aimed at a generalist, so that they are able to consider whether the tool has relevance and place in their organization.

Promoting wellbeing

This section aims to connect the tool to some research about employee wellbeing, demonstrating how it can support positive wellbeing initiatives and programmes. Here you'll read about trends and statistics and should be able to connect implementation of each tool with an increase or improvement in employee wellbeing.

Approach

This is not a step-by-step guide, but instead aims to provide some guidelines and key pointers about how to implement the tool simply and effectively. In some cases, there may be just a few key pointers. In others there may be a number of steps or a range of options to be considered. You'll need to consider which steps might be appropriate in your business, and whether you need to adjust them to make sure they are fit for purpose in your cultural environment.

Outcomes

This section gives an indication of the potential outcomes, connected to wellbeing, that you might expect as a result of utilizing the tool. Of course, they are not guaranteed but are indicative.

Measuring impact

In this section the book makes suggestions about how you might evaluate the effectiveness of the tool once implemented. The impact can take place at various levels:

- Individual: Assessing the impact that an individual or collective initiative has had on people within the team.
- Team: Assesses the impact of initiatives on a broader team.
- Organization: Assess impacts on the whole organization.

The evaluation of its effectiveness is also multi-layered. In some cases, it may only be feasible to consider a cursory or high-level evaluation – what did people say, are they happy or unhappy, did they like it or not like it, did they feel it had an impact? This qualitative evaluation relies on employees being forthcoming and honest. That said, in some cases it may be the most appropriate option, or the only one.

A more in-depth and quantitative analysis would give consideration to changes and trends in relevant and core business metrics. The flaw here is that metric shifts may not always be fully attributable to the tool itself, but they can be indicative, and provided the trends are aligned to the timing of the initiative some degree of correlation could be assumed. Typically, you might consider absence statistics (days lost, absence reasons), productivity, profitability, customer engagement or net promoter scores and employee survey responses. Promoting changes in such statistics should carry a disclaimer – claims about the impact of tools could be quickly challenged, impacting the credibility of your initiatives or programme. Be honest about what is or is not directly attributable or assumed.

Templates and examples

Some of the tools provide you with templates and samples, too, so please feel free to use these if they work in your organization, or adapt them so that they can work for you.

Introduction

What is employee wellbeing?

Wellbeing can be defined as being happy, comfortable, healthy, safe and secure. Its definition suggests a positivity of physical and mental health, mood and emotion. It encompasses a wide range of factors that are impacted by an individual's health, lifestyle, responsibilities and preferences, as well as person-centred factors such as age, gender, genes, personality, etc. Whilst some of these factors are in the individual's control (eg some aspects of lifestyle or preference) others are less preventable or manageable (eg some aspects of health). Additionally, whilst some of these factors, and their antecedents or effects, can be attributed to their personal life, they undoubtedly flow into their professional lives too.

The workplace can have a significant effect on wellbeing. It can be the main cause or a contributory factor in changes to an employee's wellbeing, or it can be the environment in which the consequences of negative wellbeing are played out regardless of cause. Organizations can certainly be proactive in their approach to wellbeing, providing health promotion information, choices that can meet their physical, mental or lifestyle needs, and an environment that responds in a supportive and responsible way when wellbeing is deteriorating.

Wellbeing factors

This book has structured tools around a number of key factors for employee wellbeing.

Leadership and advocacy of wellbeing at work

The approach that leaders take to wellbeing in organizations can be a wellbeing factor in itself. If leaders demonstrate an interest, commitment and active involvement in activities or interventions that promote wellbeing, employees will respond positively. This will have a positive impact on employee engagement, and on the employer value proposition. Well-promoted well-being strategies can also be a positive aspect for the employer brand, and can be seen externally as employers acting responsibly. Visible commitment can come in various forms, from a published strategy statement, to the implementation of a simple initiative or two, but what will be important is leadership sponsorship and advocacy. If an organization's leaders are actively supportive of wellbeing initiatives, willing to commit resources (however big or small) and are seen to be participating themselves, it will carry a great deal of weight with employees who may otherwise consider wellbeing to be a PR initiative. The tools in this book offer suggestions on developing and launching a strategy and a programme, and using champions and committees to keep wellbeing alive in the organization.

Career wellbeing

Employees want to be assured that there are options for them to develop their career, whether that is a promotional path, a depth of specialism, or developing or maintaining their knowledge and capability within their current role. For some, this also connects to issues of job security, and self-confidence in their performance in the workplace. Negative influences on these issues (lack of security, limited development) can create feelings of insecurity, anxiety or frustration. Whilst career development could cover a wide range of topics, in this book the focus is on career matters that might link to employee wellbeing directly. A section on career growth provides tools that enable people managers and team members to perform at their best, through a focus on strengths, learning opportunities and regular communication. A short section on recognition highlights the importance of non-financial recognition, particularly how feedback can have a positive impact on others, and the value of regular performance conversations. Finally, getting people involved in the business can support wellbeing. It offers the opportunity for people to understand and maybe shape the business direction, to commit to it, and to proactively support changes that happen.

Physical/mental wellbeing

Physical wellbeing

Whilst organizations and their people managers may not have a strong influence over their employees' health or their lifestyle choices, their physical health will have a strong influence on their wellbeing whilst at work. Physical health issues, from short-term sporadic sickness to more chronic

Illness and disability, become business issues when they affect the employee's ability to perform their job. People managers will need to take action, offering support, guidance, flexibility, etc, to enable the employee to continue to perform, whilst acting responsibly, and acknowledging the need to care for their health. Physical wellbeing also includes health promotion at work. Organizations can take some actions or decisions that might encourage (not enforce) different choices through availability of options, including food choices to support healthy diet, accessibility of a variety of activity options for all levels of ability and enthusiasm, travelling healthily on business, and relaxation techniques.

Mental wellbeing

Workplace mental health is a significant issue in business, but it is also a complex and sensitive one. Whilst many of the treatments for mental health, stress, anxiety, etc, are specialist interventions, there are some actions that people managers can take to proactively reduce the risk of them occurring, or to manage the situation effectively when they do. This may require medical or specialist intervention, and it is highly recommended that non-specialists or unqualified leaders do not try to diagnose, treat or address the medical issues, but do take notice, take care, empathize and support when employees are struggling with mental health issues in the workplace. The tools included in this section aim to give leaders and team members coping strategies and easily implementable techniques or approaches to ease mental strain. They also recognize that not all mental health challenges are work-related, but that the same empathy and support could still be beneficial.

A positive environment for wellbeing

The working environment can play a role in employee wellbeing. Factors such as layout, light, noise and colour can influence mood and temperament as well as efficiency and performance. Creating the right environment for people to perform at their best can be challenging when individuals have their own individual preferences for how and where they work best. There is just one tool here, but it is an important one, and it offers suggestions that are practical for those who don't have the option to fully redesign the office environment.

Balance

An employee's wellbeing can be heavily impacted by conflicting demands on their time and availability. According to the Carers UK website, 1 in 8 employees are also acting as unpaid carers, and for them, flexibility about how, when and where they work will be important to allow them to balance their priorities whilst still be able to commit to and deliver for an employer. This section of the book offers tactics for flexibility and remote working, which could offer benefits to employees with conflicting priorities, parental or other carer responsibilities or just simply be the preferred approach for some employees. Of course, it is recognized that the business need also has to be considered, and in some cases such flexibility may be impractical. However, this is not always the case, and the tools could offer the opportunity to reconsider 'traditional' working practice in favour of more agile options.

Social and community wellbeing

Given that people typically spend one-third of their lives at work, it is unsurprising that relationship problems with people at work, the seriousness of the workplace and the intensity of the work itself can have a negative impact on employee wellbeing. Employee engagement surveys often show that employees want to have a friend at work, and that they want their employers to be socially responsible. Providing the opportunity to build positive working relationships, have fun, give back to society and make the workplace a pleasant place to be are all likely to improve how employees feel about coming to work and spending time in the workplace. Tools are offered in this section that touch on inclusion, community and collective activities that help to provide an environment where employees can feel comfortable, relaxed and sociable, having fun, but remaining productive.

Financial wellbeing

Financial wellbeing is a challenging issue to address in a short and usable tool for people managers, but it can have a significant impact on the overall wellbeing of employees. Whilst the tools in this section don't attempt to offer any financial advice or education, nor encourage employers to do so, they offer some options and considerations for employees. Flexible benefits allows employees to have more choice about how their total reward package is made up, allowing them to match their pay and benefits to their priorities or lifestyle choices. Pre-retirement planning acknowledges the concerns that employees can face in the years and months leading to retirement, both financial and social, and offers some suggestions about how employers can help employees to prepare mentally, financially and socially for this significant life change.

Leading wellbeing

Whilst people managers are not expected to become experts or specialists in any of the fields that connect to wellbeing, they should be expected to lead responsibility and to take action to minimize detriment and optimize strengths and opportunities for their people, enabling them to perform at their best, and to work in ways that are both mentally and physically healthy. As such, leaders should at least have an awareness of the key wellbeing issues, and an understanding of how they could be impacted by the organizations processes, policies and key activities, as well as a leader's own style, their behaviours and their actions, and the individual's own skills, knowledge, attitude and awareness.

Role modelling is an important part of that advocacy, but authenticity is also important. Recognizing that some of the positive wellbeing actions connect to lifestyle choices (eg food and exercise), leaders may choose not to adopt or follow them, and that should be ok. However, there should be some active demonstration that they are supportive and are actually using some of the techniques or tools in the wellbeing strategy or programme. This might simply mean giving great feedback, or inviting direct reports to a walk-and-talk meeting, rather than a desk-based one. These visible actions will demonstrate a commitment to the wellbeing programme, and the leaders involved will also be able to advocate the benefits of adoption.

Talking about the impact of wellbeing will also be a key advocacy action. Ongoing evaluation of wellbeing initiatives is key to ensuring their success – knowing the feedback, impact on wellbeing and business outcomes of implemented programmes or actions will allow them to be changed, expanded or developed to ensure continued success.

Making it happen

At the top

If you are a senior leader in your organization, you need to set the standard, and act as a role model for wellbeing in the workplace. Working with your senior peers, you have the influence to set the tone for how the organization works, and to determine the prioritization for wellbeing in your business goals or your objectives. Collectively as a senior team, you can assess the costs and benefits of wellbeing strategies and programmes, and be clear about the connection to your employer brand, your core values and your service offering.

A focus on emotional wellbeing will need a collective responsibility at the top to make it happen and to make it stick. But someone has to start the conversation, and prompt the education, involvement and advocacy of the leadership, so that not only can your organization be considered a strong performer in its field, but also a responsible employer of choice. Determine who that person is to get started – and bear in mind, it could be you.

With peers

Whether you are senior manager, a team leader or a team member, as an advocate for wellbeing you can influence your peers. You can provide information and opportunity to encourage peers to take responsibility for their own wellbeing, and to advocate any organizational programmes or initiatives delivered in-company. You can operate as a role model, demonstrating the accessibility and the value of wellbeing ideas, from as simple as a short walk at lunchtime, or taking some time to work alone in a quiet space, to health and fitness regimes that take more effort, stamina and determination. Inviting others to join you, to copy or to challenge you may evoke some new habits in your peers. And since you have this book, share, and encourage others to try some things out.

Bottom up

You don't have to be in charge to set the tone and the standards in your own part of the business. By adopting some of the more simple and accessible tools in this book, you can just start working or behaving a little differently. Why not try taking the pile of papers you have to read down to a coffee lounge or coffee shop for an hour to get a change of scene, take a walk at lunchtime, bring apples instead of cakes. You can start small fires – try out some of the more simple or individual tools and techniques, and see if they work for you, then talk about and advocate them if they do, and watch them spread in usage across the broader organization.

Using these tools

Knowing what you have to do is only part of the story. Knowing how to do it is often harder. Developing the skills and knowledge for ensuring employee wellbeing can be difficult.

Within this set of tools, I have tried to provide many that require little specialist skill, and can be implemented using the guidance within the tool. In some cases there may be a few specialist skills, or some specialist knowledge that some organizations may already have in place (eg Health and Safety, Occupational Health), and in other cases, there is a suggestion that external resources be brought in to the organization to provide specialist support or training (for example, masseurs, or trainers on resilience or mindfulness). Some of those specialists have also been able to contribute their own stories or experiences, and have provided their contact details for inclusion in the back of this book.

It is also useful for you to consider some of the following questions before you get too far in developing your approach to employee wellbeing.

Organizationally

- What is the organization's approach or attitude towards employee wellbeing? Do you have senior managers who are advocates or sponsors, and are they willing to invest in it?

- What is currently being done to support wellbeing at work?

- Is there anything else going on in the organization that might highlight some of the issues or bring them to the fore (ie downsizing, major projects, office relocations etc.)?

- Are there any experts or specialists in your organization who might be useful to you – ie facilitators, health or fitness advocates, etc?

- Does the organization measure employee engagement? Does that make any reference to what leaders or employees want, need or expect in relation to wellbeing?

- If you have union or employee representatives, are they on board?

Wellbeing

- Do you know what wellbeing really means, and its potential business benefits?

- Do you have sponsorship in the organization to pilot or test out a wellbeing approach?

- Is there an appetite among staff and managers to improve the wellbeing of workers?

Your own capabilities

- Could you be considered as a credible advocate of wellbeing?
- Are you clear on the costs and benefits associated with implementing wellbeing initiatives?
- Have you benchmarked, or networked with other companies who are strong wellbeing champions, to find out what works and what doesn't?
- Are you able to influence the key stakeholders – not only senior ones – about wellbeing at work? Do you have the information you need, and the interpersonal skills to stand up to the challenges?

Your employees

- Do they want this?
- Is the timing right?
- Are they open to being educated and challenged, and to new ideas, new thinking, new ways of working?
- Do they believe that you genuinely want to help them?
- Will they at least just try it?
- Who are the early adopters? How can you work with them for mutual benefit?

Selecting the right tool

Wellbeing is not a workplace challenge that has one solution. Leaders are working with people, and those people bring differences of all sorts into the workplace, whether that be connected to personal and lifestyle choices, ambition, responsibilities, strengths, health or tolerance for challenge or stress. As a result, organizations need to be agile in their responses, providing a range of interventions, policies, approaches, etc, with the aim of enhancing the wellbeing of everyone at work. However significant factors in which tools to select will be:

- The wellbeing challenges your organization faces;
- The budget available for wellbeing programmes;
- The size and practicality of the tools.
- The cultural fit of ideas or tools to the way in which your organization works in practice.

To help with the selection, a table is included at the back of the book which identifies whether each tool is best suited to larger or smaller organizations, and whether the anticipated cost is high, medium or low.

In most cases tools can be applied whatever the size of your business. There are very few where the practicality is better for big or small.

With regard to cost, the assessment of anticipated costings is only estimated, as it will depend on the approach you take – for example bringing in expertise from outside organization may incur cost, but using internal resources will be a cheaper option. In some cases both the medium and low cost columns are ticked, which represents the choices you can make for that tool.

Complementary tools

Wellbeing is not a simple issue to address in the workplace, and you will find as you identify issues or challenges in the workplace, that they overlap in many cases. Physical health issues for example can quickly lead to wellbeing concerns or stress about finances or security. As such you may want to consider adopting complementary or multiple approaches to address challenges within your organization, or specifically for individuals.

Whilst the tools are categorized by a typical 'type' of wellbeing, it should be considered that this is exclusively the connection – eg whilst getting organized may promote mental wellbeing, it may be that issues are in part caused by the environment, not just the individual.

With this in mind, there is a table at the back of this book that identifies the complementary or connecting tools. Here you will be able to identify a tool that you have identified as appropriate for your wellbeing challenge, and any other relevant tools that you may find beneficial in the identification, implementation or evaluation of your initiatives or programmes. This table is indicative only. You may be able to make your own connections – and if you do, you're encouraged to note them on the table for yourself.

Don't forget the small stuff

Below are some quick wins – some top tips at very high level that you might focus on – things that every people manager should be doing to improve staff wellbeing. None of these alone will make an impact on wellbeing, but think about what suggestions from the list might be help you in a broader wellbeing approach:

- Advocate – champion wellbeing at every opportunity – selling the business benefits to senior stakeholders, and the health and wellbeing benefits to everyone.

- Benchmark – find out what happens where your friends work, or in similar or nearby organizations. They may have some great ideas that you can 'borrow' – and you might share yours too.

- Collaborate – if you have other organizations in your building, or other divisions of your company, pool your resources, and your employee base, to make the most of external services, such as fitness classes or training sessions.

- Greet people – Good morning. Goodnight. How was your weekend? A disengaged boss can quickly disengage employees, so take the time to chat informally during the working day. It doesn't have to take long – a minute of your time could make people feel noticed and more valued.

- Listen to ideas, suggestions and feedback and act on what you hear

- Quickly respond to the things that you notice – somebody upset, an argument, an employee staying late, or inappropriate behaviours. You don't have to take full action until you get the right advice, but immediately recognizing something like that will let the employee know that you care.

- You may want to bring the treats in for your birthday or to recognize a job well done, but to advocate wellbeing choices, mix up the cakes and doughnuts with some fruit, nuts or protein bars.

- Zone your workplace – it can be a simple and cost-effective way to set up different working environments – a relaxed area, a meeting zone and a play zone for example. Use what you have already, but lay it out differently, label it, and get people to try it out!

Leadership and advocacy

01

Creating a wellbeing strategy

Introduction

Employee wellbeing can be one of those organizational development initiatives that is seen as a 'nice to do' activity, not requiring real investment, and without any clear business case to support it. It is often seen as a 'fluffy' human resources (HR) activity, which is managed by a senior HR representative. However, there are some clear business benefits and it is extremely useful to demonstrate your commitment to wellbeing in the form of a strategy document that confirms your intent, sets your goals and clarifies responsibilities.

Promoting wellbeing

The publication of a strategy document will demonstrate the intent of an organization to promote wellbeing through its employment practices and its employee benefits packages. In a 2016 report, Great Place to Work stated that wellbeing is a key driver for employee engagement for many 'employers of choice' and reported that the number of employers offering wellbeing strategies is increasing, with half growing their activity in the previous 12 months. In order to stay competitive as an employer of choice in an increasingly active marketplace, employers need to consider their wellbeing strategy as part of their way of working and their benefits package.

Approach

Embedding wellbeing into your business strategy

Your wellbeing strategy should not be a standalone, but should be an integrated part of your overall strategy setting and business planning processes. It should align with – and complement – your strategic vision, and you should certainly make sure that neither conflicts with or pulls in a different direction to the other, or even sounds contradictory. The wellbeing strategy should support what your organization is aiming to do and, importantly, how it intends to do it. There should also be alignment between the wellbeing strategy and the core values of the organization. Incongruence between the two will result in either one or the other not being met.

Strategy content

Your wellbeing strategy should include your statements on the following.

Vision and goals   Set out your vision for employee wellbeing in your organization, and a small number of key goals that will contribute towards the delivery of that strategy. Your vision should be inspirational but achievable, and should cover a breadth of wellbeing issues, including career, mental, physical and financial wellbeing. The vision might also set out the key benefits that the wellbeing strategy is expected to bring, not only to employees, but also to customers or other key stakeholders.

Defining wellbeing   You should take the opportunity within your strategy document to define what wellbeing means for your business. You might include some of the categories that are included in this book, and provide some idea of the scope that you will cover for each one.

Responsibilities   The strategy document should set out who in the organization has overall responsibility for employee wellbeing, any the associated responsibilities of others, including the board, senior leadership team members, and specialist functions. In particular, it should include the wellbeing responsibilities of

- the chief executive officer (CEO);
- senior executive leadership team;
- people managers;
- individuals;
- specialist departments such as occupational health, health and safety and HR.

Committees and action groups   Describe any committees or action groups that will be established to ensure ongoing commitment to and implementation of the wellbeing strategy. These might include governance groups to monitor budgets, review progress and compliance, and take overall responsibility for the strategy, and smaller more local focus groups, who may contribute to putting plans in place, generating ideas, and evaluating progress in their own local environment.

Describing a programme   The strategy may also go so far as to identify key streams for a wellbeing programme, defining at high level the focus for each of them. For example, streams could include:

- career and development;
- physical/mental wellbeing;
- social and community;
- financial wellbeing;
- health promotion;
- occupational health and safety.

Resources   The strategy should also detail the resources that are allocated to the delivery of the wellbeing strategy – which may include any allocated budget, available resources such as premises that might be used, specialist expertise and access to services such as occupational health and employee assistance programmes.

In addition, the strategy may make connections and highlight dependencies to relevant policy statements or strategies, including health, safety and environment, social responsibility and employee engagement.

Evaluation and review   The strategy statement should indicate how employee wellbeing will be evaluated using key performance indicators and business metrics.

Measures might include statements relating to employee engagement scores about wellbeing and employer responsibility, as well as people metrics about absence, days lost to mental health or other absences, participation in initiatives and programmes, grievances raised, etc. In addition, there may be an opportunity to consider other business measures (which may be more indirectly connected to wellbeing) such as productivity, customer service ratings, quality measures, etc.

Make sure that your strategy document is easily understood and written in plain, jargon-free language, suited to the culture of the organization and adaptable should your business change, and lastly, but most importantly, that it is communicated to all relevant people – employees, the board, customers and stakeholders, and particularly to the suppliers of any products or services that connect to wellbeing.

Outcomes

Having a strategy does not ensure that wellbeing is prioritized and cared for within your organization, but it will make your strategic intent transparent, and as a result, the appropriate parties can be held to account for budget allocation, for delivery and for action.

Measuring impact

As above, the publication of a strategy itself does not result in changes in attitudes or behaviours alone, and so the evaluation has to be at a more individual, programme or initiative level. However, it can be useful to benchmark the defined strategy with other organizations, and consider what is 'best practice', in line or missing from the strategy and intent.

It is also useful to seek feedback on the strategy from across the organization – at all levels and in all functions and locations, to validate whether it meets the wellbeing needs, and whether it is seen as practical and value-added.

Workplace wellbeing assessments

Introduction

Having a strategy and intent around employee wellbeing is a great start to kick off a programme of initiatives if you have been able to develop one, but it is useful to know how good your organization currently is at promoting and enabling wellbeing at work, and be able to assess the gap between that and where you want to be in the future.

Completing a wellbeing assessment of your workplace and your work and employment practices will provide you with that gap analysis. It may be appropriate to invite an external assessor into your organization to carry out an independent assessment, and to provide recommendations for your wellbeing programme. Where budget is not available to do so carrying out your own internal audit will be a really great starting point, provided it covers all the key areas of importance, is done transparently and that there is genuine intent to make a positive difference.

The following information provides guidelines about how to conduct an assessment, and provides an initial template for you to consider, but this will need to be adjusted to be relevant to your business, your priorities and your wellbeing strategy.

Promoting wellbeing

Sixty-one per cent of employers are more reactive than proactive in their approach to wellbeing, according to a CIPD report (2016b). Completing an assessment provides the opportunity to consider what changes need to be made in the workplace – both to start positive actions towards wellbeing and also to stop actions or behaviours that might negatively impact it – and what could be introduced to add value and choice to a wellbeing initiative. This allows organizations to take a proactive stance, identifying preventative strategies, but also to accommodate reaction to wellbeing issues, by establishing infrastructure, process and capability to manage issues as they arise.

Approach

Independent assessment

There are many organizations that can complete an independent workplace assessment for you to assess your current levels of alignment to health and wellbeing initiatives, highlighting potential risks and opportunities for your organization, and recommending clear actions. Whilst these will require some investment, there is a clear benefit in an independent perspective from an organization that is specialist in health, safety and wellbeing – they may identify areas to address that you wouldn't naturally consider as important, valuable or even useful, and it is likely that they will be able to offer solutions and interventions for your organization with great expertise and experience behind them, albeit at additional cost.

Self-assessment

The self-assessment route is cost-effective, but is likely to be more limited in its value. This is primarily because you are reviewing your own organization, your initiatives and your employees, but also because it is unlikely that the person completing the assessment, and those reviewing the outcomes, are specialists in the area of wellbeing. However, the self-assessment route does demonstrate that as an organization you want to know and understand your current wellbeing status and how to change that.

Selecting assessors

First, you should give some thought to how long it might take (which will depend on the size of your organization, the scope of the audit and the depth of the approach). Consider, too, whether assessors need any specific skills or knowledge to complete the assessment – for example, are they simply reviewing documents and known practice, or are they being asked to interview employees and managers as part of the assessment? You may want them to do some external research and benchmarking, to find out what experts in the field are recommending, and what other organizations are doing. And finally, be clear about the expectations you have of the assessor – for example, that they need to be honest in reporting their findings, they need to make recommendations and to present those to a leadership team, and they will become ambassadors or similar for wellbeing in your organization.

It might be appropriate for a member of your leadership team or a senior manager to do it, but the outcomes may be more widely appreciated if you were to ask an employee representative (or union representative if you have them) to carry it out for you. Creating a small, cross-functional and multi-level team of assessors might share the workload, and bring different perspectives and knowledge to the audit too.

For a reassessment after 6 or 12 months, it might be beneficial to use a fresh assessor or assessment team.

What to assess

The following questions or statements provide a useful set of prompts for your own wellbeing self-assessment, but rather than simply copy them, you should review them and ensure that they are appropriate, or appropriately worded for your organization. That is not to say that you need to remove questions where you don't think you will 'pass' – quite the opposite. However, there may be some questions that don't feel appropriate for a small organization, or for certain types of industry.

The question set provided below is structured in line with the contents of this book and covers key categories of leadership, individual development, recognition, involvement, mental wellbeing, physical wellbeing, balance, social wellbeing, community, environment and financial wellbeing, and concludes with a review of relevant policies and procedures.

Leadership   This section of assessment seeks to identify whether the leaders in your organization are advocates and sponsors of wellbeing, and have the necessary capabilities to lead effectively.

Example questions:

1 Is there a wellbeing strategy in place?

2 When was the last wellbeing assessment carried out?

3 Who is the most senior sponsor for wellbeing in the company?

4 Do employees perceive that the organization is concerned about their wellbeing?

5 Is there a wellbeing committee?

6 Are wellbeing champions visible and accessible around the organization?

7 Have all senior leaders attended a leadership development programme?

8 Is there a development programme for employees progressing into people management roles?

Individual development   This section of the assessment looks at the company's approach to career development and training for individuals.

Example questions:

1 Does the performance review include discussions about future career development and training?

2 Does the company provide informal opportunities for learning (eg in-house seminars, e-learning, etc)?

3 Is there a training budget?

4 Does the company encourage job shadowing, job swaps, etc?

5 Is there a mentoring scheme in place?

Recognition   This section of the assessment considers the company's attitude and approach to employee recognition.

Example questions:

1 Is there a performance management process in place in the company?

2 How often are people participating in performance discussions with their manager?

3 What is the perception of how performance is managed?

4 What approaches are used for informal recognition (eg bonus scheme, small token awards, etc)?

5 Are those approaches consistently applied across the organization?

Involvement   This section of the assessment will review the opportunities for and extent of employee involvement.

Example questions:

1 Does the company provide opportunities for employees to make suggestions or improvements to ways of working?

2 Is there an employee representative group or committee at which ideas or concerns can be shared?

3 How well does the company prepare employees to react positively to change?

4 Does the company measure employee engagement? Does it take action as a result?

Mental wellbeing   This section of the assessment will review the steps taken by the company to promote and enable positive mental health.

Example questions:

1 Do employees have access to a confidential employee assistance helpline?

2 Is there an occupational health service provision that employees can access?

3 Are managers trained to spot the signs of stress in employees?

4 Have there been any complaints of bullying or harassment at work? How were they managed?

5 Does the company actively promote mindfulness programmes in the workplace?

Physical wellbeing This section of the assessment will review the steps taken by the company to promote and enable physical health.
Example questions:

1 Does the company encourage participation in physical activity or exercise during the working day? How does it do that?

2 Are there any fitness facilities or classes on site?

3 Do managers conduct return to work interviews with employees who have been absent?

4 Are healthy food and drink options available for employees on site?

5 Are any healthy food and drink options provided free of charge?

6 Does the company provide subsidized gym membership?

7 Does the company do anything else to promote physical health?

8 If employees have to travel internationally for work, are they offered health advice before travelling?

Balance This section of the assessment will consider the ways in which the company supports a healthy balance between work and other priorities.
Example questions:

1 Are employees able to work from home if necessary?

2 Do employees have access to the appropriate technology to enable them to work from home?

3 Is there flexibility of working hours and working patterns?

4 Is there an emergency leave policy? How well is it utilized/supported?

5 What are the company's expectations about people working outside of normal hours?

6 Typically, are people working excessive hours?

Social This section of the assessment will look to how the company provides opportunities for social interaction and connection at work.

Example questions:

1 Is there music or a television in the workplace?

2 Are there any social groups or committees established in the workplace?

3 How often does the company organize social events?

4 Are there any special interest or hobby groups set up in the company?

Community   This section of the assessment will consider the company's internal communications, external networks and involvement with community initiatives and programmes.

Example questions:

1 Is there a communication strategy or plan?

2 Are there regular employee briefings?

3 Are employees encouraged to network internally?

4 Are employees encouraged to network externally?

5 Is the company associated with any charities? Does the company offer volunteering opportunities or volunteer days?

6 Does the company encourage participation in national charity events (eg Children in Need, Comic Relief, Macmillan Coffee Morning, etc)?

7 Does the company operate a matched giving scheme for charity fundraising?

8 Does the company encourage 'give as you earn'?

Environment   This section of the assessment will review the working environment, and how it supports wellbeing.

Example questions:

1 Does the working environment have natural light and fresh air?

2 Are there break-out areas or informal spaces where people can access natural light and fresh air?

3 Does the working environment have spaces where people can work quietly, privately and alone if necessary?

4 Does the working environment have spaces where teams can collaborate well together – shared environments, whiteboards, etc?

5 Does the workplace have a rest area where people can remove themselves from their work?

6 Does the workplace have any recreation space?

7 Is the workplace a safe working environment? Are hazards identified and managed?

8 Does the company offer workspace assessments, with flexibility on the provision of desk type, screen size, chairs, etc?

9 Is the environment accessible for people with physical disabilities?

10 Does the workplace include plants and flowers?

Financial   This section of the assessment considers the level of support offered by the company to ensure financial wellbeing is promoted.

Example questions:

1 Does the company offer a flexible benefits package?

2 Does the company offer benefits that are considered to promote wellbeing (eg gym discounts, private health, etc)?

3 Does the company offer long-term incentives (eg share schemes)?

4 Does the company offer support for people preparing for retirement?

5 Are any company loan schemes offered (eg to support employees who want to invest in their further education, or for season tickets, etc)?

Policies and procedures   This section of the assessment invites a review of the company's policies and procedures, to ensure that appropriate policies are a) in place and b) take account of, and that they refer to wellbeing matters.

The following policies should be in place – and their content should be reviewed to ensure alignment to, and support of, wellbeing at work:

- absence – sickness and other absences;
- annual leave;
- discipline;
- equal opportunities policy;
- family leave policies;
- grievance;
- harassment and bullying;
- health and safety;
- maternity;
- statutory flexible working.

In addition, you may have selected to introduce some of the following that should also be reviewed as part of the assessment:

- bereavement;
- capability and performance;
- carer or emergency leave;
- code of conduct;
- corporate social responsibility;
- diversity policy;
- dress code;
- drugs or alcohol;
- flexible working and flexibility;
- performance review;
- redundancy;
- training and development;
- volunteering;
- whistleblowing.

Indicators This section of the assessment looks for business metrics and performance indicators that could help to evaluate wellbeing in the workplace – some may have a direct connection, others may be more indirect. Consider indicators such as:

- absence statistics;
- employee turnover;
- accidents;
- grievances or complaints;
- occupational health referrals;
- exit interview insights;
- employee survey results;
- productivity;
- quality;
- customer service.

Communicate outcomes

Take the time to communicate the key findings of the assessment to your employees. This is important – if you have told them you are doing it, but don't share the outcomes, the process will lose credibility and people will become suspicious about your reasons for not sharing. So be honest and transparent about your findings, and talk about the recommendations that you will adopt, and why.

Outcomes

The outcomes of the wellbeing assessment should be threefold:

1 Current status: The assessment will provide you with an as-is snapshot of the organization's approach or attitude towards employee wellbeing. Depending on the approach you have taken to the assessment, some outcomes may be factual and data driven, others may be drawn out of perception or anecdotal evidence. Either way, this provides a view of the current approach.

2 Direction: The assessment should seek to confirm the company's intent to raise the profile of wellbeing. This could be taken from a strategy document, and/or values and goals of the organization and its employer proposition. However, the statement of intent could also be sought as part of the assessment, through discussion with senior leaders. The assessment findings should reiterate the company's intent.

3 Action plans: Finally, with a current status and an intent clarified, the assessment can deliver a gap analysis, and provide some recommendations and action plans to enable the organization to close that gap.

Measuring impact

There are two key ways in which the impact of the wellbeing assessment can be evaluated.

First is the impact of completing the assessment. It may be valuable to gather feedback from those involved about employees' and managers' overall views about wellbeing, the attitude towards it in the company, and the reactions to the assessment taking place. This will give a high-level anecdotal view of whether people feel it is valuable and valued.

Second, the impact of the assessment itself should be evaluated. Having taken a view of current practice and set some actions in place, their implementation should be considered. You might want to review how many of the recommendations were implemented, and where they were not, why not? Where actions were implemented, what impact have they had on wellbeing at work? Seek out anecdotal evidence of the impacts (what feedback are you hearing, what are people saying about it) and support it with any relevant business metrics (eg absence data, productivity data).

Developing a wellbeing programme

Introduction

With a strategy in place to set and commit to a vision for employee wellbeing, and an assessment completed to understand the gaps, leaders should be able to put in place a wellbeing programme that seeks to meet the needs of both the business and its employees. However, this programme is not dependent on the strategy – it should be aligned, and send the messages to employees about the organization's commitment – but if a strategy is not developed, or if an assessment has not been completed, a programme still can be.

The programme should demonstrate the tactical execution of the intent to deliver wellbeing in the organization, acting as a programme of events or initiatives that work towards the achievement of the wellbeing vision.

The wellbeing programme is a significant output from your strategy and/ or assessment process, and will be seen as a clear commitment by the organization to delivering its vision. As such, there needs to be careful consideration given to the content, and the leadership and financial commitment that are required to fulfil its promises.

Promoting wellbeing

Employees will want to see that the company not only has intent, but demonstrates that intent through concrete actions to deliver wellbeing. They will have more confidence and trust by seeing actions planned and delivered than from the rhetoric alone, so being able to develop and communicate an action plan is likely to secure more engagement to the wellbeing strategy and/or programme. The delivery against those actions builds trust, as employees see commitments being followed through, which in turn garners further support for contributing to and participating in wellbeing initiatives.

Approach

The wellbeing programme is your action plan that will deliver your wellbeing strategy or intent. As such, it should be clear about what will be delivered, who is responsible for making it happen, the timeline, budget and resources needed, and, where you are able to, a statement about how you will evaluate it. Some of the content in this book will be useful in the creation of the programme.

Be sure that if you put something into the programme, you are willing and able to work hard to make it effective. To publicly state that you'll implement something and not do it, or to stop doing something part way through because it costs too much money, will have a significant impact on how employees perceive the leadership of the organization, and its commitment to and concern for the employees' wellbeing. The recommendation is to start small, focus on initiatives with low or no cost and evaluate and commit to them if there is commitment from employees. For any initiative with an unpredictable uptake or value, communicate it as a pilot or trial programme, but be clear about how you will evaluate its future (ie is it dependent on cost, take-up, etc?).

As well as establishing actions as a result of an assessment, you could also involve teams or focus groups to generate new ideas and suggestions.

Make sure that your programme offers a diverse range of initiatives, covering the breadth of the wellbeing agenda, a variety of interest areas and catering for a mix of abilities.

A template for your wellbeing programme is shown in Table 1.1. Some suggestions of the actions you could include are:

Leadership and advocacy

Define what steps your organization will take to ensure that wellbeing is understood, advocated, role modelled and actioned by your senior leaders. Your programme could include actions such as:

- wellbeing focus groups, assessments, committee meetings, etc;
- training wellbeing champions and advocates;
- training leaders in stress management, resilience and mindfulness;
- training leaders in fair, safe and legal employment practice, and ensuring that they fully understand and utilize the company's employment policies.

Career

Explain the policies, procedures, resources and support available to employees to help them develop their capabilities and progress their career. Your wellbeing programme could include actions such as:

- performance conversations;
- training all employees on how to give great constructive feedback;
- training people managers to coach;
- establishing a mentoring scheme;
- availability of training resources (eg a library, TED Talks, e-learning subscriptions etc).

Physical/mental

Describe the activities or interventions that you will introduce to support mental and physical wellbeing. Your programme could include:

- training on resilience and/or mindfulness;
- fitness activities, clubs or classes for all employees to join if they wish (eg running at lunch time, after work Pilates);
- unchtime talks from specialists (eg dietician, personal trainer, counsellors, etc);
- allocation of a quiet office space for employees to use as and when needed.

Social and community

Describe activities that you will implement to encourage more social interaction, inclusion and to allow employees to 'give back' to charities or communities. Your wellbeing programme might include:

- get involved with high profile charitable events (eg Children In Need, Comic Relief, Macmillan Coffee Mornings, etc);
- a cake sale or similar to fundraise for an employee's chosen charity;
- a Christmas party or summer barbecue;
- problem solving workshops bringing together cross-functional teams;
- internal or external networking events.

Financial

Describe any actions or initiatives that might support an employee in their financial wellbeing. Your programme may include:

- using external expertise to help employees to manage their finances;
- flexible benefits;
- give as you earn schemes.

Review

Be transparent about when and how you will review your programme. Stay open to suggestions and ideas from others for new additions to it, as well as feedback on those actions currently taking place. Regularly reviewing and changing your programme will ensure that it is kept relevant, interesting and that people remain committed to it.

Outcomes

The programme demonstrates the company's action towards its intent, and as such the outcome should be the implementation of activities and initiatives to promote wellbeing.

Measuring impact

It may be difficult to assess the impact of the programme as a whole, but the individual elements of it should be evaluated to gauge their effectiveness. Informal feedback can be sought from participants, but useful feedback can also be gained from those who choose not to participate. Understanding their reasons for not taking part may provide suggestions or ideas about future actions in which they might be more interested.

Evaluation through the use of key performance metrics might also be useful – at both a macro level and at individual action level too. The macro level evaluation might give high-level, and potentially indirect, links between the programme's launch and changes in measures such as absence, turnover and productivity.

Wellbeing committees

Introduction

The wellbeing committee is the governance structure that will oversee the implementation, development and evaluation of wellbeing strategies and programmes at work. The committee should be cross-representational, and its members should take responsibility and ownership of wellbeing within the organization.

Promoting wellbeing

The establishment of the wellbeing committee provides the opportunity for a number of employees to get involved in setting the strategy, the plan and the advocacy for wellbeing in their workplace. In turn, that involvement is likely to increase their – and their colleagues' – engagement with wellbeing, as it becomes a collaborative initiative, not a top-down one.

Approach

The purpose of the wellbeing committee is to drive the implementation, development and evaluation of employee wellbeing strategy, programmes and initiatives, and in order to do so effectively its objectives will broadly be as follows:

- to carry out a wellbeing strategy review and evaluation;
- to plan, implement and evaluate new ideas for wellbeing initiatives and consider any necessary changes to continuing activities;
- to review and evaluate any available benchmarking and consider any new trends or issues in the wellbeing field;
- to review feedback from employees and participants of existing activities or initiatives;
- to review the relevant metrics to evaluate the effectiveness of the wellbeing strategy.

The committee constituents should be representative of the breadth and depth of the organization. There should be participants from across the hierarchy, representatives from different functions and locations. The committee should have a chairperson, whose role is to set and issue the agenda and any pre-read materials, lead the meeting, encourage all participants to have a voice, and approve the final action plan coming out of the meeting. The chairperson should not necessarily be the most senior person in the room, in fact it can be beneficial to have an employee representative to act as the chair, or an independent party.

The committee should meet on a regular basis, but the time between committee meetings should be sufficient to allow actions to have been implemented, tested and initial reviews completed. This may mean that quarterly or twice per year could be appropriate timings.

The committee should act as a funnel for ideas and information about wellbeing. The committee will learn, review and evaluate incoming data, and a key outcome will be the amendment or introduction of initiatives or actions that take account of that data. It should be seen as a forum for employees, leaders and specialists to provide insight, input and feedback.

Outcomes

The establishment of the committee ensures that there is regular review of the wellbeing programme and strategy in the organization, and that the programme is in line with external best practice, new industry insights and employee expectations, whilst still meeting the needs of the business.

Measuring impact

The effectiveness of the committee meetings should be evaluated by the participants to ensure:

- meetings are well administered (pre-read and agenda are timely, rooms are booked, invites are issued) and that there is good attendance;
- the agenda meets the committee's objectives;
- there is a good balance of internal and external insight and feedback;
- there is contribution from all participants;
- each meeting has a clear set of outcomes as a result of the discussion.

A further level of evaluation should consider the impact that the committee has on the wellbeing approach within the organization. An evaluation should consider whether the committee is actively shaping the wellbeing agenda, proactively addressing issues and trends, and responding well to employee feedback.

Figure 1.1 details a possible mandate for the committee.

Figure 1.1 A sample mandate for the wellbeing committee

Wellbeing committee

Purpose: To drive the implementation and evaluation of the employee wellbeing strategy, programmes and initaitives

Objectives
- Wellbeing strategy review and evaluation
- Planning, implemention and evlaution of new ideas and continuing activities
- Benchmarking and identifying new trends or issues
- Reviewing feedback and metrics
- Learning lessons

Input	Key agenda items	Output
• Wellbeing strategy • Wellbeing assessment • Benchmarking outcomes • New insights • Feedback • Business metrics • Engagement or opinion survey results	Current programme status, feedback and review • Include informal feedback and metrics • Review budget Share new insights and benchmarking outcomes • Include suggestions 'from the floor' Brainstorm new ideas or actions Evaluate against cost/benefit Check programme is aligned to strategy	• Revised strategy • Updated programme of activity • Communicate key messages to employees • Budget adjustment/focus

Participants and roles		Reports and metrics
• Wellbeing sponsor • Senior representatives • H&S manager • Occupational health • HR • Wellbeing champions	Frequency: Quarterly Duration: 2 hours Location: tbd Time horizon: Next 2 quarters Focus: Review and plan	• Wellbeing assessment • Activity reports • Participant feedback reports • Business performance metrics • People metrics (eg absence, turnover, etc) • Budget status

Table 1.1 A wellbeing programme template

List your own headings in this column	What	Who	When	Budget/ resources
	Identify the initiative	State who has responsibility for making it happen	Target date or frequency	What resources are needed or committed
Eg leadership	Wellbeing Committee meeting	Chair	Quarterly	Full attendance required
Eg physical and mental	Weekly 'at desk' massage	Alex	Every Wednesday	Company will subsidize 50% cost of massage
Eg physical and mental	Netwalking – monthly internal networking club on a 5k walk	Alan	2nd Tuesday of every month at 12 noon	No cost

5 Championing wellbeing

Introduction

Identifying supporters at all levels in the organization will be a key success factor for the employee wellbeing strategy and programme. Whilst at a senior level the strategy will define those responsible and who the key sponsors are, championing and advocating wellbeing and your organization's supporting initiatives will be important to spread positive messages, engage people in the programme, provide feedback and contributions, and secure commitment toward the initiatives and activities within it.

Promoting wellbeing

The identification and promotion of champions across the workplace demonstrates the organization's commitment to wellbeing, and provides accessible sources of information and insight as well as a friendly ear to offer feedback to or raise concerns. This proximity – geographically and hierarchically – is more likely to encourage feedback from the floor that will ultimately shape the wellbeing agenda and deliver its success.

Approach

Identifying champions

Regardless of the size of your organization, identifying an individual or a group who can really connect with all employees across your business (all departments, all levels, all locations) about employee wellbeing will be valuable. They should be well connected around the organization, open and approachable to a wide range of employees.

These champions will still be engaged in their day job and the champion role is an enhancement to that. As such, you may need to account for them spending a small amount of time away from their day job so that they can give the commitment needed to be an active champion.

Provide your champions with the opportunity to learn about wellbeing, and about your strategy. Give them access to the assessment that you might have completed (or ask them to take part in the assessment in the first place) so they can understand the background, and involve them in the creation and development of your wellbeing programme. It is important to remember that you are not expecting them to act as experts, so a full training programme is unlikely to be necessary, but some basic information on what wellbeing is, why it matters, why your organization is prioritizing it, and what you want from their role will help to set them off in a positive direction.

Communicate to others who they are and their role as champion, including what people can expect from them, and how to utilize them. Consider providing 'Wellbeing Champion' T-shirts or badges for the designated champions, particularly during periods where you are launching the strategy or a new initiative.

On a regular basis, ask them to provide themes and feedback to you and your management team or wellbeing committee. They'll need to bring feedback, ideas and suggestions from across the organization, and they must have the confidence to be able to speak up about those themes to the senior managers in the business.

You might also task them with some benchmarking, to find out about current best practice, what specialist organizations, charities and health advocates are promoting or recommending, and what other companies are doing. They should use this information to provide insight to the leadership team, alongside practical but valuable recommendations. Encourage them to network with other similar wellbeing specialists and advocates, and to bring ideas back for consideration and implementation. Sending them to local or national business expos to find new service providers (eg for training, massage, gym membership, etc) could be really useful, and asking them to attend any local or national wellbeing conference, breakfast meetings, etc, could bring new insights that you might be able to use.

Recognize the efforts of your wellbeing champions, thanking them for their commitment and acknowledging that they play a key role in the wellbeing programme. It may be a letter, a bottle of wine or cinema tickets – it doesn't have to be costly, but the gesture will no doubt be appreciated.

Outcomes

A key outcome of establishing your wellbeing champions is an improvement in communication fed informally up and down the organization. You'll be able to use the champions to ensure effective communication of intentions, of initiatives and any outcomes, and at the same time champions will be getting feedback, suggestions and ideas to help the business with its wellbeing programme.

In addition, the organization should sense a greater level of engagement with the wellbeing strategy and programme.

Measuring impact

You should consider a number of factors in evaluating the effectiveness of the wellbeing champions.

You could consider the performance of the individual champion themselves – have they remained an advocate, talking positively about wellbeing, and providing a supportive two-way communication flow? Listen to their feedback about what works or doesn't as a champion, and work with them to make it as effective as possible. You may need to provide more resources, more information or more time – or to re-set expectations about how they balance their day-to-day role with the tasks of being a champion.

You might also consider the volume and quality of feedback received through the champions. Have the champions enabled that feedback to flow more freely, and what kind of feedback is being received? Note the themes of the feedback and how they have helped to shape the wellbeing programme, initiatives or evaluation.

Career   02

Growth and development

Strengths-based people management

Introduction

Strengths-based management was born out of the concept of positive psychology, which asserts that people thrive based on strengths, and want to give the best of themselves through things that they enjoy and are good at.

Based on this concept, strengths-based people management focuses on the positive aspects, characteristics and skills that employees can bring to the workplace. Brook and Brewerton (2016) describe a strength as a quality that we have that energizes us, and that we are good at, or have the potential to be good at. They suggest that if managers focus too much on the negative aspects of performance – an employee's weaknesses or development points – they will only prevent failure, rather than creating success. This focus on turning around weaknesses will remove focus from the positives of performance and the strengths that can be optimised.

Promoting wellbeing

Negative thoughts can programme an employee's brain towards negative emotions, and these can prompt the individual to take specific actions, usually to take precautions or for survival, and as such their thoughts are narrowed and focused on that negativity. In an employment context, a discussion about weaknesses or development points might make an employee defensive or lower their self-confidence, and the ensuing thoughts and actions can be based on either protecting their job security, protecting their place and reputation, or ensuring that those skills that were seen as weak become the focus of their attention to show improvement. These emotions may drive negative behaviours, and the focus on negativity detracts from their existing strengths and positivity. However, people do typically pay more attention to negative feedback and comment than they do positive feedback, but we all respond much better to positive feedback.

Positive thoughts and comments keep the brain open to possibilities, and encourage individuals to develop themselves, gathering new skills and capabilities. In an employment context, this attitude towards development can only be beneficial to the employee, as they seek to improve their capability, their employability and, if they want it, their promotability.

Employees who experience more positivity at work are more likely to feel confident in their work, develop their skills and capabilities to progress their performance and their career, and are less likely to feel stressed or out of their depth.

Approach

There are a number of areas of employment and management where a strengths-based approach can be beneficial.

Recruitment

Strengths-based recruitment uses the application and/or interview process to find out about people's interests and strengths, rather than focusing on their current abilities. This means asking questions about what people like or enjoy, how they prefer to work, etc. Rather than selecting on the grounds of what a candidate can or cannot do, or does or does not have experience of, it focuses on where their strengths and preferences lie to assess their match to the job requirements. Candidates are much more likely to become energized and speak positively about their experiences or preferences, than they might if they felt they were being tested on ability alone. For successful candidates, it is thought that they will be more comfortable in role, and perform better than those selected through capability alone. This approach is really useful for candidates with limited experience, who have less concrete examples to call upon in competency interviews.

Some typical strengths-based questions are:

- What are you really good at?
- What really excites you about work?
- How do you like to spend your spare time?
- Do you prefer starting projects or getting them to the finish line?
- Do you prefer the big picture or detail?
- Tell me about an achievement you are proud of.
- How do you think this role will play to your strengths?

Performance management

Performance management processes typically tend to consider how an individual has performed against a set of objectives, the expectations of their job (usually through a job description or similar) and specified competencies or behaviours. One of the features in a normal performance evaluation is to consider what has not been achieved, alongside what has been delivered, and to consider both the strengths and the weaknesses, putting development plans in place for the latter.

A 2005 Corporate Leadership Council study found that focusing on personality and performance strengths had one of the strongest impacts on employee performance of all line manager actions, improving performance by almost 40 per cent. A strengths-based approach to performance management becomes a more future-focused one. Rather than looking back to what should have been achieved and hasn't, the focus instead becomes about looking to what has been achieved and what needs to happen going forward. This may of course mean addressing things that haven't been delivered to date, but instead of looking at the negative perspective of this – why hasn't it been done, what stopped you, what are the consequences – the performance discussion is instead focused on the next steps and the strengths that can be used to make it happen. More frequent performance conversations mean more regular check-ins on progress, and instead of longer-term annual goals, the focus is on near term deliverables (about three months).

The tendency to focus on weaknesses and how to develop them into strengths should be avoided – managers need to be realistic about how much an individual's personality can be changed, and the degree to which someone might have an appetite for adjusting their preferences. The focus on developing strengths will not only be a more positive discussion, garnering confidence and a positive mindset, but may also keep the employee's mind open to new possibilities and developing new capabilities. However, where weaknesses or mistakes do need to be discussed, the focus of the discussion should be on the learning opportunity they present, what can be done differently or better in the future, rather than criticizing or punishing the employee.

Talent management

The approach to assessing talent should be considered along the same lines as for recruitment – that internal and promotion interviews should include strengths-based questions. In addition, the processes for developing talent should look to utilise strengths in projects, coaching, training and in development roles.

Recognition and reward

Make your recognition schemes and strategies a key part of your strengths-based management approach. If you have bonus schemes, reward schemes or employee recognition schemes in place, or if you intend to introduce any, then make sure that your qualifying criteria and assessment or judgements are based only on positively framed strengths.

More broadly, encourage people across your organization to talk openly about strengths – theirs, others, yours, the company's, the customer's, the supplier's, etc. Discourage any focus on weaknesses or mistakes, and instead reframe comments, challenge negativity and actively encourage positive story telling.

Outcomes

The use of strengths-based approaches in recruiting, selecting, developing, assessing and recognizing employees should improve the outcomes, and encourage employees to feel more positive about their suitability, contribution and value within the organization.

Measuring impact

The evaluation of strengths-based processes can be considered through the success and tenure of those recruited, assessed and rewarded using this approach. Consider how long new recruits or internal promotees have remained in role, and how well they perform.

Peer coaching

Introduction

Coaching as a method of workplace development has grown in popularity in recent years, with many organizations now developing internal coaching capability, as well as using external experts, to coach employees, developing their leadership capabilities and interpersonal skills, as well as technical or functional capabilities, among other things.

Peer coaching is also becoming more popular in organizations that are keen to develop a stronger coaching culture. It encourages small groups to coach each other. This removes the need for an external resource (though you may use an independent professional to facilitate the session) and encourages the peer group to coach collaboratively.

Peer coaching requires that all members of the peer group are trained and capable as coaches, that the peer group are empowered to take time to meet, that the connected peer group is an appropriate one (they are comfortable coaching each other) and that the ethics of coaching, particularly around confidentiality, are clearly agreed at the start of the process.

Promoting wellbeing

A report by Action Coach (2012) stated that research on the benefits of executive coaching included greater job satisfaction, improved teamwork, effective conflict resolution and improved working relationships with manager, peers and other stakeholders.

Approach

Communicate your peer coaching initiative

You should share with your employees the rationale for the introduction of the peer coaching initiative, focusing on your organization's desire to encourage learning, self-development and a coaching culture. Explaining the process for setting up peer coaching groups, how people can get involved, and what skills might be required or developed, will help to get the attention of those who are interested in development through coaching.

Train potential group members

Those employees planning to participate in peer coaching should be equipped with skills to be effective in their role as coach. Whilst they do not necessarily need to be formally qualified for the internal coaching initiative, they do need to learn what coaching is (and isn't) and some of the core skills that make for an effective coach – this training could be provided in house or by an external coaching skills professional.

Enable the process

As a manager, you need to provide the time and the space for peer coaching to take place. Encouraging peer coaching to take place is a positive step, but you also have to be prepared to cover the workload to allow the time for coaching to happen without creating greater pressures for the participant.

Providing an appropriate space for peer coaching is also important for it to be successful. Open plan offices, coffee shops or canteens are not ideal, and the preference would always be to provide a safe, confidential space, such as a meeting room, or if you are really investing in the process, an off-site venue.

Establish the group

Your earlier communications plan should have created some interest from employees keen to participate in a peer coaching initiative. The next step is to establish a peer coaching relationship or group. Peer coaching can be just two peers coaching each other, or it could be a small group (probably a maximum of four to six participants) who take turns to coach or take the role of coachee.

Connecting peers together in pairs or small groups can be done in a couple of different ways:

- Volunteers: Invite those who are interested to connect with each other. Make sure that you have permission from the individuals themselves to share their names with fellow participants. Encourage the volunteers to connect themselves, identifying someone or a small group of people that they would like to work with. This could be effectively done at a launch event as mentioned above, where you could encourage voluntary 'matching' of peer coaches.

- Selection: An alternative approach is to specifically match participants into peer pairs or groups based on some predetermined selection criteria. These selection criteria should be carefully considered and might also be communicated beforehand, but you might make selections based on:

- Function: Grouping people of the same function (eg finance, HR, operations), potentially allowing for a strong functional collaboration and greater understanding of each others' roles, or deliberately mixing functions to encourage diversity of thinking and new perspectives.

- Location: Grouping or pairing people based on the fact that they work in the same geographical location, or intentionally grouping people from different locations.

- Learning and development objectives: It might be beneficial to mix up the learning objectives for the members of the pair or group. Focusing on the same learning objectives might lead to a 'group think' mentality, and the group may not be as creative or diverse in their thinking as a mixed learning group.

- Coaching capability: You might consider matching experienced coaches with those who have recently trained or have less experience. This will help to develop the exposure and experience of those new coaches, and can help the group or pair to deliver effective coaching.

The group then needs to form, and agree its 'ground rules' and its ethics. In particular, you should encourage them to consider and agree:

- the frequency of their meetings (monthly or quarterly is recommended);
- who will coordinate logistics (the time and place for their session);
- confidentiality and ethics factors – what level of confidentiality they expect and how to maintain that;
- what issues to tackle – whether it is an open forum, whether coaching goals are submitted beforehand, etc;
- which coaching model to follow (for example the GROW model);
- what support they might need from coaching experts, HR or senior leaders to establish and maintain the group.

You may want to agree the lifespan of the group. This avoids issues of co-dependency and of excluding others from the benefits of the process or the wisdom of those in this group, but may disrupt a well-functioning group of people. Consider the benefits and limitations of a fixed term group, involving the group members in the discussion.

If the group comes to an end, then celebrate its ending. It's important to formally close the group and take time to reflect on its successes and its learnings, rather than let it drift away. The group can agree what they want to happen in the future – a more informal network or other collaboration, or simply going their separate ways.

Evaluate its effectiveness

Check in regularly with the participants for their informal feedback about the process, the effectiveness of the coaches and to get a sense of the difference their coaching may be having on their work, their challenges and their relationships.

Encourage the group to share feedback with each other so that the process can be improved.

You might also want to seek feedback from the participants' managers and colleagues about changes in their performance. But do so with the permission of the employee.

Resources

It's likely you'll need to provide some training on at least an introduction to coaching, and some coaching skills development before kicking off a peer coaching initiative, and this will require some initial investment. However, the costs should be set against potential future costs of providing external coach support for any employees, and should be considered as a wider benefit of up-skilling staff, enabling self-development, etc.

Once established, the process requires only the time investment for a peer coaching circle to take place. This could be a couple of hours each month, so whilst not a massive time commitment it may still need to be carefully planned to ensure full commitment.

Outcomes

By implementing a peer coaching approach in your organization you have the potential to achieve a number of very positive outcomes.

First, by introducing any form of coaching, you are demonstrating to employees that you are keen to support their development, and to equip and enable coaches to provide that opportunity.

Second, peer coaching can build trust, empathy and collaboration among colleagues. By using coaching techniques they will be able to help each other to solve problems and see things from different perspectives.

And finally, there are various organizational benefits, identified through research reported by Action Coach (2012), which include increased productivity, retention, and customer service and quality.

Measuring impact

The effectiveness or impact of the peer coaching group will be somewhat dependent on what the participants are seeking from the process, and as such your primary evaluation should be an assessment of the achievement of the goals set out in the coaching group or in each coaching session.

However, you might also consider feedback from the participants on:

- the process;
- the coaching capability of the group – what worked well, what didn't.

In addition, you may see changes in the number of people wanting to participate in peer coaching, and might consider that to be an assessment of its success or otherwise, based on informal feedback.

Finally, consider some of the organizational benefits outlined above. Whilst it would be difficult to directly attribute any positive trends in the areas of retention, customer service, quality, etc, to the peer coaching process, you may be able to identify a positive correlation (albeit indirect) dependent on the individuals involved and the timing of changes in trends.

Overall, the intention should be to provide an opportunity to employees, enabling them to seek support and counsel from their peers. Consequently, if feedback from participants suggests that the support is welcome, meaningful and impactful, then the peer coaching process can be seen as successful.

8   Promoting learning

Introduction

Investing in the development of skills and behaviours of your employees is good business sense. It ensures that they are able to perform at their best, and have relevant and up-to-date skills, knowledge and experiences. From the employee's perspective, investment in their development allows them to continue to learn, to develop their own expertise and optimize their potential and career goals, whilst also staying relevant in the employment marketplace. There are of course mutual benefits in terms of the quality, efficiency, creativity, etc, of services or products that your organization can offer, for example. But, most importantly for this discussion, developing knowledge also makes people feel good, valued and that they are worth your investment.

Promoting wellbeing

Workplace learning can have a positive effect on employee wellbeing and this evidence is both clearer and stronger where that learning is directly related to developing skills or raising awareness about wellbeing matters (eg stress management or mindfulness). Researchers have, however, been challenged to find strong evidence connecting a broader range of learning subjects and an impact on wellbeing.

Nevertheless, for those employees who are keen to develop their skills, knowledge or experience, or to enhance their education, support from their employer can only be a positive thing. For others, the training room or the classroom can be a stressful environment, whether or not they have an appetite for development.

Whilst some development may be mandatory or preferred for specific roles, projects or activities, the provision of employee-directed learning opportunities, through a range of delivery methods designed to be accessible to the majority rather than the minority, can encourage employees to grow, develop, collaborate and contribute. In addition, the arising positive view of the company can help to improve employee engagement and commitment, and add to the value of your employer brand.

Approach

Encouraging continuous learning

Aside from the formality of learning experiences, leaders can encourage a positive and reflective learning culture within their own teams. Rather than looking at performance deficiencies, mistakes and faults, the leader can use such incidents as learning opportunities. They should present a future-focused approach to such issues, looking at what can be learned, what could be done differently in the future, etc, rather than apportioning blame and critique.

70:20:10 development

The 70:20:10 learning model was developed in the 1980s by Morgan McCall, Michael M. Lombardo and Robert A. Eichinger working for the Centre for Creative Leadership. The model holds that an employee's development or learning journey should be 70 per cent from experiential learning, 20 per cent from learning through relationships, and only 10 per cent through formal classroom learning or training. These three types of learning can be defined as follows:

- Experiential learning: Learning can be achieved through gaining experience, whether that is on specific projects, tasks or activities. This type of learning activity is effective because it is practical and therefore easily transferred into the learner's own environment and work activity.

- Relationship learning: This type of learning relies on the employee building effective relationships with mentors, coaches, managers, colleagues and specialists within the organization. Learning may be less structured, but does provide a cost-effective and easy-access way to share and obtain knowledge throughout the organization and beyond.

- Formal learning: Formal learning activities are typically classroom-based, whether it be technical training, interpersonal skills or leadership training, or academic programmes.

Personal development funds

Allocating a small training budget for each employee in your business is one of the more expensive options, but the cost can be controlled and the rules for defining and approving appropriate training can be quite explicit if preferred, and the benefits can be significant. Providing the opportunity for every employee to learn something new, regardless of its relevance to their role, the company or their future career, can keep their minds active and engaged, and can encourage their appetite for learning to be mirrored in the workplace. This can potentially lead to greater productivity, more innovation and greater engagement.

Some companies provide each employee with a fixed amount learning fund – a set amount per annum – that they can use for any formal learning experience. This could include evening classes for hobbies or crafts, business training courses, or formal education and qualifications, although the employer may choose to set some boundaries around the legitimacy of the training. Employees can then decide if they want to use it, and how. Often the fund acts as a contribution, not a full cost, and this could be based on the relevance to the job, or a return on investment prediction.

You may need to check whether a personal development fund would be considered a taxable benefit, and if so, whether to offer it as part of a selective flexible benefits scheme instead.

Learning about wellbeing

Employees respond well to learning topics that can benefit them, such as on matters around wellbeing, managing stress, mindfulness, etc. Investing in short training sessions can bring added value not just in developing the knowledge and skills of employees, but also in helping them to manage their own stress and anxiety levels, potentially leading to less absence, improved productivity and a greater sense of loyalty to the organization.

The simple things

There are some really low-cost ways in which you can encourage and enable learning to take place in your business, providing benefit for employees with some return on a low-level investment for yourself. For example:

- Set up a library: Provide self-help books, skills development books, e-learning, books on leadership management and theory, etc, and allow employees access to borrow books for learning in their own time. If you want to save cost but like the idea, set up a book club or book swap instead.

- Guest speakers: Guest speakers can be expensive, so instead of hiring them, invite employees with a hobby, interest or specialism to share some of their top tips, skills or knowledge with an interested audience over a lunch break or after work.

- Videos: Social media and websites are full of fantastic free resources, so instead of long and expensive training programmes, why not provide the opportunity for employees to meet, watch and discuss some topical videos from sites such as TED Talks, You Tube or slide shares from LinkedIn. You just need to check their sharing and broadcasting regulations, but most of these will allow access to their content for internal use.

- Job swaps, work shadowing and back to the floor schemes: These are all great ways for people to pick up new skills or knowledge 'on the job'.

Outcomes

Providing opportunities for employees to learn at or through work can offer many advantageous outcomes for both the employee and the employer.

For the employee, the opportunity to learn and develop skills, knowledge and experiences can enhance their commitment to your organization, build their confidence and capability, and encourage them to develop and optimize their potential. Learning can increase curiosity, help to maintain an active mind and prepare and help people to adapt to change, both at home and at work.

For the employer, some of those benefits already mentioned are considered mutual – developing the competence of employees to improve collective organizational performance, developing adaptability to improve the responsiveness to organizational change, and developing curiosity and creativity to encourage more innovation and improvement. The positive effects on individual mental health may also offer advantages to the business in terms of employee retention, employer brand and reputation, and reduced absence due to stress or anxiety.

Measuring impact

The evaluation of specific training events can be managed at various levels:

- Take-up: A simple assessment of how many people volunteer for certain learning activities or events will give an indication about whether the topics listed and the selected approach to developing them are attractive or of interest to your employees.

- A 'happy sheet' evaluation will provide a review of how enjoyable participants found an event – providing insight about whether it met their learning objectives and feedback about the quality of trainer, content, materials, etc (see Table 2.1).

- Harder to assess but perhaps more meaningful is to consider the impact of the training on overall organizational performance, eg is it having a material effect on how employees are working, their behaviours, their results, etc. This could be reviewed through your usual business performance metrics, and your engagement or employee opinion survey data may also offer some useful feedback.

Table 2.1 A typical happy sheet

Title of the workshop or course	Name of the workshop facilitator/trainer
Date	Location

Please indicate your level of agreement with the statements listed below:

	Strongly agree	Agree	Neutral	Disagree
The course/workshop was relevant to my needs/my job				
The objectives of the course/workshop were met				
The course/workshop followed a logical structure				
Materials used and provided were of good quality and relevant to the content				
There was sufficient time for this workshop/training				
I enjoyed the course/workshop				
The trainer/facilitator was knowledgeable				
The trainer/facilitator was well prepared				
The location and room were adequate for this workshop/training				
The facilities and refreshments were good				
What did you like most about today's event?				
What could make it even better?				
What are your main takeaways from today's event?				
Any other comments				

Finding purpose

Introduction

We work with the basic assumption that everyone comes to work to do a good job. No one plans to come to work to deliberately underperform, upset others or perform irrelevant or timewasting tasks. With that starting point in mind, what becomes important is making the connection between what an employee does in their daily work, and what the overall business goal is. Creating that sense of significance for people – a sense of purpose — highlighting that their tasks, however big or small, really matter is likely to foster a greater sense of engagement among employees. And in addition, knowing the importance of the work carried out for other people in the organization can also encourage improved collaboration and communication.

In a study by Grant (2008), it was determined that managers need to communicate the importance of specific tasks, or improvement of a task, to others. In doing so, the manager is explicit about the value of that specific piece of work, and this helps the employee to understand the impact of what they are doing and therefore improve their performance of it. It's useful to note, however, that this study showed the significance of doing so at a task level, and not an overall position or role in an organization.

Promoting wellbeing

A study in the US, reported in the *New York Times* (Schwartz and Porath, 2014), found that 50 per cent of survey participants across a range of US companies felt that they lacked meaning and significance at work. It also reported that those employees who do feel a sense of significance are more likely to stay with their current employer, and report greater job satisfaction and higher levels of engagement. The counter suggests, therefore, that those 50 per cent who are not connected to the importance of their job are flight risks, are unhappy and are disassociated from the work they do, and that of the broader organization.

Approach

Connect tasks to dependencies

When seeking to communicate the significance of specific tasks, the line manager must first be clear and explicit about the task, offering as much information as possible so that expectations on both sides are clear. The employee will want to understand its significance in order to connect to and engage with it. This can be achieved by a discussion centred around the dependencies to the task, for example:

- Who/what processes are feeding the task to this individual (ie where is the work originating)?
- To whom or to where does this piece of work go next (ie who is the work being done for?)
- What are the quality expectations?
- How does the task contribute to the bigger picture?
- Who else is influenced by the outputs from this task?

These and other similar questions can help the employee to piece together the importance of the work, and the overall discussion is likely to encourage them to give their best in completing the work.

Connect tasks to the bigger picture

Enabling employees to make a connection between the work they do on a daily or task basis, and the broader goals and achievements of the organization will offer that sense of importance that can encourage greater commitment and engagement. Typical 'line of sight' or strategy cascade processes are an organizational approach to ensuring that connection can be made, and are extremely effective at doing so if the process is well implemented. To make sure this is the case, all employees have to be involved in the process, and encouraged and enabled to make those connections, as they do not always appear obvious or directly connected.

This point is well made in the much-told story of President Kennedy's visit to NASA in 1962, when he introduced himself to a member of the cleaning staff and asked the gentleman, 'What are you doing?' The cleaner replied, 'Well, Mr President, I'm helping put a man on the moon.'

In addition to these team-based activities, the line manager must also focus on helping to make those connections on a regular basis at an individual level, task by task with each employee when required. This helps the employee to understand the impact of their work, the effects their output has further down the line, and the opportunities that may arise to improve, change or optimize what they are doing. Spending a small amount of time to describe that significance to the employee can lead to improved processes, better quality and greater collaboration, through the task and beyond.

Outcomes

Outcomes include:

- improved retention, job satisfaction and higher engagement;
- improved quality and performance;
- greater collaboration among teams and individuals;
- attractiveness as employer/employer brand as we are able to promote corporate social responsibility/meaningful work.

Measuring impact

Engagement surveys should show that employees are able to make the connection between their work and the company goals. They should indicate that employees feel that they are participating in meaningful work and that they are able to make a difference.

In addition, you should look for improvements in quality of work outputs, in commitment to solving problems, and in collaboration with work colleagues as well as overall performance measures on the increase.

Externally you might see impacts on your customer feedback, your net promoter scores, and ultimately your bottom line.

Measures such as retention and overall engagement scores should increase positively.

10 Communicating

Introduction

A CIPD factsheet (2016a) on employee communication states that 'Effective internal communication is important for developing trust within an organization and is shown to have significant impact on employee engagement, organizational culture and, ultimately, productivity. Yet CIPD research suggests that many employees feel they receive limited or very little information.'

It can be the case that although you have shared information with your employees, the message hasn't been understood, or hasn't been delivered effectively or consistently. Alongside no communication, this miscommunication can be demotivating and disengaging for employees.

Promoting wellbeing

Continuous, relevant and authentic communication can have a significant impact on how employees feel in, and about, the workplace. Feelings of uncertainty, low motivation, low self-esteem can arise when employees are not informed about the future of the business, its performance, its purpose and impact, and their own contribution, performance and impact.

Approach

Your communications plan should be an ongoing part of running your business. It is recommended that you prepare an annual communications plan that provides a regular heartbeat of communications to your employees (including media such as newsletters, team briefings, and annual company meetings). The communications plan should be an ever-changing document in term of content and key messages, one that evolves with unplanned or unforeseen company news (eg acquisitions, downsizing, relocation, changes to customer base or products/services, staff changes, to name but a few).

Your communications plan should cover all employees, at every level across your business. The communications plan encourages you to consider the different needs of the audience groups, however – whether that is by seniority, by function, by product line or customer segment. Tailoring one core message so that the different impacts for different audience groups are clear will be an effective and engaging way to communicate across teams.

Your basic communications plan doesn't require any resources. You will need to allocate time to prepare communications messages and materials, and you will need to consider the time required for people to attend meetings and briefings. At its simplest form, communication is simply people talking to each other, and is free.

The annual plan

The annual communications plan itself pulls together your business' regular events and activities to share this information with your employees, and provides a further level of clarity and detail on the communications methods and frequency. Completing a planning template provides a structure that can be reviewed and amended over time, regularly reporting on issues such as performance, results and delivery against targets, and adapting it to include breaking or important news.

Please see Table 2.2 at the end of this tool for a sample annual communications plan template.

As delivering the messages contained in the plan in the most effective way is a key part of the tool, it is worthwhile spending some time thinking about how different stakeholders might prefer to communicate. For example:

- Will they want a chance to discuss their reactions with you, straight away, so they can clarify them, or will they want the information in writing in advance and then have time to process it quietly and in their own time before engaging in any discussion?

- Will they ask you for compelling data, reasons, proofs, facts, answers to how and why a change is necessary, or will they think about the bigger picture, focusing on the end goal and the driver behind the change?

- Will they try to understand the logic and analysis behind decisions you communicate, or will they want to focus on the impact of the information or announcements on all involved, demonstrating more of a people focus?

Giving some thought to the different preferences and using what you know about your team members to plan your communications can ensure that you optimize your interactions with them. When you are preparing materials for a more general audience, try to cover the different preferences as much as possible.

Outcomes

As mentioned in the CIPD quote above, effective communication with your employees can build trust, lead to greater levels of engagement, and may encourage improved productivity. As employees feel more informed, they may also feel more involved, more trusting of the larger organization and its leaders, and so their commitment and engagement towards the organization may grow. At an individual level, employees who experience more open lines of communication have less reason to feel insecure or anxious about their future, as the organization shares information with them openly, and their manager provides continuous feedback about their own performance at work.

Overall, employees who are more informed are more enabled – they understand why they are doing what they do, the future direction of the business and the work, and their role within it. They understand how they are performing, what changes need to be made, and what feedback is being received. All of this free-flowing information and the two-way exchange contribute to employees feeling confident, valued and secure.

Measuring impact

The intended outcome of the annual communications plan is that employees hear, understand and connect to your messages. It is therefore valuable to measure the effectiveness of the plan regularly, and to be aware of what messages have landed and with what interpretations. This will help you to consider any necessary reiterations.

The simplest way to do this is to ask people:

- What have they understood from the communication?
- Do they understand the relevance of the messages for them?
- What else would they like to know?
- How did they feel about the medium used to communicate it (ie email, face to face, etc)?

Gathering this feedback informally will provide some indications of the effectiveness, and help you to shape future iterations and future communications more generally.

Ideally, at each stage in the communications plan, you will see a deeper understanding or interpretation of the messaging.

You may want to consider different methods of delivery using a greater variety of media, of presenter, of format, and a different way to promote the same key messages so that the plan doesn't lose its impact.

Table 2.2 Annual communications plan

Month	Who?	Info to share	Breaking news	How?	When?	Need?	Owner
Eg Jan	All call centre employees	Team metrics Company performance	Approved 50 new vacancies for call handlers	Team briefing Follow-up email Include headlines in newsletter	25th at 10am Newsletter on 30th	Alan – prepare slides Need AV kit in meeting room	Susan
Eg Jan	All line managers	Performance data	Expansion – new office	Senior staff Awayday	20th	Pre-read prepared by Lee	Susan
Jan							
Feb							
etc							

Key:
Who: Who is the audience? Size and location of each audience group? Any issues in reaching them effectively (eg shift patterns, locations, time zones, language, etc)?
Info to share: Note the regular news items that can be repeated for this audience.
Breaking news: Leave this open for breaking news to be added if and when it arises.
How: How you will communicate – note the channels you will use (eg team briefings, local newsletters, SMS, intranets, TV screens, etc.), and also consider what scope you have for more innovative channels such as panel discussions/open forums, focus groups, one-to-one engagement with key stakeholders.
When: Note the specific day/date of the communication.
Need: List the people/budget/resource requirements to make this happen.
Owner: Identify the person accountable for making this communication happen.

11 A walk-and-talk

Introduction

As a manager, you will need to have regular one-to-one conversations with team members who report directly to you. You might have to meet with them to discuss their goals, their progress against those goals, challenges they are facing, opportunities or just general updates or catch-up conversations. These might need to be formal, taking place in an office or meeting room, or you might make efforts to establish rapport in a more informal environment – maybe a breakout area, a coffee lounge or staff restaurant, or off site in a coffee shop.

However, if you have the opportunity to get out of the office and have a walk-and-talk session, this can bring some great physical as well as mental benefits to both yourself and your team member.

Promoting wellbeing

The charities Ramblers and Macmillan report that getting active isn't just good for health and wellbeing – they go so far as to suggest it can save lives, reporting 'we could prevent 37,000 deaths a year just by taking a walk' (Walking for Health, 2014). The Walking for Health report added that people who stay active are less stressed, have a lower risk of depression, stay sharp, improve memory and generally just feel better.

As well as the obvious benefits of being more active, getting healthier and losing excess weight, the UK National Health Service (NHS) websites suggest that regular walking can reduce risks of some chronic illnesses particularly heart disease, high blood pressure, diabetes and asthma. It strengthens the heart and lungs as well as simply toning up legs, bums and tums. Research also suggests that that walking can aid sleep and help people to feel more refreshed during the day.

There are also some great advantages in getting some fresh air into your lungs. Yourstandardlife.com reports that fresh air provides you with a steady supply of clean fresh oxygen to increase energy levels, and to enable you to breathe out releasing toxins from your body. Huffington Post research (Wise, 2014) suggests that that spending time in fresh air and nature increases energy by 90 per cent.

If you stay in the office, you breathe the same air throughout the day, and the oxygen content goes down. The result is that breathing stale air won't supply your body with the fresh oxygen it needs and you may suffer from headaches, fatigue, dizziness, etc. Providing your body with more and fresher oxygen can help to bring a greater clarity to the brain – when you breathe fresh air you automatically think better compared to being inside for long periods.

Serotonin is a compound within the body, present in blood platelets and serum, which is thought to influence feelings of happiness and wellbeing. Our levels of serotonin are affected by the amount of fresh oxygen inhaled, so the more fresh oxygen we can get into our systems, the more serotonin we have available to help us to lighten our mood and promote happiness and feeling good.

Approach

Invite your meeting attendee to join you in a walk-and-talk. It is suggested that this is not a mandatory approach, but an option for both parties to consider. Some may feel uncomfortable, or want to discuss issues that you are not aware of that may not be appropriate in the walk-and-talk environment. Make sure your team members know that it is ok so say no, but offer information about the benefits that they might also want to consider.

It's useful to have considered your route in advance so that you have a rough idea of a route for 10, 20 or 30 minute conversations. Bear in mind you may not want a busy road, or a quiet country lane. Take into account safety and comfort issues when planning your route.

Consider your meeting attendee's comfort with spending time away from the office with you, consider their fitness level and consider the safety of the route and environment. Check that you and your meeting attendee are appropriately dressed for a walk – walk-friendly footwear, the right outerwear for the climate etc.

Think about pace – too slow for you may be too fast for someone else, and it's not easy to engage in discussion if you're out of breath. Pay attention to your fellow walker and adjust your pace – and maybe your route – accordingly.

The challenge of the walk-and-talk is that there is no meeting table, so there are unlikely to be notes to refer to, or a place to keep notes of the meeting as you talk. This might mean that more sensitive topics or formal, recorded discussions are not appropriate for the walk-and-talk.

Outcomes

The information above highlights the longer term benefits of walking and fresh air. Walking outside in the fresh air, instead of meeting in an office environment, can bring health benefits for both the mind and the body.

It can encourage benefits that we would want for our employees, and that can we can optimize too – we want our team members feeling healthy, feeling fresh, feeling happy and feeling energetic.

In addition to these scientifically proven benefits, we must also recognize that the walk-and-talk creates the opportunity to remove barriers and break down the formality of an office discussion across the desk.

Measuring impact

Initially, you should consider gaining some immediate and high-level feedback from your walk-and-talk participants. Find out how comfortable they were taking your meeting on their feet, how the distance/pace was for them, whether they were able to cover all the agenda items that in the duration, and in the environment.

The next level of evaluation could be more medium term – taking a view about whether you are seeing or experiencing some of the health and wellness benefits. Do they seem happier, less stressed and are absence levels low or reducing?

Longer term health benefits may depend on the individual, and may be more difficult to establish, assess and measure, but you can always ask!

Enabling flow

Introduction

You know that moment when you feel totally focused, when you forget to drink your tea because you are so engrossed in – and enticed by – the task you are working on? You might refer to yourself as feeling 'in the zone'. Mihály Csikszentmihalyi, a Professor of Psychology, became associated with the key research works on such working environments and named it 'flow' (Csikszentmihalyi, 1990). Similarly, in 1964 humanistic psychologist Abraham Maslow introduced the phrase 'peak experience', describing similarly intense and exciting events or periods of individuals.

Flow is a state of complete emersion, where your focus is so intense, so strong, that you don't notice you are tired, or hungry. The factors that enable flow are many and varied, and often individualized and personal, but here it is considered as a tool for you to use to encourage your own and others' wellbeing at work. As such, it is important that you know how you might 'engineer' that flow – how you can create the environment that allows an employee to get into a flow state.

Promoting wellbeing

Research suggests a strong correlation between employee wellbeing and working in a state of flow. In these peak or flow moments, we feel more whole, integrated, aware of ourselves and deeply happy. Csikszentmihalyi suggests that when we are in flow we feel happier and more successful (Csikszentmihalyi, 1990). The advantages of flow are clear – increase happiness and wellbeing, persistence and achievement, self-development and self-awareness – and it can lead to higher levels of performance.

Approach

Flow is an individual thing. What sends one person into a state of flow could be very different to their colleagues, and so engineering the environment does not mean one size fits all. In consideration of this individualization, a first step should always be to ask your team members what makes them work in a flow state. You might use some of the suggestions below as prompts for those not sure, but the list below isn't intended as a to-do list to work your way through.

Research suggests that flow is likely to occur when the following conditions are in place. When your team members are able to describe their preferred conditions for flow, think about when it might be appropriate, or necessary, to enable them, if it's not all the time.

1 Clear goals that are attainable, but that provide the opportunity to stretch or challenge oneself.
   For some people it may be that describing just the task is enough to enable them to grasp it. Others may want more description or a clear connection to the 'why' – the bigger picture. For some, one task at a time is more likely to encourage flow. For others, the whole objective will be motivation for them, even if they have to break it into tasks themselves.
   The key here is that goals must be challenging, but achievable. Challenge that is not realistically achievable – whether it is the timeline, the goal itself or the available resources – is more likely to create a barrier for employees, or simply to be frustrating. If the task or goal is perceived as too difficult, employees are more likely to become anxious, but if it's too easy they may get bored. It will be important that you judge carefully the balance between the two for each individual to encourage a state of flow.

2 An environment that allows for strong concentration and focused attention.
   That environment may be different depending on an employee's sociability or thinking preferences. For some employees, it will be important to have a quiet space, devoid of interruption, without noise, and with access only to the information really needed to complete the task at hand. Others may find that being in an active environment, with other people around them who they can share ideas and brainstorm with, will help them to get more focus and deliver the goal. Some may want to work from home, others may find that extremely distracting. Ask the question, and as far as is practical, provide the environment that works best for them.

3 The ability to have a complete focus on the activity itself.
   If you want to encourage flow, regularly interrupting your employee with a long to-do list, changing deadlines, or requiring immediate responses to your emails are not helpful. If you are really engineering flow, make sure they have the space and the freedom to really focus on the specific task. Clear their diaries as much as possible, and provide 'air cover' for them so that they are not interrupted by colleagues, stakeholders, etc.

4 Reassurance and encouragement that the task is achievable.

Support and coaching will be invaluable to the employee during flow. Offering them real-time and regular feedback will help them to maintain the right level of performance to negotiate changing demands and will allow them to adjust their own performance, and environment if necessary, to maintain the flow state.

5 Manage it.

Remember that when in a real state of 'flow' the employee is likely to lose track of time, forget to take a break, to eat or to drink, and may not interact with others for long periods. The effect of all this is positive, but it's not a bad thing as a manager to keep your eye on the employee, encourage them to take a break now and again, and get some fresh air!

Group flow might also be achievable, although in different ways to the individualized approach mentioned above. Consider a group who 'jam' together, or dancers who feel they know what their partner is going to do without being told. When groups cooperate to agree on goals and patterns, social flow is much more likely to occur.

Csikszentmihalyi suggests several ways a group can work together so that each individual member achieves flow, including the creation of informal working environments, creative spaces, visual boards for data and results and a strong focus on outputs and deliverables.

Outcomes

Performance and success

As mentioned above, there are several positive outcomes of an employee experiencing flow, which include feelings of happiness and success, and ultimately leading to better individual performance. Research has connected the flow experience to more persistence and achievement in activities, as well as the lowering of anxiety.

Learning

To maintain a flow experience, employees are continually learning. The balance between achievability and challenge is critical to flow, and as a task becomes easier, an employee risks slipping out of flow as it becomes easier. Providing continuing challenge and learning experience will enable the employee to stay in flow for longer. This continued learning and development is likely to become a strength for the employee and an advantage for the team and the organization.

Measuring impact

In evaluating the impact that the experience of flow can have, both the individual and the organizational impact should be considered.

Individual impact should take into account the employee's experience of flow, in the short, medium and long term.

Getting feedback from the employee will be important, to raise your own awareness of the impacts that the environment and conditions you enabled had on their ability to experience flow. This can help to ensure you continue or improve those conditions in the future.

Getting an understanding of how productive the employee is during flow can help to establish the value of enabling it. Were they more productive, more creative, thinking deeper or more focused? How do they assess the output – and how would you assess it? Was the output limited by the conditions set, or only optimized? For example, could it have been more effective if others were involved?

Organizational impact should also be considered from a short- and a long-term view.

Similar to the employee perspective, it would be interesting to consider the impacts of creating the conditions for one employee to achieve flow on the rest of the team or the business. Was there a cost or a compromise that others had to bear – and is the return on that cost worthwhile? Do the conditions set have any negative or positive effect on others?

And what is the overall impact on the wider team or business? Does the output from one person's flow experience have a positive impact on the productivity, creativity, thinking or focus of the rest of the organization? Does the flow experience of one inspire the performance of others?

Typically, these are very generic and qualitative measures, but the individual feedback and consideration at organizational level can provide you with a steer about whether there is benefit in consciously engineering flow for employees, or whether to just be appreciative when it happens naturally.

Encouraging a growth mindset

Introduction

Our mindset is the way that we think about things, defined by our attitudes and our beliefs, and it determines how we react to or deal with things in our world and the world around us. Carol Dweck, a Professor of Psychology at Stanford University, has carried out significant research into mindsets in individuals, seeking to discover why people with similar talents and capabilities don't always perform the same, and presented these findings in an extremely popular TED Talk (Dweck, 2014). She found that those who were successful and motivated thought about the world in a different way – they had different mindsets to those who were less successful. Her research led to two categories of mindset being defined: the fixed mindset, and the growth mindset.

Fixed mindset

Those with a fixed mindset typically believe that intelligence, talents and capabilities are stable, which leads to a desire to look clever or talented. They will be limited in their effectiveness at work because:

- they don't recognize that learning and development will play an important part in their career, or that of others;
- they are ineffective coaches, as they believe talent to be stagnant, rather than evolving;
- they are less likely to solve problems creatively, and are more likely to consider that if their talents can't solve it, then nothing can;
- they are more likely to celebrate and promote their own success than the development or contribution of others.

Growth mindset

Those displaying a growth mindset typically believe that intelligence, talents and capabilities can be developed, which promotes a desire to learn. Employees who demonstrate a growth mindset are more likely to be effective because they are:

- proactive in seeking constructive feedback, are open to hearing it, and more likely to act on it, and they'll offer it too;

- persistent in trying to solve problems – they are less likely to give in, and will keep learning from previous experiences, and from others experiences to keep trying and find new ways. They will see failure as an opportunity to learn;

- great coaches and people managers – they demonstrate a real belief in the potential of others, and seek to help them develop it through opportunity and challenge. They are likely to recognize the strengths, development and contributions of others, not just their own;

- strong negotiators, as they are much more likely to work through problems and challenges to get to solutions, rather than see fixed barriers.

Within this context we should also consider self-limiting beliefs and their connection to mindset. Self-limiting beliefs are the constraints we put upon ourselves, restricting our opportunity to progress or develop based on our own reservations.

Promoting wellbeing

There are several aspects of our working lives that can have a potentially negative effect on our mental wellbeing, such as receiving negative feedback from colleagues, customers or managers, relationship challenges among the team, or a workload or work challenge that we don't seem to be able to conquer. Such issues can lead to anxiety and stress, which, if not proactively addressed, can lead to worsening conditions.

Approaching such adversity at work with a fixed mindset can exacerbate the situation, leaving employees feeling out of control, and that there may be no solution to the challenges being faced. Fixed mindset employees are more likely to blame themselves, and withdraw, feeling that they are unable to make any change, as they don't have the ability or the talent. They may also find themselves covering up or hiding from their self-imposed limitations, adding to the anxiety they may be feeling.

Adopting a growth mindset in such situations can make a significant difference to how these issues are perceived and managed. Employees with a growth mindset are likely to be proactive in seeking help, advice or information from others. They will see the challenges or failures as learning opportunities, and feedback as a platform for development and change.

Encouraging employees to adopt a growth rather than fixed or self-limiting mindset will clearly offer advantages to employee wellbeing, reducing anxiety and stress and boosting opportunity and development.

Approach

Train leaders

Encourage the development of a growth mindset in leaders, and as a style of leadership, by including it in leader training modules. In smaller organizations, consider how you could ensure your managers are aware of mindset matters through self-learning, books, videos and short courses delivered in house by external providers.

Advocate of a growth mindset

First, be aware of your own mindset. Listen carefully to how you communicate (to yourself as well as to others) and challenge yourself to be more growth focused.

Talk about the different mindsets among your teams. Encourage them to think about their own mindset, their attitudes and the language they use, and to consider the difference that a more growth focused approach might bring. Recognize that we have all had learning experiences. Remind your employees that their growth mindset had at one time helped them to learn to walk, or ride a bike, or drive, and had they not done so, they would now be more limited. This same analogy applies to them at work.

Review how you communicate some of your business results and news to employees. On reflection and with mindset in mind, are there some messages that are not growth focused? If there are, can you rephrase them in a way that offers growth, development and progression potential? For example, if you tell employees that the company met its financial targets and congratulate everyone, the mindset is fixed, suggesting we did what we had to do. If, instead, the achievement is recognized, but the messaging also suggests we could do things better, faster, and more efficiently next year, the opportunity for growth is presented.

Giving great feedback

Tool 15, 'Giving great feedback' (page 71) offers some advice on how to ensure that feedback is delivered meaningfully and effectively. This is an important aspect in developing a growth mindset, as the language you choose in feedback can either be developmental and encouraging or (without intent) be self-limiting. For example, offering feedback that suggests 'you did well' represents a fixed mindset, where as commenting on the development, the progression and the achievement (eg 'your research to date has been thorough and your arguments have developed well') represents a growth mindset.

The power of 'yet'

In her 2014 TED Talk, Carol Dweck highlights the power of the simple word 'yet' by describing a school grading system where it is used for students who have failed a course. This immediately turns a limiting situation or statement into one full of opportunity. Consider the difference between telling an employee 'You have not demonstrated the skills needed for that promotion' and the same sentence with 'yet' added to the end. It suggests that there is not a limit or a restriction, but that there is some sense of opportunity to still develop and demonstrate those skills, and achieve that promotion. Consider how you can include this incredibly simple technique into your everyday conversations and feedback.

Recognition

A growth mindset compliment praises effort rather than natural skill. For example, rather than a focus on the outcome – 'you got some great customer feedback' – focus on the efforts made to achieve it – 'you worked really hard to achieve great customer satisfaction this week'.

Outcomes

The encouragement of a growth mindset is likely to develop a learning organization culture, in which development, progression and transformation are key features. Learning organizations typically facilitate the working environment such that employees are actively encouraged to learn, develop and challenge. This has obvious benefits for the employee, but can also bring great advantage to the organization – increasing their likelihood of business success, their ability to change and adapt to external factors, and greater creativity and innovation.

Measuring impact

The impact of developing a growth mindset in employees across your organization is difficult to assess. Much of the change sought happens at an individual level through changes in thought patterns, behaviours and responses of employees. Whilst this can contribute to career development, skills and knowledge acquisition and organizational growth, this can be somewhat indirect and not easy to quantify.

Appropriate measurement may therefore need to focus at individual level, and be reliant primarily on informal feedback, hearsay and storytelling. Consider:

- the uptake of training course places and requests for support for further education;
- utilization of online learning platforms;
- requests for coaching, performance feedback, promotion, etc;
- leader feedback about employees' attitudes towards learning, feedback, goal setting, setbacks, etc.

Overall you might consider team or organizational productivity, quality, efficiency, etc, as a measure of the impact. Positive trends may indicate some correlation between changing mindsets and improving business metrics, but this should be seen as suggestive or indicative unless a quantifiable connection can be made.

14 Mentoring

Introduction

Mentoring is defined as 'off-line help by one person to another in making significant transitions in knowledge, work or thinking' (Megginson and Clutterbuck, 2007). A mentor is usually someone at a more senior level to the employee to be mentored, with experience, knowledge and networks that they can share with their mentee. A mentor can take on several different roles in the course of a mentoring relationship, depending on the requirements of their mentee – from learning advisor (helping the employee to reflect on their experiences and draw out learnings) to counsellor (helping the employee to gain insight into their own processes, or to remove internal barriers to progression or work) or the critical ally, challenging assumptions and providing constructive and critical feedback on issues.

Promoting wellbeing

In the context of wellbeing, providing mentors for your team members can offer several advantages.

It provides the employee with a confidential sounding board, a safe space for exploring challenges, issues or causes of stress at work. The employee can share their frustrations with a view to getting advice, suggestions or coaching from a more experienced mentor, who may themselves have experienced similar issues, have ideas about how to overcome them, or be able to make connections to people or resources who may be able to help. This may offer not only an immediate next step towards finding a solution, but also a learning opportunity that provides avoidance or coping strategies for similar experiences in the future.

In addition, the mentor may be able to offer feedback to the employee about the stimulus for the situation, about its impact on the individual, their work or relationships, and about how they have handled it to date. This feedback provides more information for the employee's learning experience too, allowing them to reflect on different or better ways to handle situations.

Approach

Training mentors

You may want to invest in some formal training for your proposed mentors, or you may be able to run a short introductory session in house. As a priority you need to ensure that proposed mentors understand the process, the expectations and some of the core skills required to make mentoring effective (questioning, listening, feedback, objective setting, etc).

Training mentees

It can also be extremely useful to mirror this training with some for the mentees themselves, so that both parties are aligned as to the process and expectations of mentoring in your organization.

A nominated individual might be useful to coordinate a mentoring scheme, but this could be part of a training or HR co-ordinator's role.

Identifying mentors and mentees

Prepare a list of those employees who might make good mentors for other employees. Consider the strengths and experiences they have and how those could be utilized through mentoring.

Identify employees who may benefit from a mentor as they approach retirement. Consider what their learning or development needs are, and what personality type or preferences they might have.

Matching mentors to mentees

There are a number of ways to do this, which include top-down selection, based on your knowledge of both parties or, in larger organizations, you may consider a matching event that facilitates the meeting of numerous mentors and mentees, leading to self-selection between them (coordinated centrally to ensure a spread of workload).

Allow the mentoring relationship to begin, with the setting of some learning objectives as the starting point of the process. How the process works logistically (timing, location, duration, etc) should be left to the two parties to manage themselves.

Ending mentoring relationships

Ending the relationship is an important part of the process. Marking the close of the mentoring process will ensure that both parties can formally review the intended outcomes or objectives, and can consider from both sides the successes and lessons learnt from the experience. Simply allowing the process to drift may impact its credibility, and can leave participants feeling unfulfilled. Mark the ending and celebrate the successes.

Outcomes

Introducing mentors in the context of employee wellbeing is intended to provide support for employees who may be struggling with stress or other problems by offering mentoring as one element of a broader support package. The transfer of knowledge, skills and experience will help to develop the resilience of the employee, but also to provide a confidential environment to explore and discuss challenges and issues at work.

Organizationally, the introduction of mentors can bring about improved intra-department relationships and information-sharing, cross-functional collaboration, as well as improving the retention and productivity of key staff (as they feel valued and developed).

Mentors can get some good outcomes too. Many report that they feel re-energized through acting as a mentor for more junior team members, and feel value in imparting their knowledge and experience. Some feel that the learning is reciprocal – that as much as the mentee learns from the experience of the mentor, so the mentor can also learn about things from a different perspective, with mentees' knowledge drawn from different departments or functions, access to other projects or tasks, and with experiences from a diverse range of skills and from different generations.

Measuring impact

Inviting feedback from both the mentor and the mentee will provide some high-level feedback on how they felt about the process. For a deeper level of evaluation, consider whether the mentee (and maybe the mentor too) has found the relationship beneficial in resolving problems, dealing with stress, etc.

Recognition

Giving great feedback

Introduction

Done in the right way and with the right intentions, constructive and effective feedback is a key part of the route to improved performance. Employees need to know what they are doing well and what is not going so well. But to ensure it is constructive and effective, it must not only come from a place of good intention, but must also be delivered well, and provided often.

It's important to remember that offering positive feedback on successes and strengths is as important as providing constructive feedback on things that haven't gone so well, or on skills or behaviours that could be improved. To make it useful, positive feedback should be as carefully constructed as negative feedback.

Giving feedback effectively is an important leadership skill, and one that takes little effort but lots of practice. As a manager or colleague offering feedback to others, you need to learn few key practical steps, and build your confidence through experience.

Promoting wellbeing

Research carried out by US company OfficeVibe, an employee engagement specialist, states that 65 per cent of employees would like more feedback than they currently get (Shriar, 2016). They identified some interesting statistics in their research:

Employee turnover is up to 14.9 per cent lower in companies that implement regular employee feedback.

Employees are twice as likely to be actively disengaged if they are ignored by their manager.

4 out of 10 workers are actively disengaged when they get little or no feedback.

82 per cent of employees really appreciate receiving feedback, regardless if it's positive or negative

43 per cent of highly engaged employees receive feedback at least once a week compared to only 18 per cent of employees with low engagement.

65 per cent of employees say they wanted more feedback.

58 per cent of managers think they give enough feedback.

The ACAS guide to wellbeing and workplace performance (2017a) states that 'Being clear about what is expected of staff, including feedback on performance' is one of the key factors that influences wellbeing. In addition, they quote a sense of fairness, about how they and others are treated, and supportive supervision as key factors. The provision of effective and fair feedback to employees will therefore have a direct influence on employees' wellbeing at work.

As managers, we have a responsibility to offer feedback, and our employees want to receive it. But there is another wellbeing issue here, with so many managers not wanting to provide it. The fear of giving feedback can be stressful and raise anxiety levels. The fear factor often comes from the uncertainty of a recipient's reactions, the fear of having a difficult conversation. So as a manager, refresh the facts above – that 82 per cent of employees want to receive it. That 65 per cent of employees want more. The key to the success of your feedback delivery is in the preparation, and guidance on that follows.

Approach

Intent

Your intent to deliver some feedback, or your intent to proactively seek some out from others, really needs to come from a positive place – an encouragement or a desire to focus on improvement, development and opportunity. You won't achieve that by being harsh, critical, or offensive. You'll most often get much more from people when your approach is positive and focused on the opportunity for improvement.

Preparation

In deciding that you wish to offer feedback to someone, or responding to a request to do so, you should consider the recipient in your preparation. With positive intent firmly in your mind, consider the mindset of the individual, the timing, the quantity and quality of feedback you will offer, and your expectation of how they might be able to use it. In considering all of these things, you are more likely to provide useful content that can be actioned by the recipient.

Set aside time to consider and prepare your messages – don't just jump straight into it. It won't take too long, but your feedback will be more effective if it provides evidence, and connects to a specific and recent incident that you witnessed or experienced yourself. Constructing it into a few sentences to start a discussion therefore should not take a huge amount of time.

Timing

Timing is critical in giving feedback. You need to deliver it as close to the time of the occurrence as you can, so that it feels relevant to the recipient. Don't wait, save it all up or gather evidences or occurrences over a period of time. It will be much easier and quicker to feed back about a single occurrence than it is to feed back about a whole year of examples, and you risk the recipient feeling attacked and demoralized. However, if the situation is emotional, you may want to carefully consider your timing. If a meeting didn't go well, you may want to allow some time for self-reflection first, for example.

Location

Finding a quiet and private space to deliver effective feedback will be beneficial. Positive praise in front of a group of meeting attendees is great for those who like that approach, but not everyone does, so make sure you know your audience. Certainly, for more constructive feedback, and the opportunity to coach, a more private moment is most valuable. Take five minutes to share a coffee and provide your insights in a quieter area, where you have some privacy.

Opportunity

Focus your feedback on the actions or behaviours that the recipient can actually change or influence. Remember your positive intent, and provide constructive feedback about the good things, and the development opportunities that can be changed, and can make a difference, to both the individual and to their work.

Volume

A feedback session should discuss no more than two issues. Any more than that and your employee may become overwhelmed, and be unable to process or action anything further. You should also stick to behaviours the person can actually change or influence.

Evidence

Provide tangible fact-based examples or evidence of the action or behaviour that you are feeding back about. Avoid using vague statements or judgements. Ideally, your opening evidence will be so clearly factual that there can be no disagreement about it. If you tell someone they acted unprofessionally, what does that mean exactly? Were they too loud, too friendly, too casual, too flippant, too poorly dressed? Be as specific as you can about the action or behaviour to avoid any ambiguity or disagreement. Vague feedback will not help the recipient to know what to do differently.

Use 'I' statements. Give the feedback from your perspective, rather than second hand. Take clear ownership for the messages you are offering. Avoid 'you are' because it's probably going to lead you to deliver a judgement statement. Use phrases like 'I noticed...', 'I heard...', 'You said...'.

Describe the effect of their behaviour – how does it impact on you or other stakeholders (other managers, peers, customers, suppliers, colleagues etc).

Don't read a script but do be clear about you are going to say. This helps you stay on track and stick to the issues.

Listen and coach

Allow time for the message you have delivered to be absorbed, reflected on and processed. Give the recipient time to consider their response. Don't over-talk or try to fill a silence – say what you need to then pause. Keeping your factual evidence-based feedback clear and concise will avoid confusion. Allowing silence will allow it to land effectively.

Maintain good eye contact, use non-verbal signals such as nodding and attentive body language (leaning forward) to show you are listening, interested and have positive intent.

Use open questions (such as 'Tell me more about what happened', 'Describe what else you could do').

You may not agree on everything so it is a good idea to ask the person to provide their perspective.

Use phrases like 'What is your reaction to this?' or 'Is this a fair representation of what happened?'

If it's appropriate, coach the individual to consider the feedback, consider the impacts of their action or behaviour, and identify their own course of action. Where this is not forthcoming, offer some suggestions. The main message should be that you care and want to help the person grow and develop.

Follow up

Confirm the next steps – what will be different and what does the employee and/or you need to do to encourage it? Make sure you have the same understanding of the key points from your discussion and have agreed what should to be done to improve or optimize the performance or behaviour. Make and share notes with the recipient if necessary to ensure a common understanding.

Make it regular

Feedback is a process that requires constant attention. When something needs to be said, say it. People then know where they stand all the time and there are few surprises. Also, problems don't get out of hand. This is not a once-a-year or a once-every-three-month event. While this may be the timing of formal feedback, informal, simple feedback should be given much more often than this – perhaps every week or even every day, depending on the situation. With frequent, informal feedback like this, nothing said during formal feedback sessions should be unexpected, surprising or particularly difficult.

Be positive

Don't forget to provide feedback about the positive things you have seen or heard too. It lets the recipient identify with what success looks like, and feel recognized and valued. Together you can identify the individual's strengths, and how they can push this further, utilize it more or differently, etc.

Outcomes

The intention is to provide the recipient with some useful perspectives and perceptions on aspects of their behaviour or performance. For feedback to be 'good' and 'useful' it should be phrased in such a way that the recipient can do something with it, and as such the outcome of good feedback is that the recipient can start, stop, continue or enhance their behaviours or performance.

In addition, the opportunity to provide feedback may lead to an opportunity to provide coaching, and to further develop the recipient's capabilities.

Measuring impact

The purpose of providing feedback may be to encourage a continuation of positive performance or behaviours, optimize strengths, encourage a change in behaviours or performance, seek to minimize or transform weaknesses, or development points. How each of these is measured will depend on your business, your process and your access to the recipient on a longer-term basis.

Positive recognition feedback:

- Have you seen the strengths strengthened?
- Is positive behaviour or performance connected to the feedback you provided continuing or further developing?
- Is the recipient advocating and encouraging others to do the same?

Developmental feedback:

- Are development actions being addressed by the individual in response to your feedback? What is the overall trajectory of performance for this individual?

Self-reflection:

- How are your own skills developing? Seek feedback on the quality and usefulness of your feedback.

Receiving feedback

You might want to consider how you can help to prepare your employees to welcome feedback, and to embrace it as an opportunity rather than a critique. Here are some top tips you may want to share with them:

Be proactive

Ask for feedback from a variety of your stakeholders. We can't always see our own faults, but by carefully selecting the people who might provide useful and constructive feedback, we can take on board some positives, and some opportunities, and consider how we might optimize or improve. The goal is to keep getting better and better, so keep an open mind and take what people are willing to offer you. If it's all negative, be bold and ask about the good stuff too.

Take it on board – don't argue

If you get defensive then you aren't open to hearing what the other person is saying. Don't try to defend or justify your own performance or behaviour – instead recognize the positive intention, and focus on your opportunity for improvement. Don't rule anything out just because you might not agree with it – you could always ask for a second opinion.

Listen carefully

Make sure that you keep listening, don't start commenting on the feedback too soon, either in your own mind or out loud. Reflect back what you think you heard, check your own understanding of what's being said, and if you're in any doubt, ask for examples.

Don't obsess

Accept the feedback for what it is. Some of it you may agree with and some you may not. Take what you need from the comments and begin addressing what you can. There is no need to feel insulted or to go over and over the scene in your head, even when the message is not delivered expertly. Seize the opportunity to learn more about yourself and to improve.

Reflect

Take time to think about the feedback you've received and how you will use it. Make sure that you fully understand it, and the impact (positive or otherwise) of your actions or behaviours on others before you start trying to make changes or improvements. Don't rush it.

You can't control what feedback you get, or how it is delivered, but you can control how you respond and react to it. You may choose to embrace some, and to ignore some. That's your decision. But do recognize that you have the power to change and continue to enhance your own performance, and feedback is a great tool to help you do that.

Be proactive – stay open minded – listen well – reflect – act on it.

16   The check-in

Introduction

In recent years the traditional appraisal process has been under scrutiny, with managers and employees alike concerned that the process is paperwork-driven and does not meet its objectives of providing useful and constructive feedback and keeping employees on track with performance and development goals. As a result, many organizations have now removed or redesigned their performance management processes to implement simpler, more focused and more regular reviews. Many are referring to these regular discussions as 'check-ins'.

These check-in meetings provide the opportunity for frequent, shorter one-to-one discussions, with the aim of more closely meeting the goals of the performance review process.

Promoting wellbeing

In the previous tool, we quoted research that suggests that employees want more feedback than they receive, and we mentioned research that suggests that clarity of expectations is a factor in an employee's wellbeing.

However, a bad appraisal experience – whether it is bad because of the messages you receive or the way in which they are delivered – can have extremely negative effects on an employee. Negative feedback, badly delivered, can be a cause of workplace stress, with employees left unclear about what is required, and how they can achieve it, or develop towards improvement of career progression.

Approach

The introduction of a regular check-in process will not require a full redesign of your existing appraisal process. Instead it will simply require you as a people manager to hold more regular meetings.

The performance check-in is generally a forward-looking discussion. It is not intended as a performance evaluation, but instead is the opportunity for managers and employees to check progress, to recommend actions for continuous improvement, correction or development, and to ensure that expectations are clear and can be met.

Precursors

The check-in meeting itself may not be an appropriate process for setting objectives – this is likely to need a more thorough process, such as the 'making connections' session described in *50 Top Tools for Employee Engagement* Mitchell, 2017: 199), which encourages the cascade of strategy and goals in a short cross-functional team event, or a longer, more detailed individual planning session. The important part of that process is to make clear connections for the employee between their individual goals and tasks, and those of the team and the broader organization, so that they understand the purpose of their efforts, and the impact of their performance. The check-in then allows for focus on progress against those goals and tasks.

Frequency

The frequency of the check-in should be determined by the workflow of the role that you are reviewing. If the job has short timelines and frequent deliverables, it might be appropriate to check in on a weekly or monthly basis. If the role has longer timelines, and requires time to achieve deliverables, then less frequently – eg quarterly – may be appropriate.

You should also consider the needs of the individual you are reviewing. If the role has long timelines, but the individual needs more support, guidance and coaching, then a more regular review may be required, for example.

Ultimately, the recommendation is that managers are empowered (and enabled) to carry out check-ins as they see fit for the role, the goals and the individual that they manage, without strictly rules about frequency.

Preparation

With any performance, feedback or coaching session, preparation is important for success, on the part of both the employee and the manager. As a manager, you should ensure that you are familiar with:

- the tasks and objectives of the employee;
- the progress you are aware of to date, and examples;
- relevant behaviours, values and competencies;
- any challenges that have arisen or are anticipated;
- the outcomes and actions from the last review.

The employee should be aware of the same points from their perspective.

Encouraging some preparation will enable the discussion, but it should not be the case that the preparation time required makes this a cumbersome process. A short reflection and reminder should be sufficient. The focus should be on having a valuable two-way check-in conversation that is seen as beneficial to both parties.

Agenda

1 General review: It's useful to warm up the conversation with some general questions to find out how things are, what's the mood, etc.

2 Achievements: Ask the employee to talk about the main accomplishments since the last review – and you might also want to talk about what's been happening more broadly in the business in that time.

3 Behaviours and values: Keeping the behaviours, competencies, and values on the agenda reminds both managers and employees alike that the 'how' work that is done in your business is just as important as the 'what'. During the check-in, ask the employee to self-assess their performance against these behaviours, and provide some constructive feedback, focusing on the positives as well as any areas for improvement.

4 Focus areas for the coming 4–12 weeks: Agree with the employee their focus for the period between check-ins.

5 Opportunities: Have an open conversation about where there may be opportunities for improvement (of performance, but also of process, of collaboration, etc) and how those could be achieved.

6 Support needed: Check in with the employee that they have what they need to deliver the goals set, and offer your continued support. Consider any development that the individual may need or request.

7 Close: Summarize your discussion, confirm actions, agree next steps and confirm the date and time for the next check-in.

Follow up

As a manager, and to ensure credibility of the process, you should ensure that you follow up on the check-in discussion with actions you agreed to take or support that you committed to give.

Outcomes

The check-in is intended to provide the opportunity for manager and employee to focus on expectations and deliverables for the coming period. The outcomes should therefore be an aligned view of priorities and focus areas, as well as a clear view of the support required, and any potential challenges or opportunities that may arise.

In addition, by setting aside time for a regular conversation with employees, a manager is demonstrating that they are investing time, concerned to ensure their success and willing to support, guide and coach their team members.

Evaluating impact

As a manager, assess your own capabilities in facilitating the check-in process. Are you providing constructive feedback that is well received by the employee? Are you directing or coaching, and are you able to flex your style between these two approaches as needed? Do you have enough information to be able to effectively manage the check-in – about the employee, their job, their performance and behaviours – and about the broader organization?

You can also evaluate the effectiveness of the process from a manager perspective. Is the check-in allowing you greater visibility of the progress, actions and needs of your team members? Is the process ensuring that your team meet the targets and deliverables allocated to them?

From an employee perspective, you should consider whether the check-in is useful to them – ask them directly for feedback on how it helps or hinders them, and what they might prefer more of, or less of, in the check-in discussion, to make it beneficial.

Involvement

17 Involvement

Introduction

There are so many opportunities to involve employees at all levels in change, decision making, continuous improvement, product development, etc, but often leaders feel concerned about empowering their people in case ideas are impractical, costly or raise expectations. However, people are far more likely to buy into change that they are invested in – that they initiated or contributed to.

Employee involvement activities can be highly effective at engaging employees and at reassuring them that they have some influence – which in turn can reduce their anxiety or apprehension.

The key to their success is setting clear boundaries and expectations up front about the scope of their involvement, financial limitations, time commitments, etc. With those clearly defined at the start, there should be little reason not to empower or trust a group of employees to get involved in your ideas generation or change programmes.

Promoting wellbeing

MIND (www.mind.org.uk) say that when employees feel involved and well informed about what's happening in the organization it increases motivation and helps them to see how the work they do fits with the bigger picture. Mind encourages leaders to be as open as possible, to involve staff in decision making and listen to staff when changes need to happen.

When employees are involved in finding solutions they feel more ownership of decisions and morale is likely to be improved.

Approach

There are many ways that you can involve employees to improve engagement, but essentially employees want to connect to a sense of purpose, to feel heard and that their contributions are valued. And given their closeness to the process, products, systems and stakeholders, it's highly likely that they have value to add – so taking time to involve them could be beneficial to everyone – the business, the employees, the customers and the shareholders.

Some suggestions of how to involve employees include the following:

Staff surveys or feedback focus groups

Asking people for their input demonstrates that the organization values their input, and that they have something useful to say. Managing the process by which you seek those views is vital, because asking useful questions is important, but really listening and doing something with the views and ideas you receive is the key.

Staff forums

These give employees a voice, and taking action based on what you hear will give such initiatives the credibility they need to be interesting to participants, and to be successful.

Communication

As the Mind research shows, keeping people informed is a key factor in managing stress levels and the wellbeing of employees. So an open, frequent and two-way communication strategy is important. Regular communication sessions are essential and ensure that information is cascaded. However, all too often managers worry that information is not relevant, or that people don't want to hear bad news, etc, and so they don't communicate at all. In the absence of factual information, they are likely to develop their own stories, which can often be much more worrying than the facts. In keeping communication channels open, managers can share information widely, making it relevant for the specific audience at that moment. By keeping it a two-way process, even if you have no new information to pass on, you provide the opportunity for people to ask questions.

Customer meetings

Invite employees from your team to meet with and/or get to know your customers better, and as a result of having done so they can contribute to improvement initiatives to develop better products or services that meet customer needs.

Cross-functional working

Encourage and enable team members to get to know other departments that depend upon the work of their own department. In doing so, employees can build collaborative relationships and spot opportunities to work better or smarter for the benefit of their work and that of their colleagues.

Outcomes

Using any one, or a combination, of the approaches above, managers can ensure that employees have the opportunity to contribute, to be informed and to be heard. This can increase employees' ownership of problem solving and continuous improvement and can encourage them to feel more empowered by their managers. With a valued contribution to make, employees can become more engaged, and can feel that if problems arise, they have the power to address them for themselves.

Offering opportunities for involvement can increase an employee's feelings of self-worth, enhance self-esteem and develop their potential.

Measuring impact

Each of your involvement initiatives should be evaluated independently using criteria such as:

- How involved did participants feel as a result of the event? Did they enjoy it? What feedback do they have to offer about the facilitator, the activity, etc?

- What were the specific outcomes of each activity – were there changes, improvements, problems solved, or ideas that might enhance or add value to a product or service?

- What impact have those outcomes had on the overall business – ie cost savings, profit increases, or changes to other business metrics such as quality measures, customer feedback or overall employee engagement scores?

Engagement

Introduction

According to research by Gallup (Mann and Harter, 2016), just an estimated 13 per cent of employees worldwide are actively engaged in their work. It is clear, therefore, that a significant number have more to offer their employers, with the remaining 87 per cent either actively disengaged, intentionally disruptive, or quietly disengaged, going through the motions at work. However, it's not as simple as managing performance – as line managers, we need to actively engage employees in the purpose as well as the process of the work they do daily. Leaders can struggle with how to assess the level of engagement in their organization, and how to improve upon it, but doing so can have a significant impact on the bottom line of businesses – engaged employees are typically more productive, innovative and more likely to go that 'extra mile' for their manager. In addition, if they are engaged, they are more likely to stay in your employment, and so engagement also saves you money and time in recruiting and training replacements.

Engagement surveys can be valuable, but might also be costly, and unless you know how to use the results, they will only tell you where you are today, not where you could get to, and how to do it. The EPIC engagement tool, created by Gillian Jones-Williams and her colleagues at Emerge (www.emergeuk.com), provides the opportunity for an independent audit of your employee engagement level, and offers help and support for business leaders to help them to implement changes to improve that level.

Promoting wellbeing

Employees who do not feel a connection to the business, or a sense of purpose in connection to it, will typically become bored, detached and frustrated. This impacts their motivation, their level of commitment, and their loyalty. In turn, this has a clear effect on how productive they are, how often they are absent, or sees employees demonstrating presenteeism, whereby they are physically attending work, but mentally withdrawn. This lack of professional stimulation can be at best demotivating, but at worst can begin to have a bearing on mental health, causing anxiety or stress. Where a lack of engagement impacts work performance, these physical and mental reactions could be made worse, as managers seek to address performance issues, and provide some negative or constructive feedback.

Approach

The EPIC engagement tool aims to help organizations increase their profitability and productivity, whilst retaining their talent, by helping leaders and managers to fully engage their employees. It seeks to assess existing levels of engagement, identify what's working well to engage employees, but also to identify any causes of disengagement, and work with employees on opportunities for improvement.

The EPIC model identifies four key areas of focus for organizations seeking to improve their levels of engagement:

- Expectations: In this section, employees' and employers' expectations are aligned, ensuring that both parties know what has to be done, why it is being done and how it will be done. The model helps to connect the employee to the organizational culture and goals as well as clarifying roles and responsibilities and expected behaviours.

- Progress: Here, the model explores what managers need to do to help employees to perform in their role, and develop them to reach their potential. It reinforces the importance of feedback about performance and behaviour, ensures that employees are developed to the right levels of capability and competence, and that appropriate management styles are used to get the most from people.

- Inspiration: This element focuses on how managers can inspire their team members, so that they perform at their best every day, encouraging the sharing of a compelling and exciting vision, empowerment and trust, and creativity and innovation.

- Collaboration: In this final part, the model covers the benefits of promoting and encouraging collaboration and creating the right environment for working with others. It promotes networking, cross-functional collaboration and challenge, input and feedback from employees.

Fully utilizing the EPIC model is a three-stage process – understand, grow and sustain.

First, the process enables you to get a clear understanding of your organization's current engagement practice through a health check, set goals for employee engagement, and identify key talent from within your organization to help you to define, plan and implement your journey.

Next, line managers work with EPIC consultants to develop 'sprints' – short-term plans and activities – to achieve progress towards those goals.

Finally, as the impacts of your improvement plans begin to take effect, the EPIC model encourages the use of business metrics to review and recognize increased performance at both individual and a collective level.

Outcomes

In their major report on employee engagement commissioned by the UK Government, MacLeod and Clarke (2009) were able to report on several important research studies that provided evidence of the positive impacts of employee engagement for business success. They reported that increasing employee engagement correlates with improving performance, and quoted research by Gallup, Towers Perrin and from within organizations themselves that suggest that higher levels of employee engagement can result in fewer accidents, higher customer advocacy, greater productivity and increased profitability, as well as more creativity and innovation than is typically seen in those with lower engagement scores. In addition, they report positive impacts of engagement on measures such as sickness absence, employee turnover, company pride, and Leary-Joyce (2004) adds that positive engagement and a great company culture will also lend themselves to easier recruitment and better retention.

Measuring impact

The impact of using the EPIC engagement tool will be apparent through its own metrics. Measuring and assessing pre- and post-EPIC levels of engagement will indicate the changes that have been experienced in the organization.

In addition, there may be other metrics that can be used to assess the impact of the EPIC process, including bottom line business metrics (eg profitability, sales, customer service metrics), people measures (eg absence, turnover) and anecdotal or qualitative measures of change (ie what stories are people telling, what are you hearing?).

19 Change

Introduction

As the Greek philosopher Heraclitus said, 'everything flows and nothing stays' – often translated into modern use as 'change is the only constant'. In today's business environment, change is a regular if not continuous occurrence, with the economy, technology and globalization, and indeed the nature of employment with the rise of the 'gig' economy, all having a significant impact on how we do business. This in turn impacts how employees are organized – whether that be how many workers are needed, what they do, where they do it, or simply just the quality of their work, the technology they use, or who they interact with.

Organizational change can lead to employees experiencing downsizing, upsizing, rightsizing, restructures, process change, new technology, new service or product streams, changing legislation, different work patterns. Indirectly employees may also be affected by any of those things happening in not only their own business, but also in the business of stakeholders, suppliers or customers.

The impacts of change on how we all work can be many and varied. Ultimately, it's important to recognize that much of the major change that happens to us at work is not in our direct control, that it is initiated, led and implemented at senior levels in organizations. Other change initiatives may be more locally driven, but in the main, unless we are leading the business, change is not in our control. We may be consulted, we may have an influence, but employees will not usually be able to determine the nature of a business or organizational change.

However, everyone is in control of their reactions to the change. An employee can choose how to react, and will take actions according to their own situation. As managers of people, we can encourage them to make some conscious choices about those reactions, to recognize them and learn about them, to make the change as positive an experience as it can be.

Promoting wellbeing

Whilst in some cases people may feel excited and enthusiastic about change, others may feel anxious and concerned, and this reaction can lead to a greater level of resistance. This might be dependent on the individual, their personality type and preferences, or it could be about the type of change that they are experiencing, or other factors that are going on in their lives at the time of the change. It is much too simple to categorise people as resisters or enablers of change.

Our very human nature encourages us to detect changes in our environment, and to react to them. This decision to fight or take flight will take into account our readiness to adapt, and if we are unprepared, or unwilling, for the change, it may invoke a 'stress reaction' – one that is both physical, releasing adrenaline and raising the heart rate, and emotional, causing feelings of anxiety, anger, etc.

In order to reduce these stress responses in our employees, we need to consider how we can best prepare them for the continuous change (maybe different in intensity or duration) that we are likely to experience at work.

Approach

Anyone who has experienced a significant change in their workplace over the last few years, particularly but not exclusively those mentioned above, will know how stressful, challenging or exciting it can be. In order to effectively lead people through change, or to advocate change to peers and colleagues, it's important to understand your own responses and reactions to change, and to get an understanding of other people's anticipated reactions to it.

If you are excited and energized by change, that can be a great strength. However, you must take care to ensure that, when managing others, you are empathetic to their own individual reactions to change. Appreciate that not everyone will embrace it as you do. Take time to understand the reactions of others and to ensure they have the support, guidance, information and skills to get through it and to be able to make a valuable contribution to it.

The risk is that your excitement and enthusiasm masks the concerns in your team. You may not have everyone on board, some may not be able to fully contribute if they don't fully understand the rationale. You will need to ensure that your pace is steady enough that your change enthusiasts stay engaged and your more hesitant team members are supported along the way.

The same points apply if you are naturally more resistant to, or sceptical of, change. You may feel more hesitant, have a preference to get as much information as possible or want to focus on detailed plans before moving forward. Your team members who welcome the change may appear to you to be too fast to adopt change, and may be running before they are ready to walk. However, if you try to slow them down, they may get frustrated or lose energy and enthusiasm for the task.

Finding the right balance is important, but to do so you need to be very aware of your own reactions to change, to acknowledge them and the strengths or limitations they may bring, and seek to be adaptable in your leadership style when taking others through change at work.

Supporting others through change

Bridges' Transition Model (Bridges, 1991) represents this well, essentially describing change as the need to let go of the known, and reach out for a new, but unknown, state, having faith or optimism that it will be safe or comfortable when we get there.

Not everyone will experience this space between the known and unknown as a stressful experience. Some may welcome the opportunity, relish the challenge and be excited by not knowing what is around the corner. Others will find it more challenging, and as leaders, managers and HR specialists – also as colleagues and peers – it's important that we are able to proactively seek to minimize the depth and/or duration of that uncertainty, and to recognize the signs of stress or distress in others and take some action.

If leaders fail to take care of such issues, they are not only letting down those who might rely on us as managers or guides, but we are also limiting both our organizational opportunity, and that of the individual, to really contribute. Those struggling to understand or adapt may be perceived as resistant, and managed accordingly. By taking time to address peoples' concerns, we might not only help to reduce their stress level, and improve their wellbeing, but we might also enable them to contribute to their fullest potential.

William Bridges' book *Managing Transitions* (1991) provides really useful information about what happens at each stage of the change journey – the letting go, the uncertainty, and then in finding new ground, and how leaders can provide support at each stage. The following suggestions include those drawn from or inspired by his text, and others that have been experienced or developed through practical experience.

State the case for change

Be clear with all impacted employees about the rationale for changing or moving away from the status quo. Typically, when you announce an intention to change, employees will appreciate you sharing with them the why, the what and the how of the change. All too often, we just focus on the what.

In describing why change is being initiated, tell people what was wrong or insufficient about the way things were or are, or about the opportunity you are looking to exploit. Tell employees as much as you can about the business rationale for the change, the benefits or improvements that are anticipated, and the positive impacts it will have on a range of stakeholders.

It's also useful to outline how the change will transpire – who will manage it, who will be involved in delivering it, and at what stage each stakeholder group will start to see the change happening. Understanding the high-level action plan will help to impress upon your teams how the change will be put in motion, and should describe what the immediate next steps might be.

Involve people in reinvention

Taking into account the feedback, opinions, views, suggestions, ideas, or concerns of employees in the design and development of the new future will help to secure their engagement in the process of change, and is likely to make them more inclined to make it a success. Involve them in focus groups and question-and-answer sessions with leaders and encourage them to provide written but informal feedback to help to get their views aired.

Keep collective communication channels open, and two-way

Ensure that you are regularly communicating with employees collectively, and their representatives if appropriate, throughout the change process – from the early stages of identifying a need, to the closing stages of implementation and measurement. Communication should be two-way, affording employees at all levels the opportunity to discuss and contribute to the change plans and process.

Make time for one-to-one discussions

People will react to change in different ways. You should make time for each of your direct reports so that you can get a sense of, and support, their reactions. This will enable you to identify 'champions', as well as resisters, and everything in-between, and provide the information, reassurance or feedback that you need to give.

When employees are finding change difficult, these one-to-ones will be critical to allow you to reiterate the reasons for the change, what the future looks like – for that individual as well as for the broader team or organization – and what the employee, you, the team, need to do to make it happen. It provides you the opportunity to recognize the individual where they are making efforts to support the change and to adapt, and to coach to encourage them to work through barriers and blockers.

Recognize the strengths and the legacy of the past

For some people who are strongly attached to the way things were, or who struggle to recognize the value in the future plans or approach, it will be important to recognize – not criticize – the past. Be sure that your communications plans are not overly critical, and acknowledge the rationale for the way things worked, and comment on the strengths and benefits that those ways of working have had for the organization and employees.

Be an advocate for the change, and lead your people well

As a leader, your commitment to the change will be an important signal to the people who work for you and around you. You should act as a strong advocate, able to support the key messages for the change, manage resistance proactively, and demonstrate strong leadership during the transition phase. Leaders should take time to ensure that they fully understand the change, its impact and implications, the rationale, and the benefits to be derived.

Continue to paint a picture of the future

Throughout the transition, managers and leaders can support employees by continually reminding them about the picture of the future, about what the organization is collectively striving to achieve and why it matters. It's not enough to describe that at the outset of the change, it needs to be reinforced throughout a change programme. Take all opportunities to remind employees about the vision for change, and to report on progress towards the goal – for example, you could begin every briefing presentation with a reminder slide before providing the update.

Involve people in implementation

Involving people in the process of change is likely to lower their resistance as well as their stress levels. By staying involved, they have opportunity to influence, they can appreciate transparency, see progress for themselves, and recognize the impacts on themselves and those close to them.

Involving them in the implementation or roll-out phase can take various forms such as:

- inviting them to support your communication activities as the change is shared with stakeholders and colleagues;
- involvement in testing new ways of working, or new systems;

- training others;
- involvement in determining new measures and metrics for new ways of working, etc.

Celebrate success and recognise contribution

As the change programme draws to a close, with successful implementation and evaluation of the change, leaders should take the opportunity to celebrate its success, and to recognise the contributions of all involved.

Outcomes

Proactively managing a business change can help to ensure that employees will feel supported and engaged throughout the process, and know where they can turn to for further support if needed.

People are more likely to feel prepared for change if they feel that their leaders and managers have been proactively supportive, open and transparent in communication, and recognise the various reactions to change that may be experienced within their own teams.

Employees may better understand why and how they react to change triggers and feel more informed about – and in control of their own reactions. Self-awareness – recognizing your own reactions – can really help individuals to self-manage the stress that change can create and adjust their behaviours and reactions.

Measuring impact

Consider the overall implementation of the change, the degree of commitment from employees, and the time taken to move from transition to realizing benefits.

You may be able to connect the role played by change champions and advocates to the depth of buy in and the speed execution of new ways of working.

Physical and mental

03

Physical

20 Return to work interview

Introduction

The return to work interview is a formalized approach to a one-to-one discussion between a line manager and an employee on the employee's return from a period of absence. The return to work interview is a well-established protocol in many absence or attendance policies, but one that is often paid only cursory attention, and where the real goals and full benefits are not considered.

Promoting wellbeing

The return to work interview can play several key parts of the process to enhancing an employee's wellbeing, and can also contribute to that of the employee's wider team:

- Demonstrates you care: The simple act of having the conversation with the returning employee, and enquiring positively about their health and their needs, will suggest that as a line manager you are concerned about the health and wellbeing of your team members

- Suggests that you noticed they were missing: By discussing the impact of their absence, and explaining how and why they were missed, and by whom, you are reinforcing that they play an important role in the organization, team or in context of the output, and that absence does not go unnoticed.

- Helps you as manager to understand the issues facing the employee: Whether they are health issues, personal or maybe capability challenges, you can seek to understand them, and proactively try to manage and minimize them.

- Provides evidence: If absence persists and you need to take more formal action to address it, you may need evidence of your attempts to provide feedback, to describe impacts, and to manage the absence. Notes of each return to work interview can form the basis of that evidence that you might need later in the process

- Demonstrates to others that you are paying attention: It demonstrates good leadership – both to address this individual's absence and to minimize the risk of others' inappropriate absence.

Approach

Policy

The return to work interview must form a key part of your attendance or absence policy. It should provide guidelines for the discussion and templates or paperwork that enable managers to confirm and record conversations with the employee, for their own records, for the employee and for the company record (personnel file).

Practice

Provide training and guidance for line managers on how to have those discussions. They need to be enabled through both the interpersonal skills to hold the discussion and a broad view of the legal context of such a discussion with particular focus on disability discrimination aspects.

Encourage managers to lead discussions from a positive intent of support rather than a punitive or disciplinary approach. This requires the manager to adopt a mindset that shows concern for the employee, offers support and encourages a return to work, rather than jumping straight to escalation or a warnings procedure.

This should be a key part of any line manager's role. It demonstrates an interest in their team members, but also if you take a harder line, it is about effective management of resources.

Non-attendance will have an impact on productivity efficiency and output, as well as the motivational impact on the rest of the team who may have to cover, work harder or longer to make up the shortfall.

In the short term, the return to work interview should require no more than around 30 minutes of manager and employee time. This should be sufficient to encourage open and honest discussion about the reasons for absence, its impact and any support needed, but of course it will depend on the often-unknown details of that discussion that may be introduced by the employee.

In the longer term, the ongoing commitment to addressing issues of poor performance can require a greater investment of management time. If issues remain unresolved, a continued commitment to the return to work interview and other absence management processes may begin to eat into the manager's time and cause stress and uncertainty for both parties.

Early intervention and taking proactive and decisive action to address absence causes as well as symptoms will minimize the ongoing time investment needed.

Outcomes

The return to work interview aims to quickly review the causes and symptoms of absence with a view to reducing the likelihood of recurrence. More than that, however, the intent is to ensure the continued wellbeing of the employee, whether at work or not. This may mean respecting the need for absence or recovery time where that is recommended by a medical specialist, but keeping in close, supportive contact. Alternatively it could mean maintaining or improving mental wellbeing by facilitating a practical return to work.

Measuring impact

Consider what actions have been taken as a result of the return to work interview – for example, a return to work on reduced hours, medical referrals, light duties, training whilst away from the workplace using e-learning, TED Talks or other self-learning materials. What impact have they had on attendance?

Per employee, how many absence instances have there been in any given period of time – what's the trend (increase or decrease)?

Across the team or function, how many absence instances have there been in any given period – what is the trend (increase or decrease)?

Is the ratio of absence instances to return to work interviews 1 to 1? Is there an interview for every absence?

Managing employee illness

Introduction

In the UK, where sickness absence is typically paid for a limited time period, absence rates in 2016 averaged at around four days per employee, according to statistics from the Office for National Statistics (ONS, 2016). It is worth noting that this is the lowest recorded average in recent years. In the USA there is currently no legal requirement for employers to pay their employees for sick leave (though this may vary by state), but there is provision for an unpaid period of absence of up to 12 weeks if employees meet certain criteria, but it is difficult to gather data on absence statistics where there is no payment, and limited absence tracking. There is an assumption that as absence is unpaid, the incidence is lower.

Many organizations utilize their absence management policy in a way that enables them to manage employees with short-term repeat absence, genuine or otherwise. This can mean that when a situation of genuine longer-term serious illness arises, their policy falls short of the actions that they might want to take to support an employee and encourage them to return to work in a timely but rehabilitative manner. By supporting employees appropriately in such situations, organizations, managers and employees can ensure that the right adjustments are made and that the situation is regularly reviewed from all sides.

Promoting wellbeing

In addition to the symptoms and limitations caused by the diagnosed condition itself, employees who are absent due to ill health for a prolonged period can become anxious and stressed about their job security and financial concerns, which in some circumstances may exacerbate their condition. By seeking to proactively manage the absence, and the associated issues, managers can proactively communicate and manage those concerns, and be supportive of employee needs as well as those of the business.

Approach

A legal perspective

Some conditions may also be afforded protection if they meet the definition of disability under the UK Equality Act 2010 – ie that they have a physical or mental impairment that has a substantial and long-term negative effect on their ability to do normal daily activities. Cancer, HIV and multiple sclerosis are automatically considered to meet this definition. Employees diagnosed with these conditions are afforded certain protections and can have certain expectations about how they are managed and treated by their employer and colleagues. You may also be required to make reasonable adjustments to the work, hours or environment.

Specialist employment law and/or medical advice should be sought in such situations, to clarify whether a condition meets the definition (or automatically qualifies) so that all parties are clear on responsibilities and rights.

Acknowledging illness

When an employee reports their absence and diagnosis to you as their line manager, an immediate acknowledgement, and some next steps, can be really useful for both parties. A short email letter or call to confirm that you have received the information, and what you intend to do in support of their absence will set the expectations for both sides. Your acknowledgement might include:

- thanking them for the notification and acknowledgement of any medical information provided;

- confirming that you will seek advice on how to best support the employee through this period of absence (eg from occupational health specialists, from charity organizations, etc);

- a positive intent to maintain contact by sharing company/department needs and information (see 'Keeping in touch', below);

- a positive intent to regularly review the situation together with any important advisors or parties (see 'Case reviews', below).

Case reviews

The case review should be an inclusive and transparent process, allowing all relevant parties to update on progress, table any questions and agree any next steps. It is important to emphasize that the case review is not part of a formal absence management or disciplinary process, and is not a return to work interview, but rather an approach to regularly monitor and evaluate the absence situation.

The case review could be carried out in the workplace, at the employee's home (with permission) or, if it's more appropriate, at a neutral venue.

Typical attendees could include:

- the line manager;
- the employee;

- a representative or accompanying person for the employee (in some circumstances it may be appropriate to waive the usual rules about who can act as a representative, and extend to include a family member or a friend);
- an HR specialist;
- occupational health advisor or any relevant medical advisors who can or should attend.

Typical points for conversation during the case review could be:

- status of the condition and changes since the last review, any treatments completed and outcomes, or treatments planned, update on prognosis;
- latest estimate of period of absence or return to work;
- support requirements from employer;
- what the employer needs from the employee or medical advisors;
- any opportunities to undertake light duties, or carry out limited duties from home;
- any reasonable adjustments that could be made to enable a return to work;
- update on pay and benefits during absence;
- an update on any useful 'keep in touch' information;
- actions or next steps that can be taken by either party;
- a manager should take the opportunity to remind the employee that they are missed at work, but empathetically, not in accusatory way.

Sometimes it can be beneficial for the employee to visit their team/department during the case review.

After the meeting, a record of the key points of the discussion should be held by both the employer and employee.

Keep in touch

Agree your approach to keep in touch – it is better that the employee knows what to expect from you during their absence, and what their own responsibilities are with regards to the maintaining contact. Managing expectations means that the employee is more likely to have a positive reaction to your keep in touch plans, rather than feeling concerned that you are not allowing them space that they need.

Note down any key trigger points – it might be useful to diarize them – to keep in touch with your employee (eg after important company meetings, team events, announcements, etc). Alternatively, they may be driven by the employee's issues (eg after an important appointment or at the end of treatment).

Ensure that you make regular contact, respond to the triggers identified, and remain inclusive in your communications approach. Email minutes of important meetings and, if it is appropriate, continue to invite your absent employee to major events and social activities. They can of course choose whether to attend, but the simple act of extending the invitation is likely to foster engagement.

Specialist support

At an appropriate time in the process, you may need to consider bringing specialist support into the case review to:

- assess and prepare the environment and the team for the individual's return to work;
- offer advice and guidance on pension implications, state benefits and allowances etc;
- help with other specialist matters that may arise in the course of your case reviews.

External support for specific conditions

In addition to that specialist support, there are a number of charities that can support the management of an employee suffering from an illness or condition. It is highly likely that the employee will have access to such resources, but it could be extremely beneficial for the employer to access such materials, resources and specialists directly. An internet search will quickly present results about support for employers dealing with employees with specific conditions, but some of the high-profile organizations are as follows:

- Cancer: Among other charities, Macmillan (www.macmillan.org.uk) can offer support to employers who are supporting an employee through cancer treatment, including a wide range of resources (information leaflets, sources of help, posters, etc) and clearly documented information for both employers and employees about the impacts cancer can have, employees' and employers' legal rights, how to best help, etc.
- Multiple sclerosis: The MS Society (www.mssociety.org.uk) offers guidance about education, your relationship with an employee with MS and reasonable adjustments that may need to be made.
- HIV: Among other charities, the Terrence Higgins Trust (www.tht.org.uk) provides information for employers about employees with HIV, as does

HIV Sport (www.hivsport.org), whose toolkit for employers is available on their website.

• Mental health: MIND (www.mind.org.uk) have extensive resources for employer on their website, including training and consultancy and webinars.

Outcomes

By proactively approaching significant illness using some of these practices, you can begin to work collaboratively with your employee, building a plan to support them through recovery to their return to work. In cases where this may not be possible, you can work together to ensure a mutual understanding of the issues, and the consequences of that. The key benefit of such approaches is that it is collaborative and transparent, and at no stage should the employee have any surprises about their security or financial implications. This should go some way to alleviating some of the stresses that might come about because of their illness.

From an organization's perspective, as a leader you are able to offer support and keep informed about the situation, allowing you to plan accordingly.

Measuring impact

The impact of this approach is not about business measures, but more a consideration of how an employee felt that they were treated and supported during their absence or illness. This requires some anecdotal or qualitative feedback to be sought, but in reality, as an organization and as a leader, if you feel that you have offered the best support you could to an employee during a difficult time, maybe that is benefit enough.

22 The fruit box

Introduction

Most businesses have access to snacks and drinks through the provision of vending machines, local kitchens and sometimes the addition of a local food truck or café. However, it can be difficult for employees to make healthy food choices with those options, and bringing in their own healthy foods are sometimes the only way to ensure that healthy foods are available.

Promoting wellbeing

According to an NHS report detailed in the *Telegraph* in 2017, only 1 in 4 of us are eating our recommended 5 a day of fruits and vegetables (Bodkin, 2017), and this is particularly an issue among younger workers (16–24 years old). Worryingly, some research has suggested that the five-a-day recommendation falls a long way short of the intake we really need – and suggests that we should be aiming for closer to 10 a day (Telegraph, 2017).

In addition to this recommendation, and perhaps connected, the NHS suggests that obesity affects about one in every four adults (NHS Choices, 2017b), and similar rates are experienced in the USA, with statistics varying by state, but ranging between 22 per cent and 35 per cent (State of Obesity, 2017).

The benefits of maintaining a healthy diet and making good food choices are well known – they can reduce the risk of cancer, diabetes and heart disease – and these alone should be good reasons to take care about what our employees eat. According to an article in *Harvard Business Review* in 2014, 'Food has a direct impact on our cognitive performance, which is why a poor decision at lunch can derail an entire afternoon' (Friedman, 2014). Healthier food choices can help to maintain personal energy, attention span and motivation, and can encourage people to feel happier.

Approach

Providing fruit

A study carried out in Australia by Pescud et al (2016) researched whether the provision of fruit would encourage healthier eating, and whether employees would be willing to pay for the provision of fruit in the workplace. The study found that where fruit was provided without charge, or with a token contribution towards the cost, employees were more likely to consume it.

According to one supplier, in the UK, fruit could be provided from as little as £0.29 per employee, depending on the type of fruit and the volume purchased, making it an affordable option for many employers (pricing information provided by www.jonesdairies.co.uk).

Providing fruit for free may encourage more consumption, but you might also find that a nominal contribution to support a subsidy from the business itself will help to manage the cost.

If, however, these costs are still too high for your business, then you could instead implement a 'free fruit Friday', or choose to occasionally have a health promotion campaign with fruit as a centrepiece, or celebrate days such as National Banana Day etc – although the stories told are usually of fruit being eaten really quickly, which is testament to the success of the initiative.

Competing options

In implementing a regular fruit box plan, you should also consider the availability of competing food choices that might detract from healthy eating options. Whilst it may be a step too far for some employees to remove them completely, you may want to consider making the choice clear and transparent for people (ie available in the same office area) and support the fruit choices with some healthy eating information and education.

Enablers

The study by Pescud et al (2016) also carried out some qualitative research, which concluded that key success factors in implementing fruit boxes were management support, that the organization was willing to try it out, and that there were sufficient resources (ie funding, and admin support) to make it effective. This suggests that prior to considering such an implementation, managers need to feel confident that they have those enablers in place, ie:

- that managers themselves are willing and able to support the use of fruit boxes, and will set the example to their teams by making use of them;

- that the organization's culture is receptive – running a short pilot, or working with representatives to establish the appetite would be a good step to assessing this enabler;

- that there is a sustainable budget to fund the fruit box initiative on an ongoing basis, rather than as a short-term initiative that may just fade away. In addition, responsibility will have to be allocated for purchasing, distributing and managing fruit boxes, and this resource needs to be identified and briefed in advance.

Alternatives

You might also want to consider other healthy snacking options, such as nuts, dried fruits or protein bars.

Allergy

Be sure to include allergy warnings on any foods that you are providing for your employees.

Outcomes

Providing fruit boxes is intended to encourage employees to make healthy food choices. Whilst you cannot enforce your preferences, the provision of boxes makes it easy for employees to consider options, and you may introduce them to new habits.

As mentioned above, the consumption of fruit can have some short-term as well as long-term health benefits, so employees might report themselves as being more alert, and you may see an increase in energy.

Employee feedback will be an important impact for your business. Providing fruit boxes may encourage a positive perception from your workforce, showing that you care about their wellbeing and are willing to invest in it.

Measuring impact

There are a few evaluation factors that should be taken into account to assess how effective the introduction of fruit boxes has been:

- Reception and consumption: It will be useful to identify how well received fruit boxes have been in the workplace. You can do this qualitatively, seeking verbal feedback and comment, as well as quantitatively by assessing how much fruit is consumed, and what the typical wastage is.

- Cost/benefit analysis: As a business decision, you should assess the costs and benefits of investing in fruit boxes. You will be able to identify the typical cost of a fruit box, and the frequency with which you intend to purchase them – and could therefore find a cost per employee. Understanding the financial benefits may be more difficult, as they could be indirect, but you should use anecdotal feedback as well as any of the organizational measures (below) to balance against the costs. In addition, you should consider whether the introduction of fruit boxes has had any bearing on other catering facilities, particularly vending machines or canteen services.

● Overall organizational measures: This will be difficult to measure, but you may see some reductions in the rates of employee absence, employee turnover, and increases in motivation, energy and innovation at work. Whilst it will be difficult to attribute these directly to the introduction of fruit at work, there may be some correlation, and informal feedback could help to validate any assumptions.

23 Exercise at work

Introduction

Whilst access to a huge range of health and fitness activities is now widely available in the UK, with everything from Pilates to military-style boot camps, many organizations are now offering fitness classes in the workplace. Usually scheduled to take place outside of normal working hours, programmes such as Pilates, yoga, aerobics or walking and running groups can be relatively easy to organize, and can gain great interest from employees.

Promoting wellbeing

In a 2005 study of employees at three workplace locations, employees reported that 6 out of 10 workers stated that on days when they exercised, regardless of the type of activity carried out, they recognized improvements in their own time management, mental performance and ability to meet deadlines, quoting a 'performance boost' of about 15 per cent, and generally felt more satisfied with their day (McKenna and Coulson 2005).

The UK National Health Service website reports on how small amounts of exercise can improve or maintain a state of mental wellbeing, suggesting that physical activity can help people to combat mild depression and can protect against anxiety (NHS Choices, 2017a). Their recommendation on getting active is that adults should aim to do 'at least 150 minutes of moderate-intensity aerobic activity – such as fast walking or cycling – a week'.

Of course, as an employer, you are not ultimately responsible for ensuring that your employees are meeting this recommendation, but you can encourage and advocate it, and by establishing such classes or groups in the workplace, you will be seen to be enabling it. This shows an interest not only in your employees' physical health, but also in their mental wellbeing.

Approach

Find a champion

Initially, you will need to identify someone to act as the champion for this initiative – not a standalone role, but as a volunteer, or someone who can include this activity as part of a broader remit. The champion's role will change over time, but in setting up classes and groups, will take ownership and responsibility for assessing needs and preferences, promoting and advocating, coordinating delivery, accessing resources and early evaluation of initiatives.

Establish the appetite

Simply asking questions of your workforce about what they might be interested in, what times of day, and (if necessary) what they might be willing to pay, will give you a good steer into the programmes or groups you might want to set up. A short survey, or a request for ideas via email or through managers, will give you information to get started.

Be willing to try things out and see if they are well attended, and if not, don't be afraid to scrap them and start something new. In addition, try out new things. Once you have a programme up and running, invite trainers or instructors to offer taster sessions so that your employees can try out new things – and if successful, those trainers will be keen to return for paid classes.

Find trainers and instructors

There are a huge number of fitness trainers and instructors easily found online. However, there are a few factors you need to consider when hiring a fitness instructor – as a starting point they should have:

- an up-to-date first aid certificate;
- Disclosure and Barring Service (DBS) clearance (in the UK);
- public indemnity and professional liability insurance;
- self-employed status (unless you intend to employ them).

You should also check the qualifications and certifications related to the programme or discipline they will teach, and look for professional association memberships, etc. Always take references, and if anyone is able to make recommendations for instructors, that's a great place to start.

Be transparent about the business opportunity for your instructors. If employees are paying to attend, their income will always be dependent on the popularity of the activity. If the organization is paying, that may be dependent on attendance, or a specific time period for the programme to run. Agree the approach upfront with your instructor so that expectations on both sides are clear.

Communicate and advocate your programme

Once you have established the activities, the frequency and the instructor, you can begin to promote your programme. Use testimonials of those who attend to encourage others to participate, and where feasible, offer incentives to attend (free water, a gym bag with your company logo on it, etc).

Keep people informed about changes to events, activities, groups, achievements, etc, and encourage participants to be advocates and champions around the workplace.

Consider resources

Before committing to any activity, you should consider the resources you may need to implement and maintain these classes and groups. Whilst some can be implemented at little cost (such as an organized running group) others may require investment (from a class instructor through to facilities).

As a business, you have the choice whether to fund this yourself as a benefit for your employees, subsidize it to reduce costs for participants and yourself, or charge employees a fee that allows you to cover the basic cost of the service provision, so that to you it is cost neutral.

Participants will expect changing and shower facilities on site if they are to participate in classes during working hours – this will need to be factored in to your plans.

Whilst facilities may be required, it is unlikely that the expectation will be the provision of state of the art gym or studio facilities. You will need to provide sufficient space and any equipment that the instructor won't provide (eg mats, music systems).

You may need to consider whether your offices need to be open later than you would normally expect for classes to take place, and whether security staff, cleaners or facilities teams need to provide any additional cover or services to accommodate the classes.

You should check whether you need any additional insurance to cover any risks during the classes.

If you don't have the space, consider instead whether you could subsidize membership of a local gym or fitness class for employees who want to participate.

National initiatives

As a business, get behind national initiatives that are launched to promote active lifestyles. You can simply promote programmes such as Park Run, encouraging all abilities to participate in a community spirited, free and local five kilometre run, or the This Girl Can programme, a National Lottery and Sport England funded initiative that aims to inspire women to take up sports. There is access to such a wide variety of sports classes and clubs nationally. AgeUK can provide information that is beneficial for your older or less active workers, and English Federation of Disability Sport (EFDS) offers advice, support and connections to organizations and individuals to encourage those with a disability to remain active for life.

Connecting into such national initiatives (and there are many more than have been mentioned here – the internet will guide you to a wide variety of initiatives, organizations and programmes) will provide you with additional resources, networks and ideas for your fitness classes and groups.

'Disabled people make up a large population in all our communities, so it is important for all providers to understand, involve and engage disabled people. Our insight highlights some of the ways providers can enable disabled people to access sport and active recreation wherever and at whatever level. We would actively encourage providers to visit our website to access our research, resources and training.'

Andy Dalby-Welsh, EFDS Deputy Chief Executive

Outcomes

The advantages to the employee are clear – it's convenient, it's flexible (in that it won't require membership commitments) and it can bridge the gap between work and home, allowing employees to 'wind down' from a day of working before they get back home to social activities and/or family.

There are benefits to the organization too. There are the simple advantages of being seen to promote good heath, and employee fitness and wellbeing, all aspects that, as well as being advantageous to your current employees, will be attractive to future potential candidates, and therefore add to your positive employer brand.

Including fitness activities as part of the overall benefits package can be attractive to many, and for those who use it often can be a very cost-effective way to maintain fitness.

It must also be assumed that increasing the health and fitness of employees will have a positive impact on their presence at work – not just in attendance but also in energy and focus.

An additional benefit may come from the fact that employees socialize together. They may attend fitness classes or activities with people they would not normally connect with in your business, and as such it could be the case that new cross-team and cross-functional relationships are formed, leading to greater collaboration and improved communication.

Measuring impact

You should start your assessment of the impact with some basic 'happy sheet' measures of evaluation. For example, how many people are attending the class, or how many book versus how many actually turn up? Ask participants about their enjoyment of classes, get feedback on trainers/coaches that you are using and ask what else they might like to attend.

Further levels of evaluation could consider the impacts on employee morale – assessed through an opinion survey, for example, and/or on absence statistics.

You might also consider the impact on teamwork and collaboration. As people may be attending classes with those they don't normally work with, this may have a knock-on effect in their daily work.

Workplace massage

Introduction

Massage is a term used to describe the rubbing, kneading and manipulating of skin, muscles, tendons and ligaments. The massage aims to relieve pressure or pain, encourage better circulation and foster relaxation. The pressure of a massage can vary according to the type of massage that you choose to have, and your own personal preferences.

Promoting wellbeing

There are many published benefits of a massage, ranging from improvement of sports injuries, digestive problems and joint pain to better quality of sleep and sleeping patterns. However, with a particular focus on workplace massage and employee wellbeing, the following benefits are noted:

- It can improve your mood.
- It can help to reduce anxiety and stress.
- It can reduce absence due to sickness.

A study by Engen et al (2012) considered the feasibility and benefits of providing chair massages to nurses. They concluded that 'offering chair massages for nurses during work hours, while challenging because of busy schedules, reduced stress related symptoms significantly and was highly appreciated by the nurses', with 92 per cent of the participants making positive comments in relation to improvements in sleeping, reduction in pain, stress and tension, and reduction in headaches.

Detailed research into the clinical evidence to support these arguments is limited, but more informal reporting supports the views that massage can have a positive impact on mental as well as physical wellbeing, with some commentators suggesting that simply the demonstration of value through the process is enough to raise a participant's mood and lift some of their anxiety.

Approach
Check the viability

Is it feasible for you to offer workplace massages in your business environment? You need to consider the availability of staff to take up the opportunity. If you have employees involved in continuous customer service, are you willing to release them for a short massage, or will they be required to participate in their own breaks? You should also consider your facilities – do you have some space for people to have a massage in a private space? You might want to discuss the options with a service provider to get a sense of the space needed. Many workplace therapists will offer 'in chair' massages, offering convenience for both the employer and the employee.

Agree the cost model

Decide whether this is a service that you will provide at no cost for your employees, whether you will subsidize the cost, or whether the costs must be fully funded by the employee. The decision you take will no doubt affect the uptake of the service, despite all the known health and wellbeing advantages.

Test the water

Ask your employees if this is something they may be interested in. You might also want to talk to other organizations about their experiences of setting up similar schemes. If you sense some interest, it may be valuable to offer a 'taster' experience, to see if people (and the organization) find it beneficial.

Find a provider

In countries where the massage industry is not subject to regulation, it can be difficult to know who is appropriately trained, checked and experienced to work with your employees. However, the following may be useful guidelines:

- Training courses and massage qualifications can vary significantly, and none of them are subject to regulatory standards, but you really want to see that someone has attended a good quality establishment for training of at least five days, and received a certificate of completion of that course.

- Professional indemnity insurance (PII) is a must for a masseur practising at your workplace, and you can take some comfort that a reputable PII provider will check qualifications are appropriate before committing to insure.

- Membership, or connection to, a relevant governing body may also be useful. There are a number in the UK that are relevant for massage therapists, including the General Council for Massage Therapy, Association of Massage Practitioners and the Association of Therapeutic Massage Therapists, to name but a few. Information can be found on their websites, and other similar ones, about qualifications and how to find an appropriate therapist for your requirements.

• References and testimonials should be sought – particularly if the therapist has previous experience in workplace massage, it's well worth checking with other employers about their experiences, particularly in terms of participant feedback, reliability and professionalism.

Schedule sessions

Promote the availability of the massage session, making links to employee wellbeing and the benefits of massage, and encourage your employees to book in a session. Be transparent about pricing, and whether you will make any contribution, and ask your service provider to offer information to encourage bookings, including how long a session will be, what to expect, where to be and what to wear.

Get feedback

Following on from a taster day, or your first full session, seek feedback from your employees about the massage. You'll be interested to hear about their views of the therapist, the set-up, the organization and the experience itself, and what impact it had on them during and after the massage. If successful overall, make this part of a regular programme.

Outcomes

Offering massages at work, whether fully funded or subsidized, can offer a number of beneficial outcomes, not least of which is the appreciation of employees for the provision of such a service. Employees may feel more valued and that their concerns about anxiety or physical concerns in the workplace are heard.

Employers may also see benefits connected to the research and hearsay mentioned above, including a positive change in mental attentiveness, less stress or anxiety, increased job satisfaction and reduced absenteeism.

Measuring impact

Consider both the individual and the organizational benefits that could be delivered through the implementation of a workplace massage programme.

At individual level, you should seek feedback from those who participate on:

• the quality and professionalism of the therapist;

• the impact the massage had on their wellbeing that day/that week;

- the impact on their workload – whether the massage is time being 'enabled' or discouraged by managers;
- whether they enjoy/value the experience.

At organizational level, you might want to consider:

- the cost of the programme to the organization;
- the take-up of the massage at work offer;
- impacts on employee wellbeing and absence statistics;
- informal feedback from employees and line managers about the benefits or otherwise of massage at work.

Any employee engagement or opinion survey may also provide some insight into the impacts of massage at work, and workplace health and safety audits may also be a useful source of evaluation.

CASE STUDY Workplace massage – a break from the routine

Jemma Giles runs her own massage business, and offers her experiences on the benefits of massage at work.

In general, what are the health or wellbeing benefits of massage?
Release of tight and aching muscles; release of tension and toxins.

How can massage specifically help employees in the workplace?
A lot of the employees I treat are sitting at computers all day, so taking time out for a massage helps to break their pattern of sitting. They often have neck and shoulder issues, headaches and lower back pain. Taking some time out for a quick massage breaks up the pattern of a day. Sometimes just the walk to the therapist gets them moving more than they normally would. And after their massage, my clients often say they feel more awake, can think more clearly, and that their neck and shoulders are relaxed and less painful.

Why do employers invite you and your services into their workplace?
I believe there is a huge benefit to the employers, as staff feel listened to and appreciated, and feel their hard work is being rewarded. Employers often bring a therapist in to keep up staff morale. There is some research that shows that absence is reduced when a therapist regularly comes to a place of work.

Who pays?
This varies between client organizations. I work on site for one small business employer who pays the full cost of a massage for each of their employees. In

ther cases, the employer subsidizes the services so that employees can have a
5-minute massage but they pay a reduce cost.

What do the employees say about it?

They love it. Staff say they feel better after treatments, necks less stiff,
headaches reduced. Others report feeling relaxed and less stressed. Where the
employer foots the bill, we hear that all the staff feel greatly appreciated and
relaxed afterwards.

Jemma Giles, Clinical Massage Therapist

25 Travel health

Introduction

Whilst the perception of travelling for business can be one of a glamorous lifestyle, with luxury flights and the opportunity to see the world, the reality can often be very different, with work–life balance impacts, long and uncomfortable economy flights, limited free time, and high work expectations. As a result, business travel can become a stressful and unhealthy activity for many employees, but there are steps that businesses can take to mitigate the risks, and encourage some healthy practices before, during and after a business trip.

Promoting wellbeing

In 2005 the *Harvard Business Review* reported:

> frequent business travel, especially long-haul travel, accelerates aging and increases the likelihood of suffering a stroke, heart attack, and deep-vein thrombosis … frequent travel leads to unhealthy lifestyles (eg poor diet, lack of exercise, excess drinking), while jet lag causes stress, mood swings, disorientation, sleep problems, and gastrointestinal problems, all of which impair job performance. Over 70 per cent of business travellers report some of these symptoms, even when they travel across only one time zone, and it has been estimated that jet lag recovery time may take one day for every time zone crossed.
>
> (Chamorro-Premuzic, 2015)

Whilst the necessity for business travel may be reducing, face-to-face meetings are still highly valued, and as such it is clearly important that organizations look at their travel policies and practices, and seek to mitigate the risks and issues that compromise wellbeing through the business travel journey.

Approach

Travel avoidance

As your organization develops internationally, consider your IT strategy and make sure you have the capabilities to work virtually with your international clients and teams. With the rise of technology at work, it is now easier than ever to avoid the need for international travel. Many meetings can be held instead over conference telephone calls, video calls (Skype and FaceTime) or using virtual meeting software, that allows you to see and peak to remote colleagues, but also to share slides and information. Using his technology is naturally better for an organization – it's more cost effective, it's more time efficient. It's also better for the environment (it reduces our carbon footprint significantly) and is better for employees.

Using technology

Even the implementation of such technology can have its challenges for employees, as time differences may mean that they have to work outside of a standard UK working day to accommodate colleagues overseas. In some cases this is unavoidable, but there are a few things that can be done to manage this effectively:

Rotate the requirements to work out of hours. Try not to fix regular meetings so that one country or another is regularly committed to working late at night, during the night, or early morning.

Recognize the time taken for out of hours working – if an employee has a late call, offer them the opportunity to have a later start that day or to come in later the next day to balance out the requirement.

Take into account some of the issues and solutions mentioned in Tool 37, 'Remote working' (page 168), to ensure it is effective and as stress-free as possible.

Overseas business travel

Overseas business travel is sometimes seen as a 'perk', but the reality is that it can be disruptive, exhausting and offer very few benefits for employees. However, in many organizations it is a necessity, and where travel cannot be avoided there are steps an employer can take to reduce the stress and health risks that it can cause.

Health

Inoculations: Ensure that employees are aware of the inoculations they need to have, and know where to find information about them. If you have an occupational health service, using them to inoculate travellers will be efficient and cost effective. If it is a business requirement that an employee travels to a country requiring inoculation, the company should cover the cost.

Compression socks: Provide travellers on long haul flights (typically above four hours) with compression socks. These can reduce the risk of DVT or leg swelling. Typically very unattractive, the company Happy

Socks offer a range of more cheerful looking socks. This is a low-cost gesture – between £10 and £20 for a pair of socks is a small price to pay for some risk reduction for an employee.

- In-air exercises: Remind employees about in-air exercise that can help them to stay active and fresh on long-haul flights. These are usually provided in the airline magazine, and there is plenty of information online, including downloadable exercise sheets that you could issue to travellers with their travel schedule.

- Managing jetlag/time differences: Encourage your employees to consider their jetlag and the time differences when planning their workload, meetings and schedule overseas. Wherever practical, encourage them to build in rest times rather than rush straight from airport to meetings, and to plan flexibly their start and finish times to allow for adjustment to the new time zone. Different people will respond differently to jetlag, but allowing flexibility will mean that your employees can plan for working at their best.

- Hotels: Where possible, use hotels with fitness facilities, and/or safe running or walking routes so that travellers are able to do some exercise during their stay.

Safety

- Before confirming any travel requirements and arrangements, check with your foreign office or travel organizations online for any important information about safety or health issues in the destination country. If either you or an employee has concerns, they should be taken into account, and where possible alternatives arranged.

- Arrange airport pick up: Where possible, and particularly for first time travellers to an airport or country, pre-arrange an airport pick up. This is not only much more convenient for the traveller but also avoids risks of getting involved in scams, fraud or worse. By using recommended ground transportation, you can mitigate against the risks for travellers.

- Share experiences: If other employees are regularly travelling to the same area or country, and have safety advice to share, encourage this through networking events, or online communities. Top tips can be really helpful to hear from others who have already experienced similar.

- Local contacts: Provide your employee with one or two key contacts in the receiving company (be that a customer, supplier or division of your own business) so that they can contact a local person in case of emergency.

Make sure the local contact is aware that they are a first point of contact should the employee require assistance.

Courtesy

- Currency: Provide a small amount of local currency so that your employees are able to manage any transport issues overseas (eg enough to get a taxi from the airport to office or hotel), and manage it later through your expenses policy. It's better if employees don't have to fund or arrange that for themselves – it's taking something off their busy to-do list rather than adding to it.

- Language: Encourage employees to learn some language basics, particularly with those countries your company interact with most. Providing connections to online learning, or even a small phrase book or podcast will allow your representatives abroad to make small gestures towards the locals, such as hello, please and thank you.

Convenience

- Money: If possible, provide the employee with a corporate credit card or expenses float so that they are not limited to their own budget, and are not incurring their own credit or bank charges whilst on business. In addition, should it be necessary, the card could also be used if an emergency required it. Make sure that the guidelines on acceptable use of a corporate card or a cash float are clear, and that repayments and expenses balance for either are understood.

- Travel to airports: Encourage the use of taxis to and from airports where it's practical and reasonably cost-effective, or the use of short stay or valet parking at the airport. This allows travellers to be efficient, and reduces risks of accidents when driving to and from airports before or after early or late flight times, or following long-haul flights.

- Lounge access at airports: Whilst many companies are no longer willing to foot the bill for first class or business class flights, particularly for short-haul flights, one of the key benefits of doing so is the accessibility of lounge access. If your organization's travel policy is limiting the use of business class flights, consider covering the costs of lounge access only for regular travellers. It not only provides a relaxing space before travel and during layovers, but also provides food and refreshments that might otherwise be claimed as expenses, and a quieter and productive place to do work.

- Travel times: The cost-driven need for the cheapest possible flights can result in inconvenient routings, and disruptive travel times. Wherever practical, aim to balance the two elements of cost and convenience so that travel is easy as it can be, whilst remaining within a specific budget.

- Tourism: If it's possible, and the employee is willing to spend additional time using holiday entitlement or days owed, and their own funds, consider whether you can allow them to spend some leisure time in the destination. Be clear about what is and isn't a claimable expense, and how any personal costs should be managed. There are benefits – the employee may get to know more about the destination, which could be advantageous to your business, they may engage with their hosts socially, encouraging better relationships and greater collaboration, or they may use the time for rest and recuperation, encouraging a faster recovery time from business travel.

Resilience

Refer to Tool 30, 'Building resilience' (page 137), as supporting employees to remain strong and recover quickly from some of the impacts of travel will be advantageous.

Outcomes

Implementing any one of the initiatives identified above will go some way towards reducing the stress and health risks for your travelling employees. By proactively addressing them, and taking positive action (some of which is low or no cost), you will demonstrate to your employees that you have concern for their wellbeing, and that you value and appreciate the sacrifices they make to travel to represent your business.

Measuring impact

As always, it's useful to ask people who travel regularly a few key questions:

- What do they find most challenging to their health or wellbeing during business travel?
- What suggestions do they have that would mitigate this?
- What encourages them to work at their best whilst travelling?

As you implement any of the initiatives above, ask your regular travellers about the impact the implementation has had on their travel experience, their preparation for travel, their work during the travel period and their settlement back home after travel.

Mental

Stress prevention and signalling

Introduction

As a manager, you have some responsibility for the wellbeing of your employees where stress is concerned. Whilst some stress can be healthy – some people can find it a motivator or a trigger for focus or action – much of it is unhealthy, with people suffering physical and mental effects of stress both at home and at work. Your role in simply 'noticing' – spotting the signs, raising the issue with those involved – is critical but is only effective if you are willing to then signpost support for that individual. You do need to recognize your own limitations, though, and unless you are trained or qualified appropriately, you shouldn't seek to delve deeply into either the issues or the remedy, but instead seek specialist support.

Critically, however, you have a role to play as a people manager in seeking to avoid workplace stress in the first place, by knowing and understanding your team, appropriately allocating workload, and monitoring performance and wellbeing on a regular basis.

Promoting wellbeing

In the UK, Acas estimate that mental health, which includes stress, depression and anxiety, is responsible for the loss of around 91 million working days every year at a total impact cost of about £30 million (Acas, 2017: 6). Whilst not all of that can be attributed to workplace stress (there can be many triggers) there is clearly a business case, alongside the moral responsibility, for aiming to prevent or, when it does occur, address workplace stress as quickly as possible.

A Health and Safety Executive report states the main causes of workplace stress to be workload pressures, tight deadlines and too much responsibility. In addition, they mentioned lack of managerial support, change at work and lack of clarity on roles and responsibilities as key contributing factors (HSE, 2017).

Whilst there may be antecedents or domestic factors that make certain individuals vulnerable to stress illnesses, there are clearly things that leaders and organizations can do to reduce the risks, given these contributory factors.

Approach

First, it is important to recognize a distinction between maintaining a watchful eye over things, intervening when necessary, and over-protecting employees without allowing them to face challenges head-on and work through them. It's a fine line sometimes, and the key is to know your people, the work and the challenges. Wherever possible, a manager should be encouraging team members to work through problems themselves, and to learn from their experiences in doing so. However, the line manager should be close enough to the employee to recognize when difficult or challenging is tipping over into a situation where an individual cannot cope, and should be ready to intervene with support, coaching or guidance.

Know your people

Build sound relationships with your team members so that you have a really good understanding of their capabilities (including their previous experience) and their capacity or tolerance for challenge, for ambiguity and for additional responsibility. Understand about their career ambitions, any conflicts they have on their time that need to be considered, and their level of commitment to the organization, team and task.

Knowing them well also means you can notice when behaviour has changed – ie a mood change, they have become quieter, less reliable, or working later than normal – and you can start a conversation about what (if anything) has triggered a change. It could be nothing, or it could be a private matter, but noticing will likely be appreciated.

Building the relationship is also important so that they feel comfortable raising issues with you as the team leader – that they can confide in you without fear of punishment or reprisal when they are finding things difficult. Be explicit with them that you are there when they need to talk.

Know the problems

As a manager of a team or work area, you have no doubt seen how things work over a number of years, and so you have a good idea of the hot spots and problem areas that employees face in going about their work. For example, you might know when customers can become more challenging to deal with, or when materials or supply shortages cause issues in production, or where teams' competing priorities can lead to conflict. Knowing this information means that at times of high pressure you can be proactive in preparing your team members, or offer support when it is most needed. This ould take the form of coaching, liaising between teams, additional head-ount for peak workload or help in prioritizing workload.

Know your resources

Knowing the skills, experience and capacity of your team members is essential if you are to appropriately balance them with the workload requirements of customers, stakeholders, projects etc. Before accepting any new tasks into the team, assess the time and skills required and ensure that you are able to deliver what is expected within the set timeframes. Involve employees in the discussions about taking on or releasing workload or projects to get their perspectives.

Notice

It can be difficult to start the conversation, but a simple and non-invasive way is just to say what you have seen. Start with 'I've noticed that ...' and refer to what you have seen or heard, focusing on factual information rather than opinion. For example, 'I've noticed that you have been at work until gone 7pm every day this week.' Or, 'I've noticed that you spent much of today on your own in a meeting room.' Follow up the fact with a question – is everything ok? Is there any help you need? What's going on for you right now? These open questions provide the opportunity for an employee to raise any concerns and to ask for help. And if no help is needed or wanted, then you haven't caused a major issue or any offence.

Educate

Providing formal training, or access to information, about topics such as resilience, managing stress, mindfulness, etc, will also enable those who are vulnerable or interested to recognize their own reactions, and to develop their own coping strategies.

Monitor and review

Reviews and check-in meetings with your team members allow you to monitor their performance, behaviours and temperament, and doing them frequently will allow you the opportunity to notice changes, and to offer continuous support to those who need it.

Some potential signs of stress in individuals

You should notice any of the following changes in behaviour and address it supportively with the individual concerned:

- more negativity than normal;
- self-doubt, self-critique, etc;
- a tendency to spend more time alone than they might usually;
- checking in with supervisor more often to check instructions, direction or work output;
- changes in mood;
- reluctance to engage in team activity;
- forgetfulness;
- erratic performance or quality of work;
- eating more, or eating less;
- lateness or more absence from work (planned or otherwise);
- tiredness.

This is not an exhaustive list, and it maybe that an employee under stress doesn't display any of these symptoms, but they are typical indicators.

Outcomes

In following this approach, the intent is that, as far as possible, leaders are able to anticipate, prevent and manage potential stressors at work.

Measuring impact

With significant days lost in the UK because of absence related to stress, and the resulting loss of productivity, the real evaluation of your preventative, proactive and reactive steps is the reduction in the instances of work-related stress and absence in your business. Organizationally, this may not be recorded, but you can monitor the instances within your own team. In addition to this, your view – and the view of your employees – of how some of the potential triggers are managed could be considered. For example, how do your team members react to change, to increased workload, or to additional responsibilities – do they feel well supported, or otherwise?

Managing 'overwhelm'

Introduction

When an employee experiences a strong emotional reaction to a situation at work, they may be considered – by themselves or by others – to be in a state of 'being overwhelmed'. At its extreme, being overwhelmed can make a person feel defeated, that there is no clear way to recover from the current state. In less stressful conditions an employee may feel out of their depth, stressed or concerned by their current situation.

Promoting wellbeing

Estimates from the 2016 Labour Force Survey show that in 2015/16 stress accounted for 37 per cent of all work-related ill health cases and 45 per cent of all working days lost due to ill health (ONS, 2017a). The main work issues mentioned by respondents as causing work-related stress, depression or anxiety were workload pressures, including tight deadlines, too much responsibility and a lack of managerial support.

The benefit of proactively dealing with issues such as excessive workload, challenging deadlines or conflicting priorities is therefore clear. Not only is it likely to result in a reduction in the instances of stress-related ill health, but as a consequence absences could be reduced significantly.

Approach

Recognize the signs of an employee being overwhelmed

Different employees will have different tolerance levels for workload, for deadlines and for stress in general. Whilst some may find multitasking engaging or exciting, others may find it challenging and stressful. As a people manager it is your responsibility to recognize your employees' different tolerance levels and to notice and act when that tolerance is at risk – when an employee may be becoming overwhelmed.

Help employees to reframe their language

Reframing is a coaching tool that encourages a coachee to change their language to encourage a mindset change. It can help an employee to move from a negative state into an more positive frame of mind, and allows them to focus on what they can achieve rather than on what they can't. Negative language such as 'it's an impossible deadline' or 'I'll never finish this project on time' can create mental barriers. In some cases it might provide the justification an employee needs to allow the feeling of being overwhelmed take over and let themselves be defeated.

Enable prioritization and provide 'air cover'

Taking some time to work with the employee to review their workload, re-set priorities and agree focus areas will not only demonstrate your support to the employee, but will ensure that they can deliver what it is most important, whilst reducing the stress levels they may be experiencing.

Providing 'air cover' means that you as manager act as a buffer between the employee and senior managers or other stakeholders. You must take responsibility for the adjustments to the delivery schedule or priorities. The employee can focus on delivery without fear of reprisal or concern for their reputation in the organization.

Breaks

Use some of the tools from this book that allow an employee to take a walk and a break for fresh air, short relaxation exercises, etc.

Encourage mindfulness

Use some of the techniques of mindfulness that are mentioned in this book to help employees to re-focus, and to try to regain or maintain control of their emotions during stressful periods at work. Encourage them to use mindfulness resources, and support them in taking the time to do so.

Act quickly

The sooner you can make changes to support the employee, the more effective your interventions will be at helping to address their concerns. As soon as you notice any signs of 'overwhelm', check in with the employee to find out how they are, what's on their workload, priorities etc. Be inquisitive, not accusatory; offer support not critique.

Outcomes

By simply noticing when someone is showing signs of being overwhelmed, you enable a conversation to start that can uncover the reasons for those feelings, the support needed and what actions can be taken to address the state of overwhelm.

In taking prompt, proactive and decisive action, it is hoped that you will be able to minimize the stress and anxiety felt by that employee.

As noted above, initiatives taken to reduce such anxiety may also have a preventative impact on productivity issues and time lost due to absences.

Evaluating impact

There are a number of levels of evaluation that you could consider to assess how effective you and your organization are at supporting employees through phases of being overwhelmed with workload:

- Managerial support: Most employee surveys will ask participants to provide feedback or ratings on the degree of support they receive from their managers. Scoring in such surveys will indicate whether you have the right foundations of support to be able to help employees in a state of 'overwhelm' as and when they need it.

- Impact on productivity and/or attendance: The outcomes identified above suggest that proactive intervention by a manager should have a positive impact on productivity and/or attendance. It may be worth tracking, but it is important to recognize that other factors may also impact these metrics.

- Manager feedback: As the line manager, your anecdotal stories of identifying, addressing and avoiding 'overwhelm' within your team should also be noted and recorded. Not only should your successes be shared, but lessons should also be learnt about what might be done differently in the future to prevent, as well as address, overwhelming employees and the stress and anxiety that may arise as a result.

28 Employee assistance programmes

Introduction

Employee assistance programmes (EAP) are an employee benefit offered by some companies to their employees as part of a broader reward package. A typical EAP provides a confidential telephone or internet support service by an independent third-party specialist organization, offering information, advice and counselling to employees. Some may also offer a limited amount of face-to-face support. Their services support employees in dealing with emotional, health, financial and legal concerns that they may be facing in either their professional or their personal lives.

Services are provided by an external third party, and employees can be assured of strict confidentiality with no specific reporting back to the employer, although overall statistics on usage will usually be provided.

> 'Over the years EAPs have become an integral tool in an organization's attempts to engage employees and support the health and wellbeing of its workforce. In fact, ... independent research commissioned by EAPA UK in 2008 reveals that 5,200 organizations – representing over 8.2 million employees – now enjoy the services of an EAP.'
>
> EAPA

Promoting wellbeing

Companies invest in employee assistance programmes because dealing with issues such as domestic relationship issues, legal battles, employment concerns, financial worries or health matters without support can be detrimental to an employee's health and wellbeing. In turn, from an organization's perspective, such issues can negatively impact work performance, workplace relationships and attendance, as employees struggle to balance sustained stress with work commitments. Providing simple and confidential access affords employees the opportunity to quickly seek the support or guidance they need.

Approach

Identify the business case

Before implementing an employee assistance programme, a clear business case needs to be considered. Whilst it is difficult to quantify the benefits of uch a scheme, as its use is confidential, there are some generic benefits that an be considered in the business case, such as employee reputation, connection to a wellbeing strategy, acting as a responsible employer, creating an mployee-focused total reward package, etc. In addition, you may be able o connect some key statistics to the potential service provision, for example bsence statistics, with an estimate that you will reduce absence through the AP implementation, and that less of those lost working days can be attributed to stress or mental health issues.

Another potential benefit to be explored is a reduction in insurance remiums if your organization offers health insurance cover as part of the enefits package.

According to the EAPA, the average cost of an EAP programme is £14 er employee per year (EAPA, 2013). There are likely to be additional set-up osts, and there may also be tax implications that should be fully documented in the business case.

Select a supplier

The EAPA provides a register of EAP organizations, with varying requirements for different levels of registration with the association. This is a great resource for looking at some options for EAP suppliers, but may not be exhaustive. You may also want to consider seeking referrals, asking occupational health, your professional network or other stakeholders or any recommendations they have. In selecting a provider, you should consider:

Service offering: What support and advice is covered by this provider – ie legal, financial, counselling, etc.

Service access: How do employees access the service? Is there a telephone line or internet access, and is there any face-to-face service provision available?

Service delivery: What are the operating hours of the service? Issues can arise at any time, so a 24/7 service is usually preferable.

Service quality: What are the skills and qualifications of those providing counselling and advisory services? What outsourced organizations are used for specialist advice (eg legal, financial)?

Service communication: How will the provider assist with the launch, communication and advocacy of the programme?

Service enhancements: Are there any proactive interventions included in the service, eg wellbeing seminars, or stress management workshops?

- Service additions: What additional services are available at additional cost? This may include face-to-face counselling or employee training and workshops.
- Service reporting: What information will the provider give your organization to report on utilization and issues arising?
- Service commitment: What is the contract duration?

Optimize and advocate

As well as advocating the EAP scheme in general, line managers also have a responsibility to encourage its use. Noticing that an employee is struggling, or establishing that they have issues, as a line manager you can recommend at any time that they tap into the EAP resources for support.

Often, employees will not realize it doesn't have to be a work-related matter, or they are concerned about the confidentiality aspect, so reminding them on these aspects may encourage greater use of the programme.

It is also a tool that can be used during performance or attendance discussions. Without having any specific evidence or information about an employee's issues out of work, you can easily point them towards the EAP as a resource for support if it is needed.

Outcomes

For many employees, the EAP is a benefit that they may not plan to use, but the fact that it is there is reassuring to many. For those who do use it, the access to counselling, legal and financial advice and support may also have a financial benefit to them, avoiding potential charges for services that they might otherwise have to pay for, or worse, might avoid using.

The impact of using the services can be invisible or subtle – as a manager you may not be aware of an employee's issues, or that they have used the EAP service to help them to manage those issues. The benefits to the organization – and the employee – might therefore be hidden.

For others who are more explicit about use of the EAP service, you may be able to connect the outcomes to their attendance, their work productivity or quality, and their relationships at work, seeing positive impacts as the support from the EAP helps them to deal with their issues and concerns.

The provision of an EAP scheme as part of a total reward package for employees can enhance the attractiveness and reputation of an employer. For example, 23 of the top 25 organizations in the 2013 *Sunday Times* 100 Best Companies to Work For provided employee access to an EAP scheme (EAPA, 2013).

Measuring impact

Measuring the effectiveness of an EAP service is challenging. Utilization figures are used by many organizations, and whilst use of the programme can be considered high if 16 per cent of employees use the service, it could be the case that just one short intervention could make a significant impact for that employee, that could potentially save them stress, ill health, financial losses and job security concerns, and could save the employer from productivity losses and absence costs.

Employee details and matters discussed will always remain strictly confidential, but statistics provided by EAP service providers will usually allow organizations to assess:

- utilization;
- categories of issues being raised through the helpline;
- frequency of these issues being raised.

29 Emotional intelligence

Introduction

Emotional intelligence is an individual's ability to recognize, understand and effectively use their own emotions and reactions, and to recognize and adapt to the emotions and feelings of other people. As a people manager, this is an important skill to ensure that you understand how your behaviours or actions affect others, but also so that you can see how those who work for you respond. It matters more broadly in the workplace too. Being able to effectively manage emotions is important for workplace relationships with colleagues and peers, for building effective associations with customers and suppliers, and being able to work effectively across functions and geographies.

JCA Global have developed an emotional intelligence framework (Figure 3.1), which focuses on:

1 Personal intelligence: Having positive self-regard, being self-aware and managing your behaviour effectively.

2 Interpersonal intelligence: Having a positive regard for others, being aware of others and managing your relationships effectively.

The model recognizes the underlying attitudes that underpin an individual's thinking and feeling, which then drives their behaviour.

Promoting wellbeing

In a study by Carmeli et al (2009) a connection was identified between emotional intelligence and some of the key factors of wellbeing such as self-esteem and self-acceptance. In addition, there were some findings in their

Figure 3.1   Emotional intelligence framework

	Personal intelligence	Interpersonal intelligence
Behaviour	Self management	Relationship management
Feeling	Self awareness	Awareness of others
Attitude	Self regard	Regard for others

SOURCE JCA Global (www.jcaglobal.com)

study to suggest that employees who practice positive wellbeing habits can function better than those who have less emotional intelligence.

Approach

Organizations and individuals can take a variety of approaches to develop emotional intelligence:

Reflect

Encouraging your team members, and taking the time yourself, to reflect on interactions is one of the most valuable ways to learn about emotional intelligence. Take the time to work with your team members, at whatever level in the organization, to discuss and reflect on behaviours and reactions, calling out specifically how certain actions, words or instructions made them (or you) feel. Raising self-awareness in this way allows people to mindfully consider their own responses, and to discuss how they might be able to adjust or adapt their emotions in certain situations.

Be curious

Asking others for comment or feedback about how behaviours or actions have been perceived will provide some additional information for individuals to take into account. Asking 'How did I come across?', 'How did you feel about my approach' or 'What was surprising to you about my reaction?' can uncover some interesting perceptions. Equally, offering feedback to others about how they have been perceived, using principles of giving great feedback (see Tool 15, page 71), can provide some useful information. Using this information, whether reactively sought by a person or proactively offered as feedback, can help individuals to reflect on and consider their emotions and behaviours.

Learn

External consultants and training providers offer training in emotional intelligence, and many segregate training to accommodate employees and leaders separately. Typically, training courses will include content that connects emotions and behaviour, discovering personal triggers, learning coping or adjustment strategies and developing and improving self-awareness.

External programmes run by experts or specialists are highly recommended, but are likely to cost in the hundreds of pounds per delegate.

However, running a programme in house may not only be more cost effective, but also act as a signal that the employer is acting responsibly and demonstrating care and concern for employees. Other learning strategies could include the use of self-learning materials (eg books, online videos, etc) or e-learning packages could also be used.

Measuring

There are a number of psychometric tools available that will help with a measure of emotional intelligence. For example, JCA Global can provide an emotional intelligence profile based around their six-part framework. However, in the main, whilst these types of profile can be completed online, the most effective methodology will be to combine them with a thorough one-to-one feedback session and/or coaching. There will be costs incurred, but these need to be considered against the training budget, development programmes for people managers or individuals, and the potential risk factors associated with lower levels of emotional intelligence.

Outcomes

Organizations that proactively encourage and demonstrate a high level of emotional intelligence among their people are likely to see strong team interactions, productive and supportive relationships between people managers and their team members, and sound relationships with customers and stakeholders. Employees who work for emotionally intelligent managers are likely to feel more supported, developed and coached, and recognized for their efforts. It is likely that they will be open and adaptable to change, optimizing their strengths and performing at their best.

Measuring impact

Assessing the impact of your efforts to develop emotional intelligence has to be a highly individual process. People managers should be able to notice and identify changes in behaviour, performance and reactions from their team members, and equally team members should feel a change in the levels of empathy and support offered by their manager. These changes can really only be assessed through individual informal feedback processes.

Emotional intelligence training can be evaluated using a training 'happy sheet' or assessing learning outcomes against programme objectives.

Jolyon Maddocks, author of *Emotional Intelligence at Work* (Maddocks, 2014), describes how emotional intelligence is put into practice by JCA Global and supports wellbeing and engagement at work.

Emotional intelligence (EI) is how we manage our personality to be both personally and interpersonally effective. Developing our EI enables us to manage our mindset and emotions to be more mindful in today's challenging work environment. Being emotionally intelligent involves being more aware of what is going on for us and amongst many things, underpins wellbeing and resilience.

When working with clients to develop their EI there are four key steps we invariably include in helping clients successfully meet their objectives.

The first step is to develop emotional awareness. Our programmes use activities that require participants to get used to checking in with their feelings regularly (there are several apps for doing this). The point of this is so we notice feelings early before they become too strong to manage, such as recognizing feelings of 'worry' before they grow into 'anxiety', and 'frustration' before it becomes 'anger'.

The second step is to develop mindset awareness. The foundation of EI is mindset – my regard for myself and others. Our mindset or attitude at this deep level drives behaviour very often subconsciously. For example, high levels of conflict can threaten our self regard and our regard for others. The mindset 'I am not OK' can lead to submissive or aggressive behaviour as opposed to assertiveness, which requires a mindset of 'I'm OK, you're OK'. Our work helps people to understand how attitude impacts behaviour and how to manage this.

Step three is a key ingredient in managing emotions and is relaxation, which is essential for clear thinking and problem solving. Although the term 'emotional intelligence' may sound like an oxymoron, learning to manage our emotional state is essential for making best use of our cognitive intelligence (or IQ). How we feel drives what we do, so we teach techniques for putting a 'pause' between thinking, feeling and behaviour. All too often people attempt to resolve issues while feeling angry, upset or anxious but too much emotion can significantly impair our cognitive capacity by narrowing our attention, blocking access to our rational thinking brain, making us more judgemental, and reducing awareness of ourselves and others.

The final step is taking action. Why is it that people often know what they should do but fail to put this into practice? Neuroscience tells us that the cognitive parts of the brain learn from acquiring knowledge while the emotional parts of the brain learn from experiential activity. Unfortunately, one does not necessarily lead to the other, just because you know what you should do doesn't mean you will do it. To develop emotionally intelligent behaviours we need to rehearse, practice and make it real, otherwise it just becomes another unfulfilled good intention (like many a New Year's resolutions). A method we employ at JCA Global is a habit change technique, where the individual will repeat the same specific daily activity over an extended period until it becomes embedded as a new neural network.

In our experience of coaching individuals and facilitating group workshops, applying these four steps provides an essential basis for developing EI. For individual coaching it is important the client puts the theory into practice after the session. Group workshops are a most direct route as they offer the opportunity to interact and apply these and other techniques in a real-life but safe environment.

For specific suggestions on how to develop emotional intelligence refer to Maddocks (2014).

Building resilience

Introduction

Resilience can be defined as one's ability to bounce back, adapting to challenges that people face in everyday life and recovering from those challenges in ways that are proactive and healthy, and potentially even beneficial. Resilience at work has to take into account many of the typical challenges faced by employees – business change, team conflict, challenging targets and tight timelines – but may also have to factor in the broader life challenges that can affect performance in the workplace too. Resilience isn't about avoidance of the issues that cause distress, and in fact it recognizes that different people will have different reactions to similar issues. Instead, it is about the way in which such challenges can be managed by the individual, their coping strategies and the ways in which people might learn from challenges or mistakes, and move on from them in a positive way.

Whilst it is not expected that people managers become experts in resilience, or counsellors for employees, they should have awareness about what it means to be resilient, what it takes, and how their actions or behaviours might challenge that resilience.

Promoting wellbeing

In 2016 the World Health Organization reported that mental disorders such as depression and anxiety are increasing, with approximately 10 per cent of the world's population suffering. The 2016 Labour Force Survey reported that in the UK during the period 2015–16 the key contributors to employee stress were tight deadlines, volume of work, too much responsibility, a lack of managerial support, organizational change and a lack of role clarity (ONS, 2017a). Their statistics suggest that around 11.6 million working days are lost due to work-related stress or anxiety each year. With such prevalence of reported issues, and the impacts not only for individual employees, but also on colleagues and teams, as well as the issues for an organization's productivity, profitability, quality and service, it is an issue that employers need to proactively address. Developing resilience is just one approach that employers and leaders can take to minimize the impacts of organizational pressures on individual mental health.

Approach
Resilience training

External providers and specialists can deliver resilience training for employees that helps them to understand what resilience is, how it affects people generally, and them personally, and determines some potential strategies to build their own resilience – sometimes through health and lifestyle choices, but also through their own interpersonal skills and confidence. Providing such training for employees is a proactive strategy, rather than a reactive one, that helps to build resilience in the organization enabling employees to become more self-aware and adopt strategies to manage change, uncertainty or challenge in the business. In addition, it may be seen as a privilege and/ or benefit to attend, as many will find it beneficial in their personal as well as professional lives.

Leader education

Providing people managers with some insight into resilience, its potential triggers, and how to manage people in that context will help to reduce and to manage the incidents of resilience-related stress or anxiety at work. People managers need to know how their own actions or behaviours may impact others, and with this knowledge they can adjust accordingly. Whilst it may not be possible to avoid it completely, having leaders who are aware and empathetic will no doubt have an impact on employees. Whether this is through external training, self-learning or internally led workshops, this raising of awareness should become a core part of a leader's development path.

Encouraging reflection and learning

People managers can provide opportunities to reflect on challenges and to extrapolate learnings from previous experiences to encourage greater resilience. These approaches can be tested out in regular check-ins or during coaching or mentoring sessions, or following any feedback conversation. They allow the opportunity for the employee to learn from their own experiences, and from their reactions to those experiences, and consider what they could have or might do differently in the same situation in the future, or to consider how the learnings might apply in other situations. Building this arsenal of personal tactics to approach similar challenges will build resilience.

Equally important is the reflection and learning from successes – when challenges have been overcome, or stretch targets achieved, it can be powerful for people to reflect on what worked well for them in that scenario, and how they can do more of the same in different situations. Understanding – and explicitly discussing or noting – what skills, actions or behaviours have served them well will help people to consciously use them again to their own benefit.

Preparing for change

Change is a constant in most businesses these days, and helping people to navigate positively through it is a key responsibility for any people manager. Tool 19, 'Change' (page 88), provides some useful guidance as to how this can be achieved. In addition, provision of training so that people understand their own reactions to change, leader development so that leaders understand what people need and deserve during transition, and a regular and open communication channel will reduce the level of anxiety felt by team members. Where the change has a significant impact, eg redundancy, the provision of outplacement support can be extremely beneficial to help people to understand the impacts, and the opportunities, that come from it.

Signpost support

Whilst a people manager may not be fully equipped to personally help an employee through resilience challenges, they should be aware of the support and interventions that are available for employees to access. If your organisation has occupational health services, this could be an important first step, as could an employee assistance programme, but other options may also be available, such as coaching or mentoring, training or a listening ear from a colleague or manager.

Additionally, as a manager you can signpost people towards self-help methodologies, whether these are books, videos, local support groups or health specialists.

Outcomes

The approaches above suggest mostly proactive steps that can be taken to prepare leaders and their team members for change, workload/pressure increases, etc. By using these interventions to develop their own tools and coping strategies, employees may be more able to react steadily, or even positively, to these challenges.

The 2016 Labour Force Survey (ONS, 2017a) also quoted lack of management support as a potential cause of anxiety or workplace stress. Proactive actions to develop improved resilience, and simply having open discussions about it, could go some way to improving that perception of managerial support and, as a result, reducing anxiety related to it.

Measuring impact

Measuring positive mental health, or the degree of resilience, in individual employees is challenging, but there are some indicators that could be considered:

- take-up rates and feedback from any resilience training programmes offered by the organization;

- informal feedback from leaders and employees about their own comfort with anticipated or experienced change and the rise and fall of pressure at work;

- absence rates, where possible highlighting specifically absence related to stress or anxiety;

- employee assistance programmes will maintain strict confidentiality but may be able to provide some high-level trends in the issues presented to them or support requested, which may offer an insight into the incidence of mental health issues.

Reframing

Introduction

Reframing is an approach taken to encourage an employee to change a negative or pessimistic use of language to a more positive one – and as a result to also adjust their mindset. It provides the opportunity for an employee to reconsider and reposition their thoughts, feelings and emotions about a person, a task or a situation.

You might notice opportunities to work with employees to:

turn a problem into an opportunity;

- remove a barrier or blocker in a situation;
- consider a conflict from a different perspective;
- see a lack of skill or expertise as a learning opportunity;
- embrace a change rather than resist it;
- encourage more self-confidence through positive thinking.

A few minutes of your time may be enough to prompt a rethink, and the return on that investment of time could be significant.

Promoting wellbeing

People who express negative views in the workplace may well be experiencing negative emotions such as sadness, hopelessness, fear or anxiety. These emotions can have a knock-on effect on how people behave – for example, an employee experiencing fear or hopelessness may not want to make difficult decisions at work, or may be reluctant to step out of their comfort zone, develop themselves or take a career step. Those emotions and behaviours can also affect the mood of the individual, which can have a knock-on effect on the collective mood at work, or the morale in a workplace.

Approach

Establish receptiveness. Think about the circumstances or situation you are in when you notice the trigger for reframing. Consider what caused the negative or pessimistic reaction or comments that have been made, and use your knowledge of the employee to make an informed decision about whether they might be receptive to reframing guidance. If not, note this example and come back to it at a more appropriate time, but if it is likely to be ok, find a quiet space and have a conversation.

1 Notice and reflect

Notice what has been said, how it was said and the accompanying body language. In reframing, the words people use are really critical – but they don't stand alone. You may notice negative words (eg it went badly, I'm not happy), or words that are packed with feeling or emotion (eg it was a disaster, I'm devastated). You may notice a particular tone of voice – the volume (particularly quiet or unusually loud), the intonation (which words are said with the varying rise and fall) and the speed of talking (fast and panicky or slow and controlled). These tonal differentiators considered in conjunction with the actual words used provide a good indication of what feelings might be wrapped up in what is being said.

Add to that the body language you are seeing as someone speaks and you can get some real insight. Notice eye contact – or lack of. What is their body posture telling you – how are you reading it? What non-verbal signals are you picking up – folded arms, turning away, nodding or shaking head, etc.

As you take in the signals provided by the words, the tone and the body language, note also whether they are congruent.

Having taken all this information in, you need to replay and reflect it to your team member. Tell them what you have heard – in their words and tone – and/or seen in their body language. Be objective, stick to the facts, and be constructive. For example, you might say, 'I notice that when you mentioned Bob you sighed and shook your head before you described him as ineffective', 'You said you're excited about the project but your tone of voice was flat.'

2 Challenge

Having replayed what you heard and saw, you need to challenge the thinking, to encourage the employee to self-reflect about their mindset and where it comes from. Sometimes just holding someone accountable for what you've seen or heard can be surprising to the person who said it – they may be unaware of how they are presenting themselves. Asking 'How do you feel about what I have told you?' will indicate their level of self-awareness. To get deeper into the issues, asking 'Why do you say that?' or 'Why do you see it that way?' can be useful prompts to stimulate the challenge.

3 Offer or invite a reframe

Whether you present a suggested reframe or encourage your team member to develop one may depend on the circumstances and the individual. Knowing your employee, you'll be the best judge.

To invite a reframe, encourage the employee to consider it for themselves. This may be as simple as asking 'How else could you put it?' or 'If you were to turn that into a positive what might it sound like?'

Providing an idea yourself may be more directive than you would like to be, and would ideally be a last resort after inviting the employee's own thoughts. But there may be scenarios where it is needed – if time is critical, if the employee struggles or if they don't understand, for example. Offering your own suggestion should be exactly that, though – an offer (refusable) and a suggestion (not forced, or necessarily the right answer!). Wrapping your suggestion with phrases like 'Have you thought about saying ...?' at the front end, and 'How would that work for you/feel?' as a tail end allows them an opportunity to consider it, develop it, reject it, find alternatives, or try it out.

4 Self-reflect

You might also want to take a moment to reflect on your own assumptions that could be reframed. If you're thinking that a team member is always negative or underperforming, think about how you might positively reframe that thought, what difference that might have on how you address or interact with that person and, in turn, what impact that might have on their performance or behaviour.

Outcomes

By seeking to help employees to address their negative self-beliefs or negative thinking, managers can help to improve not only the individual's attitudes and behaviours, but also the emotional environment that the team operate within.

Measuring impact

The evaluation of the effectiveness of reframing is anecdotal. You may see or hear changes in the employee's attitude or outlook on certain aspects of their working life that you can relate to reframing. Or you may want to ask them directly whether reframing has had any impact on the work, task, relationships, etc, that were the subject of the exercise.

With either – or both – of those insights in mind you may also be able to connect the change in attitude or behaviour to a change or improvement in the output of the work.

32 Mindfulness

Introduction

Mindfulness is about presence. It describes a state in which individuals can consciously and deliberately focus on what is happening in the here and now, for them specifically. It is both internal (where individuals focus on their mind, thoughts, consciousness and feelings) and external (where individuals focus on their physical being, their geographical or physical position, their five senses, etc). Mindfulness heightens the awareness of where an individual is, what they are doing and their feelings about it, without the distraction or interference of others' perceptions or opinions. This can be beneficial in all aspects of a person's life, but the idea behind mindfulness at work is to encourage organizations to enable and advocate mindfulness practices, so that people can give their very best at work.

> Even if you just use mindfulness to develop the capacity to pause between stimulus and response, you'll be making the difference between simply working and working brilliantly with your best self.
>
> Justin Standfield, Incendo Development

Promoting wellbeing

In today's modern workplace there are many distractions – open plan offices, flexibility on working hours meaning more comings-and-goings that before, remote working, technology – both personal and professional, on the go at the same time. Workloads are typically higher than our counterparts may have experienced 25 years ago, and we are more aware of our own – and others' – mental health. As a result of all of these factors, it can be difficult to really focus, and to prevent our minds from wandering. As we become distracted in this way, we can lose touch with our physical as well as our mental presence, and that lack of focus on the task at hand can lead us to stress or fret about things other than those we want to be focused on at that time. This creates anxiety. In turn, anxiety can make us at worst unwell, and at best less productive or effective than usual.

Estimates from the 2016 Labour Force Survey (ONS, 2017a) show cases of work-related stress, depression or anxiety in 2015/16 were 1,510 per 100,000 workers, with 11.7 million working days lost as a result.

Research has shown that mindfulness-based stress reduction activities can have a significant impact on the management of anxiety in individuals and there is evidence to suggest that even quick mindfulness techniques can have a positive impact on cognitive ability – on brainpower we use to think, read, learn and concentrate. This improved concentration and focus can be important at work for various reasons – not only in how we focus on work during times of stress or anxiety, but also because more of us are working in open plan, noisier environments where the ability to focus can be critical to success.

Approach

There are a number of things you can do to encourage mindfulness at work. There are endless resources online to inspire your mindfulness activities, but the following are a few of simple initiatives you can undertake.

Encourage self-discovery

Encourage your employees to use mindfulness techniques that they feel work for them. Provide information on mindfulness so that employees who are interested can help themselves. There are so many books, videos, online programmes and classes that you could provide access to, or time to focus on, to allow employees to learn about and begin to practise mindfulness for themselves.

If you have an intranet facility, or a shared employee network or database, consider including information or links on that so that people can find information and resources for themselves.

Mindfulness training

Mindfulness training will not only provide employees with some techniques they can use, it will also demonstrate your organization's commitment to wellbeing. Identify a specialist provider who can offer your employees practical and realistic tips and techniques to practise mindfulness in order to reduce stress. The case study about mindfulness by Incendo Development (page 148) shows the benefits it can have in organizations.

The working environment

Whilst you may not be able to change some elements of the physical working environment (how the building looks, its geographical position, or how many windows or walls it has) you can impact the internal environment. Provide as much open space and natural light as you can, avoiding partitions where possible, and introduce plants and greenery to the office – not only does this increase oxygen, they are also attractive to look at.

Provide spaces in the workplace that could be appropriate for mindfulness activities at work. A quiet room with informal furniture and enough floor space to meditate or lie down will be useful. Whilst many offices are open plan, finding a space for individuals to reflect, take time out, or just work quietly with focus will be advantageous.

It's also beneficial to provide spaces – and opportunity – in the workplace where people can seek solitude when they wish to. This space will enable them to practise mindfulness, but it might also be used more simply to focus, avoid distraction, or take 'time out' to refocus and recover. Time alone can help employees to balance the constant workload, interactions and smartphone interruptions, and this internal reframing can benefit not just the individual, but their colleagues too. Not everyone welcomes the idea of working alone, but as a manager, encouraging the use of time alone may bring benefits in workplace relationships, effectiveness and productivity.

Advocacy

You may not choose to practise what you preach when it comes to mindfulness, despite the benefits described, but your employees are likely to appreciate support and advocacy for mindfulness techniques in the workplace. This doesn't have to be a major public relations campaign, but could be as simple as providing information, supportive communication activities, training and spaces for people to practise techniques and, perhaps more importantly, encouraging them to take some time out to do so when they consider it necessary. This advocacy and enablement will reassure those who are already under some pressure that you are supportive of their attempts to manage the associated anxiety – and this ultimately will benefit them, you and your business.

Encouraging champions

Through the introduction of these types of initiative, you may identify employees within your workforce who are strong advocates and champions of mindfulness. If you do, it may be beneficial to adopt them as champions for mindfulness at work, or wellbeing at work, and encourage them to identify, recommend, action and support new ideas about how to encourage mindfulness in your working environment. Don't forget to recognize this discretionary effort, though, particularly where these initiatives prove popular or successful.

Outcomes

Adopting some of these approaches may enable employees to find their own ways to give their best possible performance day after day. However, perhaps more importantly, organizations that implement such practices are likely to be perceived as supporting wellbeing initiatives, and being proactive in doing so is likely to have an impact on the mental health of the collective workforce, absence is likely to be lower, and productivity and quality of work is likely to be improved.

Measuring impact

The impact of your organization's efforts to introduce and maintain mindfulness practices at work can be measured in a number of ways.

Employee feedback

Seek proactive feedback on the impact of any mindfulness initiatives during your one-to-one discussions with employees in your team. As well as a typical 'happiness' measure (did you like it or enjoy it), ask more specifically about the impact on working practice, stress levels, etc.

Listen for informal feedback in response to the initiatives you have implemented, and for other suggestions that may be coming through.

Ask for collective feedback from teams or groups who use the spaces or programmes you have implemented. As well as a typical 'happy sheet' style of evaluation, ask for comments on the impact the initiatives have had on wellbeing, on motivation, on stress levels, and on their general capacity to cope with the pressures in the workplace. You might also be interested to understand whether mindfulness is having any broader benefits for participants, including impacts they are experiencing outside work.

Organizational evaluation

At an organizational level, it is important to establish not only the feedback from those participating in mindfulness initiatives – and collating them to extract key themes from the feedback – but also to consider what return on investment your business is achieving. Whilst you may be in a position to invest in mindfulness without concern for the payback, it is not just a financial issue – it is also a consideration of the effectiveness of the initiatives you have chosen to implement. Some of the key organizational metrics you could consider would include:

- Absence statistics: Positive impacts are likely to result in an overall reduction in employee absence.

- Days lost due to workplace-related stress: More specifically, you might expect to see less absence directly attributed to workplace stress.

- Productivity, efficiency and quality measures: You may see an impact on your existing business metrics that could be indirectly attributed to mindfulness initiatives.

CASE STUDY Developing mindfulness at work – Incendo Development Ltd

The client organization – in the motor insurance industry – had recently been through a takeover; the residual impact on employees was apparent through increased instances of stress-related absence, anecdotal feedback of feeling overwhelmed, strained relationships with colleagues and general negativity.

The company asked Incendo to deliver a six-week 'Developing mindfulness at work' programme, consisting of six early morning sessions that people could self-nominate to attend before starting work. Although some participants had experienced a bit of meditation as part of practising yoga outside work, everyone in the group was new to the concept of mindfulness. Feedback throughout the programme was positive, and from the first week of practising some breathing techniques and noticing their thoughts, participants reported an increased awareness of their internal reactions to events at work.

The programme has since been repeated in two different forms within the organization. First, it has been offered at lunchtimes and evenings on the same basis as the original format, where participants attend a scheduled six-week mindfulness course. Second, a drop-in programme was offered on an ongoing basis so that people could come to as many or as few classes as they needed, as long as they had completed an initial 'induction' session on the fundamentals of mindfulness. Here is some feedback we received:

'Stopping and thinking about how I am feeling (and why I am feeling it) has really helped to build bridges with some very difficult stakeholders.'

'The Incendo course on mindfulness has provided me with some much-needed guidance to help me in my day-to-day schedule; there are many things which all professionals can relate to in the programme and implement immediately at work.'

'I have stopped being judgemental and approach people with less aggression. My frustration at work has also eased from using the principles from the Incendo mindfulness course and I am now making more informed, conscious decisions.'

33 Mediation

Introduction

Mediation is an approach to resolving disputes, finding solutions to difficult interpersonal problems and mending relationships. In the context of this book, the focus is on the resolution of workplace disputes, usually occurring between two individuals or between the organization as a whole and an individual.

Mediation is a confidential process that follows a structured approach led by an independent intermediary to encourage an open and honest conversation between the two parties, which aims to jointly resolve their conflict. The intermediary gains an understanding of the issue and works with each party, either together or separately, to understand the issue, to share different perspectives and to work towards a resolution that addresses issues raised, has shared responsibility for making changes and improvements that are robust, practical and meaningful to both parties.

The mediator is a facilitator of the conversation. It is not their role to determine a successful outcome, and the independence of their role in the process means that they should not judge or overly influence the discussion – they should remain impartial throughout the process. The specialist skills required to do so, and to get the best out of the process and participants, lead to a requirement for trained and experienced mediators to lead the process.

Many organizations train in-house mediators so that they have an internal resource they can tap into. Others use Acas mediation services where skills are not available in-house, or where there needs to be a strong sense of independence in the process – external consulting mediators can also be used for these purposes.

Promoting wellbeing

A research paper published by Cascade (2017) reports that disputes between co-workers are the most likely causes of conflict in UK workplaces, with more than a third of employees (35 per cent) saying they have experienced this type of problem in the past, and 1 in 10 reporting a conflict between the wider employee group and management. And these issues can have some very negative impacts. A report in the *Telegraph* in 2015 suggested that:

> the most common side effect of workplace conflict is stress. Employee stress can erode job satisfaction, which leads to anger, depression and anxiety. This in turn

can lead to missed deadlines, delayed projects, and low morale. Stressed employees are more likely to become ill, which can mean missed work and increase workload on other employees. At its worst, workplace conflict can cause staff turnover, damage to the reputation of the business, or even workplace violence.

Whilst it may be a challenge – if not impossible – to eliminate any workplace conflict, being able to proactively and efficiently deal with unhealthy conflict will reduce the associated stress levels and maintain a higher level of morale in the workplace. Less absence, greater productivity, improved retention, etc, will all have a positive impact on the workforce, in comparison to the risks associated with leaving conflict to resolve itself.

Approach

Ideally, mediation is not a process you will ever need to utilize, but being prepared and being transparent about its availability and how you would use it if required can be reassuring to your employees who may have to access it. The recommended approach is therefore to raise awareness of mediation as an effective intervention, put in place a clear company policy on mediation, ensure access to skilled mediation resource and regularly monitor mediation matters.

Awareness

It is important that employees are aware that mediation is available to them should they need it, but there is a balance to be struck between raising awareness, perhaps risking scaremongering, and encouraging inappropriate use of it as an intervention. Ensuring that managers and HR specialists fully understand what mediation is, and when it is appropriate to introduce it during a conflict situation, will ensure that it is appropriately used at the right time. Publishing a policy will provide a transparent approach to what mediation is and when it might be used.

Company policy

Implementing a mediation policy in your organization will signify to your leaders and your employees that you are keen to resolve issues proactively and fairly, and will resort to grievance or disciplinary procedures only when absolutely necessary. A policy statement should indicate to employees that mediation exists as part of a broad approach to managing people, rather than as an intervention that is used only when particular incidents require it.

A mediation policy should:

1 Define what mediation is and clarify the objectives of mediation.

2 Explain who can access mediation, and the circumstances that might lead them to do so.

3 Explain who might mediate (internal or external, with what qualifications to mediate, etc).

4 Describe the process, step-by-step, and the roles of the parties involved.

5 Clarify the confidential nature of the process.

6 Describe potential outcomes.

7 Describe what happens after mediation.

8 Explain how information gathered through mediation is used – confidentiality statements, and monitoring of trends and frequencies.

Mediation resources

There are three main choices for how to ensure you have skilled, experienced and available resources to support your mediation requirements:

Train in-house mediators A number of organizations, particularly in public sector, choose this approach. Acas provide training for in-house mediators, and having a pool of resources in house with appropriate training and certification can ensure that mediation matters are resourced and addressed swiftly. However, it is also important to ensure that they can act impartially, and maintain confidentiality throughout, and any concerns about this from other parties involved may impact the outcomes of the process, and the credibility of mediation as a whole.

Utilize Acas resources Acas have access to a large mediator resource pool, so may be able to support your mediation requirements. Before establishing your policy, discuss your potential requirements, your organization type, etc, to ensure they can provide timely support, and at what cost.

External independent mediators As the requirement for mediation grows, so does the number of independent consultants who are trained and experienced in providing mediation services. It could be beneficial to build relationships with one or more external mediators who can partner with your business as required. It is also the case that many law firms, and particularly those offering employment law service, have trained mediators who can act as external independents.

Monitoring mediation

Whilst much of the mediation process and conversation remains confidential, it can be important to collect data to understand any trends or patterns of behaviour that might suggest more than an isolated or personal issue. For example, as you might with grievances, you would want to know which parties are involved, and monitor for any repeat participation. You might also consider what types of issues are being raised through mediation – this could alert you to skill, knowledge or capability gaps that could be resolved through training.

This information might not be for wider communication, but could certainly act as useful indicators for you as a leader or HR specialist.

Outcomes

Proactive conflict management can reduce the likelihood of workplace conflict issues. As we have seen above, such conflict can have significant impacts on all parties – stress related issues, absence, low morale, a decrease in productivity and potentially increased turnover. At worst case, such issues could result in employment tribunals (a CIPD report in 2015 suggested that employers could typically spend approximately 20 days preparing for an employment tribunal).

Early intervention mediation can be used to avoid or minimize the stress-related impacts for people at work (whether they are the complainant or respondent). In addition, the proactivity shown by leaders to take prompt action to address such issues might have a broader impact on morale and on trust between parties and teams in the organization.

Measuring impact

Consider monitoring and evaluating the following.

To establish any wider organizational issues or leadership capability issues

- What types of conflict are emerging? What themes are you seeing?
- Who is raising issues? Consider the level or grade of individual raising the issue – is there a consistency of complaints within certain teams, are there any recurring complainants?
- What conflicts are being reported? Are there common themes – eg bullying behaviours, inappropriate banter, poor work allocation?

- What outcomes are being recommended? Is there a trend that might suggest a change in company policy, or training/awareness of certain issues or procedures need to be improved?

To assess the effectiveness of mediation

Mediation is confidential, and therefore accessing, and certainly publishing, data about the nature of the issues discussed could be difficult, and may even be unethical. However, if you can do so confidentially, and without compromising the process, you might consider:

- Are agreed action plans followed through by both parties? Do they resolve the issues presented?

- How many instances of escalation (eg to grievance, disciplinary, tribunal) following mediation have been reported?

- What is the informal feedback about the mediation process?

- Does anyone refuse mediation?

- What feedback have you received about the mediators you use?

To present a case for mediation

- Prepare statistics reporting the number of disputes, the percentage of mediations that end in agreement, and the percentage of participants that report it as beneficial/helpful in addressing issues.

Mediation in action

Sharon Crooks, mediator, describes how mediation can aid conflict resolution at work.

The secret of an effective mediator is to help the parties to see underneath the surface reasons for the conflict. Typically, people can very easily articulate their position – the reason they are right and the other person is wrong! The mediator will ask lots of questions to understand what each person's interests are – what would solve the problem from their point of view, to enable them to move on into a conflict-free future. But even deeper down underneath the positions and interests are the parties' needs.

As social animals, humans have the usual biological needs for safety, food and shelter, but we also have what David Rock (2008) labels as five primary social needs, which can drive our behaviour. When these social needs for status, certainty, autonomy, relatedness and fairness are threatened, which can often happen at work, we may react with a fight or flight response, just as we do in any conflict or threatening situation. We either fight to protect ourselves, or simply try to avoid situations where these needs are threatened.

At work this response could manifest itself as ducking out of competitive team activities, blaming others, making excuses or derogatory comments, raising grievances, bullying or even a very directive management style, escalating to raising a grievance or taking disciplinary measures, rather than having a constructive conversation. A skilful mediator will unpick the story of the conflict, help the parties to see the underlying reasons for their behaviour, and prompt them to think about ways they could rebuild their relationship. In a mediation, the parties have equal status, and equal power. They formally and confidentially contract with each other about how they will work together in future, and unless the parties request some external support from the organization, the only other person who knows the details is the mediator. Mediation focuses on finding solutions that meet the needs of the people involved, and it can be empowering and motivating, because there are no winners and losers.

Sharon Crooks is an accredited Civil and Commercial Mediator and trainer in mediation skills. She has resolved conflicts in a variety of contexts including charities, multinationals, education and communities as well as teaching restorative justice in prisons.

34 Switching off

Introduction

For many reasons, the world of work has become something of an 'always on' culture, with people checking their phones, tablets and laptops continuously throughout the day. Research has suggested that we check our phones up to 85 times a day (Woollaston, 2015). And in many cases this is prioritized above interpersonal interactions. Whilst much of this may be for social media, personal email and recreational use, many of us operate from one device, making the separation of home and work more challenging.

Add to this the increased flexibility of working patterns and locations. It is becoming more common to work remotely (be that from home, a coffee shop or a virtual office environment) and/or with flexible working patterns that accommodate our other commitments in life (volunteering, children, the gym, etc). Our team members may not be working flat out from 9 to 5 – they might start later, finish earlier, take an extended break in the middle of the day. These factors mean that 'normal' or 'standard' office hours are becoming more unusual, and flexibility may mean that we appear to be 'always on' – or maybe we just *feel* that we need to be always on.

Promoting wellbeing

Whilst the precursors to this 'always on' culture can have some really positive effects on employees – flexibility, continuous connection, information availability, etc – there are also negative impacts. They may find it more difficult to switch off and relax, or enjoy social activities or hobbies. Not being able to switch off means that our minds can be overactive, they don't stop working, and in turn this can cause tiredness, reduced sleep, less energy at work, less creativity, more mistakes and an overall loss of productivity.

Approach

Lead by example

You may feel that as 'manager' you have to put in the extra hours, and be clearing your email or your to-do list outside of typical working hours. However, in doing so, consider how the recipient may be feeling or reacting – they may feel a need to instantly respond, or that because you are working, they should be too. But just because that pattern of working suits you, this doesn't mean that it will suit others, and the stimulus to respond might be one of fear or stress. Instead, consider:

alternatives to making a call – can you draft an email or a handwritten note instead?

preparing your messages or emails, but sending them during 'normal' working hours from your drafts folder;

whether you need to send an email at all, or whether you can add it to a discussion list for when you next meet that person.

Set the tone

As the manager, your team members will follow your lead. If you are constantly on your phone, tablet or laptop during meetings, one-to-ones, or just through the working day, there may be a feeling that it is an appropriate way to work and behave. Set the tone by having time away from your devices, particularly when you are in discussions with team members – individually or collectively, or formally or informally (over lunch for example).

Be clear on expectations

As a manager, one of your key roles is to set the expectations that you have of your team members, and this includes any expectations you may have about flexibility of working hours, responsiveness etc. At a more macro level, if you have to send a request outside of normal hours, be explicit about whether you need an urgent or immediate response, or whether the matter can wait until they are back in the office. Encourage your team members *not* to check emails or messages whilst on holidays or weekends. Setting these boundaries will make clear that it is ok, and will relieve any perceived or self-imposed pressure for the employee.

Keep a log

In an environment where flexibility is encouraged, it may seem to be counter-cultural, but it is useful to log the hours worked. This is not about measuring input or attended hours, but more about understanding how much you or your team members are working, managing excesses, readjusting workload and encouraging them (and you) to maintain a healthy balance between working and home. Don't think of it as a clocking on and off, but more about noting the time spent outside of traditional working hours, particularly when a reciprocal flexibility is not part of the arrangement.

Step away

For meetings or tasks that require specific concentration or attention, particularly those where accuracy is important or you are in face-to-face discussion, leave devices behind. Encourage team members to do the same – to put it in a drawer, or not bring it to a meeting, so that the temptation to check it, or the noise of notifications, cannot distract you from your focus at that time.

Outcomes

The primary aim is to recognize a change in the way we work, the responsiveness we expect and the impact that can have. For many, the 'always on' working that technology enables means that employees don't take the opportunity to switch off and rest their minds. By encouraging some of the above actions and enabling those rest periods and reasonable breaks away from technology and work demands, managers are more likely to see employees take breaks, rest their minds and as a result, feel more alert, energized and productive.

Measuring impact

Individual impact

Asking employees about the difference their 'switch off' makes to them and their lives is an important first level evaluation. Responses to this could go either way – for some the switch off strategy may be one that allows them to regain control of their own time, and to focus on what matters at appropriate times, prioritizing work in accordance with expectations. This could leave them feeling more energized and productive during working hours. Others may find that switching off leaves them feeling more stressed and anxious due to workload build-up, but is the counter true – that because they have not switched off they feel tired, less productive, etc? Understanding the preferences and impacts of different individuals will allow people managers to adapt their approach to meet them and ensure the best strategy for each person. Ask employees at key times – before and after their annual leave, or their weekends, or when they are having a day of flexible working, to understand in the moment what impact technology and their availability is having on their productivity and how they feel about work.

Team or functional impact

It may be interesting to observe behaviours and ask questions to see whether there is any impact on the collective team – for example, switching off may negatively impact collaboration and communication, but it could positively impact interpersonal relationships and improve the quality and amount of face-to-face communication. If you decide to switch off technology during meetings, does this have any impact on the length, focus or contributions during the meeting?

35   Getting organized

Introduction

In today's typical working environment, people can feel busier than ever with increasing competing demands both on and off line. Offices don't see the same quantity of paperwork in the in-tray anymore, but there is still plenty of administration, paperwork, technology and screens to work through, to manage and to keep track of. As the old expressions goes, 'tidy desk – tidy mind'. Whilst it's not in everyone's nature to work in the most organized way, with schedules of tasks, lists and immaculate filing, there are some top tips that everyone can take away that could help to reduce levels of stress just by being more organized.

Promoting wellbeing

By getting organized, you and your team members are likely to feel much more in control of the working week, the environment, and the priorities. If an employee perceives they have control at work, they can feel less stressed and more satisfied. In addition, employees may feel that they are making a better impression on co-workers and bosses, and this in turn can improve their self-confidence. But it's not just about appearances – it can also be the case that being organized can improve an individual's productivity – that if you write down goals and objectives, they are more likely to be achieved, not least because you are able to define a plan that will drive their delivery, and monitor and check progress. Being more focused on delivery means knowing what needs to be done and when, and knowing this, employees are much less likely to experience those negative thoughts about the task or how to deliver it that can drain mental energy.

Approach

There are a couple of different factors that could be the focus of your plans to improve organization – organizing yourself, organizing your stuff and organizing your time. The following suggestions are guidelines that you can simply follow, regardless of your natural tendencies for organization, or that you as a manager can share with and use to encourage your direct reports to enable them to feel more organized, more in control and more prepared.

Organize your time

- Plan your diary: Make sure you include time in your diary to do the day-to-day or weekly tasks and activities that need to be completed, as well as time for meetings. If you book meeting after meeting, you'll find yourself having to do the daily tasks outside of your normal working hours. So always try to block out an amount of time each day or each week for just doing 'stuff'. A to-do list – on a notepad or on screen – will help you to know what you have to achieve each day.

- Schedule your workload: Plan head. Think about your priorities for the week, about what is urgent or important, and what could be delegated, held for now or is waiting for a response from someone else. Taking a few moments to categorize your weekly or monthly schedule at the start of whichever period will help you to prioritize what is important, and make sure that the right things are done. At the end of the week, make a quick note of things you need to achieve next week, and use that as the basis of your planning at the start of that week.

- Set goals: Writing down your goals makes it much more likely that you will achieve them. So take some time to think about your goals, whether they are life goals or professional ones. Review them regularly to ensure that you are working towards achieving them at the right pace, and celebrate when you succeed.

Organize your stuff

- Declutter: Even if you are not the tidiest person, and it's not your normal way of working, a regular declutter of your workspace will help to keep you organized. Spend a few minutes working through all the paperwork on your desk will help you to organize it (filing or shredding what you don't need), identify priorities (or remind you of outstanding commitments) and feel prepared.

- A place for everything: Use folders, boxes or online filing to keep important documents or information related to a specific project, task, customer etc all in one place. If you're not the type to file as you go, block time out 15 minutes in your diary each week to put things in the right place, so you can find them easily when you need to.

Organize yourself

- Manage home and work commitments together: It is often more effective to maintain your work and your domestic/social diary in one place.

It may appear to give a better separation of the two to manage two diaries, but this can result in unexpected conflicts when the two are brought together. It might consequently be easier to see whether or not you can meet a tight work deadline if your domestic and social commitments are set out in the same place.

- Use reminders: With smart phones and devices on our person most of the time, it couldn't be easier to set reminders for the things that really matter to you, either on a regular basis, or as a one off.

- Don't beat yourself up: If you're struggling to focus, take a break. Get a coffee, take a walk outside in the fresh air, and then come back to your desk and take a fresh look at your to-dos, your diary and your priorities.

Outcomes

By taking time to consider a plan, and to get your work and that of your employees organized, filed and prepared, you will have a clearer idea of what has to be achieved, the priorities and any potential conflicts. With these conflicts or limitations made apparent, they can be proactively managed or planned for, and in your role as leader you can work with your direct reports to ensure that they have the support and resources they need.

Measuring impact

The effectiveness of getting more organized is subjective, as it is primarily about how the individual feels about their own management of their workload and achievement of their goals. The key to evaluating it will therefore be to ask them about the impact any experimental changes have on how they feel about planning and structure, and what impact it has on how they work. As a manager you may also observe changes, and it is important to provide constructive feedback about these to your employee so that they are aware that the impact is valuable.

Environment

Designing the working environment

Introduction

Whilst there are many factors that impact how an office may be furnished and laid out, there are some factors that can influence the factors connected to employee wellbeing. Whilst we have seen an evolution of office environments over the decades, from small offices to cubicles to open plan, the optimum solution is to provide a workspace that encourages flexibility in where and how people work. However, organizations have to balance the need for employee satisfaction and the business needs of the working environment.

Whilst considering the size, layout, fixtures and fittings of your workplace may sound like an expensive project, this tool will focus on some of the small steps that you can take to offer a positive and productive working environment for all employees.

Promoting wellbeing

A study by US firm Steelcase found that there is a strong connection between employees' satisfaction with their workplace satisfaction and their levels of engagement. In particular they reported that employees who are able to choose where they actually work within the office environment are significantly more engaged that those who have no flexibility (Steelcase, 2017).

Changing or adapting the working environment to promote wellbeing factors and to become more 'person-centric' will no doubt positively impact some of the main employee health issues that are faced in the workplace – for example, lack of activity during the working day, stress, healthy eating, etc.

In addition, some of the changes that might be made can have a direct impact on health issues too by considering office furniture and how it might be able to accommodate conditions such as back pain, visual impairments, etc.

Approach

Accommodating difference

It is important for employers to recognize that different people work with different preferences, and it can be beneficial not only to the individual but also to their productivity and temperament at work to consider how you might accommodate those differences. Some people prefer to work alone to enable them to think and focus, whereas others prefer to be in open plan areas, able to interact with others and work with a buzz around them. However, most organizations operate on open plan office spaces, which means some preferences are ignored.

Here are some suggestions for accommodating people's different preferences:

- Provide a few small areas where people can go and work in private or in quiet at times when they really need to focus. Whilst this shouldn't become their permanent place of work, allowing people who prefer this environment to spend time alone during the working day is likely to increase their productivity and improve their overall temperament or stress levels.

- For some people, working at a desk space helps them to remain more productive, but for others it can feel restrictive and not creative or inspiring. Provide some comfortable or more relaxed spaces where people could wok more informally at points during the working day if they prefer. For example, a few sofas with a coffee table, or a bar area with bar stools, can make a difference to how people feel when they are working.

- The opportunity to collaborate informally can be important for the organization's productivity, quality and innovation needs, and can also be an important social factor for employees at work. Whilst open plan offices go some way to enabling people to meet, interact and work together, there is more that can be done to actively encourage and enable it. The sofas and bar areas mentioned above can be useful spaces for this to happen, but providing the opportunity to use technology in that space (eg USB plugs, iPad docks and screens to connect to laptops or tablets) will enable sharing of information during discussions.

- Provide 'stand-up' collaboration areas – space in the office to stand around a board or chart and engage in discussion or brainstorming.

- Creative spaces can be important, too, particularly where that is required in the team or the role, and so the provision of an inspiring or creative space that is stimulating and interesting to be in can be valuable. Setting up a creative or idea hub in the office can be beneficial. This doesn't have to be a huge space, but should be well equipped, with tools, toys and coloured pens and papers to enable creative working. Allocate a small space in the office for an 'ideas hub', and stock it with creative work materials (Post-Its, pens, cards, flipcharts, write-on walls, etc) and other stimulating things such as Plasticine, stickers, Lego, etc.

• In addition, the provision of whiteboards, flipcharts or write-on glass walls or splashbacks can enable brainstorming in collaboration spaces.

Reducing stress

There are some simple initiatives you can consider that will help employees to reduce stress in the workplace, in addition to the other suggestions included within this tool:

• Encourage organized and decluttered office spaces: Provide ample storage space for employees to use, and for office stationery, equipment, filing and storage.

• Add plants and flowers to the work environment: They have a calming influence on employees and create positive emotions, as well as making the office look nice.

• Add ambient lighting as well as – or ideally instead of – fluorescent lighting: As well as adding atmosphere and looking more pleasant, it can create a more calming environment.

• Make light refreshments available (coffee, bottled drinks, fruit, biscuits, etc): This not only encourages people to take a break, but might also encourage some interaction and collaboration.

Addressing health issues

Availability of adaptable workplace furniture and equipment is important for those employees with health concerns. Adaptable chairs, height-adjustable desks, appropriate IT hardware or any equipment that is required to support a disability will ensure that employees are able to work at their best and minimize disruption or discomfort.

• If you have an occupational health advisor, or a health and safety advisor, involve them in the assessment of individuals' workspace to ensure that they are comfortable and safe, and to make recommendations with or on behalf of the employee.

• Inform employees of the availability of adaptable furniture or equipment if required, and the process to use to request and/or justify any requests.

Optimizing engagement

Employees like to have a feel-good factor when they arrive at work – after all, they spend most of their day there. This feel-good factor can translate into engagement, too, and engagement is not only beneficial to the organization's bottom line, but is also a key factor in ensuring the employee's wellbeing. Some of the workplace features mentioned above will have an impact on their engagement and wellbeing, but you could also consider the following:

- Put up posters and wall art that promotes your company vision, mission, goals, etc, and/or that focuses on your products (especially in use) or customers (using products or services).

- Provide real-time updates on screens of your business metrics, sales, calls, etc, so that employees can see how much is being achieved.

- Brand office spaces with logos and corporate colours, providing corporate items like mugs and pens, etc, to enable employees to connect to the brand.

- Use motivational artwork and word transfers on walls to inspire and motivate employees.

- Make the space attractive to employees through the use of colour, shapes, variety of furniture, etc.

- If you have space, and the right culture in your organization, providing leisure facilities like table tennis, football tables or game consoles can help employees to connect, de-stress and switch off from work for short periods of time.

- Consider the use of music in the workplace to stimulate engagement (see Tool 48, 'Music at work' (page 218), for more information).

Outcomes

By providing a variety of options for employees' working spaces, and ensuring that they are light, fresh and inspiring, employees are more likely to enjoy their presence at work, and be inspired by their surroundings.

Measuring impact

The benefits of a flexible approach to the working environment may be highly individualized but there are still some things managers can be done to evaluate how effective it is, and what impact it has. For example, you could consider:

- Room/facility utilization: Gather information about how often, and by whom, the specific spaces in your office environment are used. This will give an indication about whether the space is effective or not, and you can follow up by finding out what might be more useful.

Meeting effectiveness: Ask for views about how effective meetings are in the spaces provided, and establish what could make them more effective – eg open or closed spaces, different or better equipment or stationery, etc.

Employee feedback: Ask employees for feedback on the overall office environment, and for any suggestions they might have about what could make it better (perhaps within given constraints, such as budget, or without substantial redevelopment).

Occupational heath audit: If you have occupational health or health or safety teams on site, it can be extremely valuable to get their assessment of the workplace from a health, safety, environment and adaptability perspective, and particularly relating to overall stress reduction or the health matters of specific individuals if they are known. This audit will then indicate whether there are any further actions that should be taken to ensure the workplace is fit for purpose for those with specific needs, and what else could be done more generally to make it a healthy and inspiring workplace.

Balance

37 Remote working

Introduction

As organizations become more technology dependent, business becomes more geographically spread and employees call for a better work–life balance, so the need and demand for effective ways to work remotely and/ or virtually come to the fore.

The virtual workplace is not a traditional office environment, but rather one that has no boundaries about where people work from. Some individuals may select to work virtually or remotely, whilst some organizations choose not to have an actual office environment, instead asking all employees to work remotely. Yet still there will be a need for cohesion, for teamwork and for collaboration. The changing spectrum of technology has enabled these new ways of working, and forward-thinking organizations do embrace them, with some proactively encouraging them. And whilst there are many great advantages and benefits to virtual working, there are some pitfalls too, and some of these pitfalls can have a negative impact on employee wellbeing if not carefully managed.

Promoting wellbeing

According to a TUC report in 2014, employers should be concerned about employees doing too many hours of work. They stated that long hours and overwork cause issues for people's mental health, causing employees to feel stressed, making carer responsibilities more challenging, and leaving them tired and burnt out – all factors that the TUC say are bad for business. Virtual working does in many cases allow employees to schedule their own working time, and as far as is practical, to work around other personal commitments, carer responsibilities or personal interests.

A 2011 study carried out by Staples in the US found that 86 per cent of remote workers say they are more productive, reporting that they were 25 per cent less stressed working from home than working from the office, with 73 per cent eating healthier at home than at work. Eighty per cent of the workers they surveyed said that they had a better work–life balance since working from home.

However, other research studies claim that a balance can be harder to achieve when people work from home as the boundaries can become more blurred. There are other factors that might negatively impact well-being as employees work remotely, such as a lack of support and visible leadership and less social interaction. These need to be carefully managed to ensure that the positive health benefits are optimized, and the risks are minimized.

Approach

Leadership

Traditional approaches to leading and managing people become irrelevant when workers are remote or virtual. Typically, employees and their workload has been managed 'visually' – you are able to see the employee is in attendance, whether they are actively working, and you can see the outputs of that work easily. In virtual working relationships, there has to be a strong element of trust between the leader and the employee, strong lines of communication, and much more focus on outputs and deliverables, rather than on hours worked.

This focus on outputs requires clear and collaborative objective setting, with short-, medium- and longer-term targets set out with expectations defined and understood by both parties. Regular check-ins will ensure that deliverables are on track. In check-ins and outside of those meetings, employees will need to know when and where they can turn for support. In an office environment, they can immediately reach out. Remotely this can be more difficult, so providing quick and effective access to guidance, advice and coaching will be reassuring to the employee when they need it.

Balance

Whilst many remote workers find a better work–life balance, some find it more difficult to set clear boundaries between work and personal time, and the blurring of these boundaries can result in people working longer hours and losing their balance. As a leader, you should take a proactive role in checking in with your employee regarding their working patterns and working habits when they are remote. Check your own behaviours to ensure that you are not passively encouraging longer working hours, and instead actively encourage people to shut down from work at specific times, don't set short-term deadlines that will see people working late, and review workload to ensure it is realistic and they can maintain a balance.

It can be beneficial to encourage remote workers to check in and check out of the working day. This should not be seen as a necessity to confirm working hours, but rather an approach that sets boundaries for the employee on the start and finish of the day.

Social

With remote workers usually located at home, the opportunity for social interaction with work colleagues is limited, and this can cause some to feel isolated and detached from the workplace. Finding ways to encourage that social interaction is important, and there are a number of suggestions about how that can be done:

- Chat: Web chat technology allows people to chat more informally at work, and this can be very effective when workers are remote. It is a simple way for people to communicate with each other one-to-one or in groups.

- Informal interactions: Build in time during conference calls and webinars for ice-breakers and informal chats. The usual office-based conventions of finding out about people's weekends, holidays or how they got on in a sports challenge are often missed as people dial into a call and immediately start working. Allowing some warm-up or warm-down time at the start or end of a meeting can facilitate this kind of interaction, and encourage team members to feel more connected.

- Social activities: Building social activities into evenings or weekends will provide opportunities for those who want it to interact on a social level with their colleagues and friends at work.

- Regular office-based meetings: Calling the team together at the office for a regular interaction face-to-face will help to maintain connections and build relationships.

If in doubt, ask your remote workers what methods of social connections they might value, and trial them.

Technology

The success of remote or virtual working is highly dependent on having the right technology for your business and for the employee's role. This doesn't mean they have to be provided with every piece of kit that is available. However, as a minimum most will require a laptop, internet access, and reliable access to your email and company systems (eg finance, HR or payroll systems, etc), and access to a phone line. Some companies now have a 'bring your own device' policy, asking employees to purchase or provide the required technology in return for a small cash allowance. Many, however, refer the comfort of providing their own assets, ensuring appropriate security and safeguarding can be applied.

In addition to hardware requirements, collaboration tools are really important. This could be access to shared folders allowing access to information, policy, data etc that can be updated and accessed in real time, or communication tools. Telephone conferencing is the simplest form of collaboration technology, and whilst it is useful, it does have limitations. Advancements now mean that video conferencing is a well-used technology, and at the next level webinar technology should be provided and accessible to all to encourage virtual meetings, in which employees can communicate, collaborate and share slides. In some newer technologies, this includes sharable whiteboard space that can be accessed by participants.

Providing the technology is key, but encouraging, enabling and training employees to use it effectively when working virtually is critical.

Office

Take responsibility for ensuring that your remote workers have an appropriate, safe and healthy environment to work from when they work remotely. If you have occupational health and/or safety specialists, a risk assessment of the working environment should be carried out. In particular, pay attention to the safety of any electrical equipment provided for work, and the furniture (desk, chairs etc) that people use. Offering advice and recommendations to ensure employee comfort, safety and health will minimize the risk of future absences due to illness, and will demonstrate your ongoing commitment to employee wellbeing. It is likely that many virtual employees are working remotely from flexible locations – from home, a coffee shop, pop-up office environments, etc, and it can be beneficial to be transparent about any safety or health issues related to these environments.

Outcomes

Virtual working has some significant benefits for all parties. For organizations, it is more cost-effective. Those who establish a fully virtual workforce have no office-based overheads, for example, and have ultimate flexibility in where they recruit talent from – they could recruit from an international field without concern about relocation, eligibility to work, etc.

Employees are likely to feel more in control of their working pattern, and typically remote workers will feel that they have a better work–life balance and less stress.

The environment benefits too, with fewer employees commuting on a regular basis, less business travel to and from meetings required, and much more work carried out online, rather than on paper.

Measuring impact

There are several aspects you can consider in the evaluation of your remote working policy or approach:

- Cost: Is there any cost impact on your business? Are you saving money on facilities? Is it more costly to provide appropriate equipment to remote workers? Is there any impact on your travel budget (are people travelling to meet each other more often)?

- Productivity: What impact do you see on the productivity of your team? Are there any impacts on the quality of work, products or services?

- Collaboration: Does remote working impact the ability of your team to work effectively together? Are you seeing benefits from regular virtual interactions, or is your team's performance limited by their less frequent discussions?

- Employee perspectives: Do employees prefer working remotely? Are they confident they have the support they need?

- Manager perspectives: Are people managers confident in the outputs of the team? Are they able to offer supervision, coaching, direction etc using remotely technologies?

Flexible working

Introduction

Approaches to flexible working arrangements can vary greatly across different organizations and different sectors. Whilst some businesses may be able to operate in a fully flexible way, others will have customer or stakeholder requirements as part of their business operating model that require presence (virtual or onsite) at specific times.

Some typical approaches to flexible working might include:

- Flexitime: Variable start and finish times, and flexible lunch periods, with core hours for attendance explicitly specified.

- Autonomous patterns: No working pattern is determined, but a contractual number of hours may well be agreed. The core focus, however, is on the output of work rather than input of hours.

- Compressed hours: Whereby an employee works a specific number of hours but over a reduced number of days.

- Annualized hours: Whereby an employee is contracted to work a specific number of hours per annum, but has some flexibility about when these hours are worked. Often – though not exclusively – this is seen in roles connected to education, allowing for more working time during term time, and more leisure time during school holidays.

- Job sharing: Allows for two employees to share a role, enabling both to work part time hours.

- Virtual working: Encourages employees to work in flexible locations – with facilities available in the office, but with technology provided (eg laptop, phone, conference call and webinar facilities) such that the employee can work anywhere, and at any time, at their convenience, provided that they can meet the deliverables of their role.

Promoting wellbeing

A NICE report (2009) into mental wellbeing at work identified flexible working as a key recommendation to enable improved employee wellbeing, stating that 'such opportunities can enhance employees' sense of control and promote engagement and job satisfaction'.

Acas (2015) report that an imbalance between work and life can result in an increase in employee stress, may impact attendance at work, and can knock on effects to productivity, and this can impact the quality of work done and workplace relationships.

Employees can often find it difficult to achieve a work–life balance, and those who do may feel guilty or concerned that they arrive at the office late after looking after a dependant in the morning, or that they have to leave early to take care of personal matters. A more flexible approach to working hours and/or location can encourage a guilt-free equilibrium, removing the inner conflict that may be felt, and enabling a better balance.

It is also worth noting that employees may prefer working at certain times that are not conducive to a standard nine-to-five operation. Some employees are highly motivated and productive in the morning, whereas others are night owls. Providing options allows them to work at the time when they are at their best, and when they know they don't have other distractions or concerns.

YouGov research reveals that British people feel they would be more productive with a shorter working day, which currently averages 8.6 hours based on a five-day week. Asked how many hours at work would be most productive, most people (56 per cent) choose a length of up to 7 hours. In the US, the majority also say a shorter working day is most productive.

(YouGov, 2015)

Approach

First, an organization needs to decide whether it intends to offer a blanket approach to flexible working, or an individualized one, responding to specific requests and needs as they arise. Whichever is applicable, the organization needs to consider some of the following factors.

Business drivers/operating model

Is the organization one that has core operating hours on which customers, suppliers and other stakeholders are dependent? For example, roles in the customer service industry may need to be tied into certain opening hours such that customers know when they can contact the company. Such arrangements may call for employees to be present in a contact centre, on site for those fixed hours. Other organizations, such as creative agencies, are less likely to be tied to specific daily working hours, and indeed may find that creativity is stifled by such practices. As such, many encourage a much more relaxed approach to hours of work, and will focus instead on project timelines and delivery to ensure that customer needs are met.

Organizational culture

Connected to the above, the organizational culture will influence the way in which employees are managed and led. If the culture of the organization supports freedom of responsibility, it is more likely that working hours can be relaxed. A more controlled culture, or one where strong governance is vital, may see a more restrictive approach to working hours. It is important that the culture and the working practice are aligned.

Technology

Real virtual working, and optimum flexible working, can only really be effective when technology is in place to fully enable it. Whilst today most people have some technology skills and equipment to enable them to access work content remotely, not all wish to use their own devices (preferring to keep work and home separate) and not all companies have the required security infrastructure to be able to make it happen. Companies therefore need to pay good attention to the elements of their IT strategy that would enable – or hinder – virtual working. This means providing appropriate equipment and devices, enabling remote access into company servers and email accounts, and (often forgotten) providing solutions for conference calling, video calls and virtual meetings that can include document sharing. Equally important is that all employees are trained and able to use these remote access and virtual tools.

Facilities

This technology investment comes at a significant cost, and some organizations are now balancing this investment with reduction of overheads for office facilities, by encouraging agile working. Agility in this sense refers to the fact that employees are not required to attend the office, and as such are not allocated a desk space. Space is available as hot desking, or in informal work areas. The challenge here connects back to cultural issues, and the need to rethink how people connect at work. If colleagues are no longer certain to be physically present and visible, leaders need to ensure that trust is strong, and the communication is robust.

Implementation

For each of the flexible working approaches mentioned in the introduction, here are some issues that need to be considered prior to implementation. All of them have to be practical for business, and whilst aspirational, you may decide that now is not the right time to introduce a new way of working. The notes below are not exhaustive, and will vary depending on the operating model, culture, technology and facilities issues mentioned above, but give some indication of the issues you will need to consider.

Flexitime

- What core hours do you need employees to work? Consider starting time windows (eg 8–10), finishing time windows (eg 4–6) and lunchtime windows (eg 12–2). Check that this will not be too disruptive for your clients or customers, and that you will always have sufficient cover.

- Will you allow people to accrue additional hours worked and take time off in lieu? What limitations will you put on this?

- What additional costs or time will be incurred by monitoring or managing time and attendance? Are systems required to make this effective, or are you willing to work on trust?

- What is preventing you from adopting a fully autonomous pattern of work?

Autonomous patterns

- Would flexible working be more appropriate?

- How will you measure employees' effectiveness and performance? You should consider how you will now set goals and targets, as attendance and timelines are no longer relevant.

- How will you ensure that as a leader you are updated on progress, risks and issues?

- How will you manage absence or illness issues?

- How will you build trust and collaboration among your team, and with yourself?

- What new skills and behaviours will your leaders need to demonstrate to effectively manage employees working autonomously?

Compressed hours

- Is there a gap in cover when the employee is not in the office – if the work is not being done on that day, who or what is impacted?

- Will you need to adjust your regular meeting schedule, or similar calendar events, to ensure that the employee can still participate?

Annualized hours

- Are there specific times of the year that the employee needs to work at peak, and other times that are lower or have no requirement to work? Be explicit about that in your arrangements with the employee.

Job sharing

- Is the allocation of responsibilities or tasks clear?
- How will you ensure effective handover and open communication between the jobsharers so that the role is executed smoothly?
- What additional costs or risks does job sharing create in having two employees for one role? What additional opportunities or benefits does it present?

Virtual working

- What investment in technology is required? Are you willing to make it? What is the cost/benefit?
- Are there specific roles where this approach would be valuable (eg jobs requiring a great deal of travel)?
- Are your customers, suppliers, other office locations and other stakeholders also technology enabled? If not, it is unlikely that this will be an effective way of working.
- How will you build your team, when they are working remotely?
- What training do your line managers need in order to enable them to effectively manage virtual teams?

Legal responsibilities

In the UK, legislation gives employees with certain qualifying conditions a legal right to formally apply for flexible arrangements. These 'statutory applications' must be put in writing to the employer, who must consider the request and respond within three months of the application being made. Agreement is likely to result in a change of terms and conditions, whilst any intention to reject the application must be explained to the employee, who subsequently has the right to appeal against the decision. Employers should have a robust policy and procedure that outlines the statutory responsibilities of both the employer and employee in these applications.

Outcomes

Acas (2015) says that employees who have a better work–life balance often have a greater sense of responsibility, ownership and control of their working life.

Measuring impact

Feedback, whether formally through employee satisfaction surveys or similar, or informally from your team members and colleague, will indicate whether the implementation of flexible working approaches is having the impacts you intended, or those that are specified in the outcomes section above. You should also look for quantitative measures too, such as:

- Absence should be reducing, as employees can use flexitime to schedule appointments, fulfil carer responsibilities, and as health impacts of stress or mental wellbeing are minimized through better working patterns.

- Productivity should not be negatively impacted, and indeed you may see positive impacts.

- Quality and creativity should be improving, as you offer people flexibility to work at their best times.

- You should also keep a watching eye over issues such as team conflict, grievances or performance management issues, which can arise as a result of perceived unfairness, blurred boundaries or unclear expectations.

Social and community

04

Motivation

Introduction

Theories of motivation have been well discussed in business for many years, but have rarely changed to incorporate recent developments in how we work, what we work on and why we work, or what we want to get from our lives, both inside and outside of the workplace. Traditional models of motivation may still be valid, but there could be more to an employee's drivers or triggers than those models explain.

Motivation triggers are a highly individualized matter. Generic theories may make assumptions about groups of people, but actually it is our individual personality, lifestyle choices, drivers and needs that impact how we feel about work and what makes us want to get to it every day. Understanding these at an individual as well as a collective level will be key to tapping into them, and meeting employees' needs wherever possible.

Promoting wellbeing

A lack of motivation at work is highly likely to have an impact on an employee's performance, behaviour and commitment to their job.

Approach

Ask

The simplest way to find out what motivates one of your team members is to ask them. Explain why you want to know, and work with them to identify how you might use the information you get to make tasks, the job or a project more motivating and engaging for them. For example, an employee motivated by achievement might want to be set stretching targets and goals. An employee motivated by social interactions might prefer to be in a collaborative and team-focused environment. Whilst it may not be possible to always meet these preferences, it can be worth the conversation about them, and you could consider providing opportunity outside the usual day job to enable the employee to satisfy those preferences.

Observe and learn

Regular reviews, check-ins and monitoring of your team members will help you to learn more about them, about what they are enjoying doing and why, and importantly what they are not motivated by. In the case of the latter, it may not be feasible to eliminate demotivating tasks or factors, but acknowledging that you recognize the issue, and minimizing it as far as possible will help the employee to manage it.

Assess

There are various psychometric tools and less technical questionnaires that can be done to point towards a person's motivations or behavioural drivers. It is worth investing in some expertise if you want to use such tools to ensure that anything you select is fit for purpose and robust and that the appropriate feedback is given. This can be particularly valuable as part of a career development process (eg coaching or outplacement) or potentially for selection.

Match

Ideally, candidates will match themselves to roles and organizations that meet their motivational preferences for certain role characteristics, be that money, flexibility, social responsibility etc. However, there may also be an advantage in making small changes (where it is practical) to tasks, roles, the working environment or pattern, for example, to make the most of an individual's motivational drivers and optimize their performance.

Review

During regular check-in conversations or performance reviews, keep the conversation about motivations alive – they can move with changes in lifestyle, ambition, education or other priorities. Continue to keep in touch with what is important to your employees, and seek to match those priorities where you can. Of course, it is a two-way street – your employees should also bring some self-motivation to want to deliver their best for you every day. This reciprocity will be key to a mutually beneficial working relationship.

There are some simple ways to encourage your employees to feel motivated. Just doing little things can make a large difference, for example:

- Show appreciation: Saying thank you is hugely underrated, but it makes a big difference to how people feel about having gone that extra mile for you. Whether it's a quiet thank you face-to-face, a short note, or thanks in front of a bigger audience depends on you and the person you're appreciating, but the two little words have big impact.

- Give recognition: Don't take the credit – share it out. When people have contributed and made a difference, tell them that, and, if it is appropriate, tell other people too.

- Delegate meaningfully: Rather than just allocate out tasks from a list, set clear goals and expectations and be clear about the purpose – not just what needs to be done, but why it matters, who cares about it, and what opportunities or benefits it offers the person you are delegating too.

- Be fair and consistent: Employees want to know that when you thank them for doing a good job, you mean it, and know that when others aren't pulling their weight, you'll address that too. Nothing is more demotivating than a broad generic thanks to a team, when it's clear that not all have contributed equally. So take time to recognize or address those contributions individually and fairly.

Outcomes

By identifying an individual's own motivators, what is important to them, managers may be able to adapt and enhance the working environment, the tasks, the methodologies of work with a view to meeting those needs, motivating the employee to work harder, smarter or to be more committed. These benefits, in turn, will influence your bottom line, as a motivated employee will want to be successful, both with you and for you.

Measuring impact

The continuous performance review conversation is the most conventional way to assess the impact of your efforts to know and to optimize an individual's key motivators. Asking about them in the first place should demonstrate the manager's genuine interest, and asking for feedback about the degree to which they are being met will be a strong indicator of the impact.

40 Harmony initiatives

Introduction

Equality legislation around the world has begun to have an impact on the diversity of our workforces. Typically, organizations are experiencing much greater inclusion of age, race, gender, sexual orientation and disability in employment. Many organizations now establish diversity and inclusion training as a key part of their employee training agenda, with some mandating attendance at such programmes on an annual basis. Others will ensure it forms part of an induction or leadership development programme.

In Australia, Harmony Day has been launched annually in March as a celebration of cultural diversity, highlighting cultural respect for all Australian residents. For them, the day coincides with the United Nations International Day for the Elimination of Racial Discrimination, and its key message is 'everyone belongs'. Harmony Day aims to engage people to participate in their community, respect cultural and religious diversity and foster a sense of belonging for everyone. The Harmony Day initiative celebrates the multiculturalism of the country, and the different, new and enriching traditions that it brings.

Implementing a similar initiative within your organization could reap the same benefits, increasing awareness of diversity, fostering a sense of belonging and inclusion, and respecting and learning about difference. There is a risk associated with a single day, or a focused event – that it is seen as tokenistic, or only relevant on that day. Although an annual celebration may be effective in a national campaign (much like International Women's Day, for example) you may want to implement a series of initiatives or ideas that promote the ongoing commitment to diversity and inclusion in your organization.

Promoting wellbeing

Whilst much of the research into the benefits of diversity and inclusion initiatives focuses on the business benefits, including improved creativity and innovation, positive bottom line impacts, etc, there is clearly a link between employee wellbeing and inclusion – as opposed to exclusion.

A positive approach to diversity at work, and increased awareness of employee equality rights, and the behaviours expected and required between colleagues, will reduce the impact of negative of bullying behaviours and harassment inside and outside of the work environment.

A report by the BBC in November 2015 stated that bullying and harassment complaints were on the rise, with Acas reportedly receiving 20,000
complaints of bullying or harassment in the previous 12 months (Milligan,
2015).

The Acas guide to health, work and wellbeing states that one of the 11
factors they put forward for a model workplace is 'attitudes and values that
can help healthy relationships to flourish' – and refer to the need for quick
action to resolve claims of bullying or harassment (Acas, 2012). The latter is
covered in an earlier/later tool, but as well as taking quick remedial action
once bullying or harassment are reported, it is as important – if not more
so – to advocate the positive impacts of diversity in the workplace, and to
aim to prevent issues arising in the first place.

Approach

Harmony initiatives, celebrations, activities and education can take any
form you wish, or that suits your organization's culture, time or budget – big
or small, simple or challenging. However you choose to celebrate, an event
creates an opportunity to think, talk about and recognize how our differences and similarities make our workplace stronger. Events can be a simple
multicultural morning tea or a guest speaker at an all-staff meeting.

The following offer some suggestions of events or activities that you
could consider to promote Harmony Day, or other diversity and inclusion
initiatives in your workplace. The suggestions were taken from Australia's
Harmony Day website, provided by the Australian Government Department
of Social Services, and have been published with their permission. More
ideas and inspiration are available on their website: www.harmony.gov.au.

Photo competition

In the lead-up to Harmony Day, encourage your staff to capture images
from around your workplace that represent the concepts of diversity, inclu-
siveness, respect and a sense of belonging. You could provide awards or
certificates for the best pictures, and they would make a great display for
your Harmony Day event.

Harmony Day Olympics

If you have access to an outdoor space, organize some traditional sports
from around the world for your staff to try. Swap the footy for Kabaddi or
Gaelic football, or have a go at Te Boiri or Ki-o-Rahi. Share photos from your

sporting adventures across your workplace, physically as well as on intranet, community or chat sites. Games are a simple way to have fun, boost team morale, break down barriers or silos and learn about other cultures. Ask colleagues to share board or card games from their cultural backgrounds.

Food festival

Ask staff to bring in a plate of food from their cultural background or a country they have recently visited. This idea can work for morning tea, lunch or afternoon tea. Ask your catering supplier to support the initiative, too, with international foods available on the day – or week.

Guest speaker

Organize a keynote speaker who can attend your Harmony Day event and speak about their experiences of diversity, and the contributions people from diverse backgrounds or lifestyles make to our workplaces. If you are able to identify individuals within your own organization who can do similar, encourage them to participate as a speaker or an advocate.

The Wellbeing Charter advocates the development, communication and promotion of diversity policies, and encourages business leaders to act fairly in pay and benefits, development opportunities, career progression and general employment practice.

Diversity and inclusion training

It can be extremely beneficial to run diversity and inclusion training for all employees on a regular basis. It can help to set expectations and clarify acceptable and appropriate ways to behave, as well as providing clarity on the protections offered to certain groups under national legislation. Because of the sensitive nature of some of the subject matter, it is advisable to consider a specialist external organization, or your HR department, to design and deliver such programmes. Typical content should include:

- information about the UK Equality Act, what and who is protected under the legislation and the penalties for offences;
- awareness of the different types of discrimination described in the Equality Act;
- how your company policies, procedures and practices align to the legislation;
- stereotypes, unconscious bias, beliefs, attitudes and assumptions – and their impacts on inclusion;

the benefits of embracing diversity;

recognizing individual and organizational responsibilities;

how your organization's competencies values and behaviours connect to diversity and inclusion, and what this looks like in action, not just in theory.

Outcomes

Research published by the Work Foundation (Jones, 2006) suggested that positive inclusion policies can have the following benefits:

improved business performance;

positive employer and brand reputation;

greater creativity and innovation, rapid reactions to stimuli for change;

innovative approaches to products;

increased customer satisfaction and loyalty when your workforce reflects your customer base.

Measuring impact

The evidence on whether diversity and inclusion training and initiatives really have an impact on the makeup and behaviours within the workforce are mixed. However, this is not a rationale for complacency. Raising awareness and setting clear expectations are critical if complaints of bullying and harassment are to be reduced, and the benefits of diversity and inclusion are to be optimized.

Evaluate the impact of your initiatives by:

asking for feedback, formal and informal, on the events and initiatives you run;

happy sheet evaluations of diversity and inclusion training;

diversity and inclusion metrics – track the percentage of various diverse groups in your organization as a general population, and in terms of pay equality.

41   Building trust

Introduction

Leaders who are authentic, ie those who value fair and ethical ways of working, are self-aware and honest, are able to build trust-based relationships with employees. Those who are trusted, in turn tend to trust – it's a reciprocal value that can offer rewards to both parties' confidence, assurance and respect. A relationship with these characteristics is likely to be a mutually successful one.

Promoting wellbeing

In a study by Long (2017), research found that an employee's trust in their manager was a factor in their wellbeing, and contributed to the level of commitment and loyalty felt by employees towards their employer. Long concluded that the managers promoting confidence, self-respect and recognition of meaningful work promoted positive mental health among employees – and that this requires nurturing and supportive relationships in the workplace.

In an article in the Harvard Business Review in 2017, Brower et al reported that employees who are not fully trusted by their manager can be less productive, put less energy into their work and are more likely to leave their employer.

A lack of trust is demotivating for employees, and those who trust managers and feel trusted by them are more likely to experience job satisfaction, and stay committed to their employer.

Approach

Care

Authentic leadership is one of the key factors for building employee trust. If an employee believes that their manager is behaving in ways that are natural and genuine, they are more likely to trust them. After all, if a leader is acting the part, faking it, why would an employee believe in them? Within authenticity is the leader's ability to demonstrate care and empathy for those who work for them.

To build trust in your team:

- Be yourself, not a controlled or false version of the normal you.
- Take time to listen to others.

- Be curious and ask questions to understand the motivations, issues and dreams of your employees, demonstrating a genuine interest.

- Coach and support wherever you can – don't allow team members to remain stuck: get involved and help them to solve problems.

Communication

Trust and authenticity are important factors in communications with employees, whether collective or one-to-one. For employees to really pay attention to what is being said, they need to feel that the communication is honest and open, empathetic and relevant. Equally, leaders and managers will feel that they are being trusted if communications from employees are delivered in the same way – honestly and empathetically.

To build trust in communication:

- Keep communication channels open, and make sure that employees and people managers are approachable and available for informal discussions at any time.

- During times of change and turbulence, communicate regularly and as openly as possible.

- Allow opportunities for open question and answer sessions so that employees can ask questions of leaders about the business.

- Wherever possible, keep communication formats informal so that people managers can tailor messages to their own audience and demonstrate listening and empathy.

Feedback

Trust can be enhanced through the delivery of honest but constructive feedback that is delivered with care and positive intent. Tool 15, 'Giving great feedback' (page 71) offers some guidance on how to ensure that feedback is effective.

To increase trust in the feedback process:

- Provide feedback on a regular basis, not just during formal review processes.

- Stick to facts and objective evidence (for both positive and constructive feedback) rather than opinion or vague statements.

- Offer feedback 'in the moment' – don't save it up for a 'better' time.

- Demonstrate that feedback is given with good intent, not just to critique, by taking time to prepare well, and offering suggestions or coaching for improvement.

- Give feedback about things that have gone well, not just where improvement is needed.

Involvement

Trust can be demonstrated and developed by empowering employees, trusting them with making decisions for themselves, and enabling them to get involved in problem solving, collaboration and idea generation.

To encourage trust through involvement:

- Find opportunities to ask employees for their ideas and suggestions. Listen to them, provide clear feedback about them, and implement where practical. Connect the original idea to the outcome delivered, and ensure that employees are recognized for their contribution.

- Encourage employees to take risks.

- Allow employees to visit customers, suppliers, colleagues, etc, with a view to finding out how things might work better, or uncovering problems or challenges that they may have. Ask them to present back their findings and recommendations.

- Encourage employees to act as 'champions' (eg for change, for wellbeing, etc), giving them responsibility for communicating messages and bringing feedback. Trust will follow if you listen to the feedback and take action.

Fairness and consistency

If an employee perceives that their line manager is acting consistently and fairly, then the level of trust will grow. Where people issues (such as performance reviews, task allocation, opportunities, disciplinary or reward and recognition) are dealt with consistently, employees are more likely to trust their manager, and as a result will be more accepting of their approach or decision.

As a manager, ensure that you are operating consistently in your own people management decisions, and where necessary or appropriate seek advice from HR specialists. It can also be valuable to check with other managers on their approaches and decisions to ensure cross-functional consistency.

To demonstrate trust through fairness and consistency:

Check your people management actions against policy or procedure statements, but also against what has typically been done in custom and practice.

Ensure your people management actions are consistent with your peers – check with them directly or liaise with HR.

Calibrate performance evaluations, pay increases and bonus pay outs – check that there is a consistently applied methodology for your evaluations, and that no one decision stands out (positively or negatively) without clear justification.

Explain your decisions rationally to your employees. You should be sufficiently confident in the decision you made to be able to defend it. If you cannot, you might need to rethink it.

Outcomes

Building trust between managers and employees will clearly result in an improved relationship between people managers and their staff. It is likely that trusted employees will be more engaged with their work, and are more likely to stay committed to their employer. Managers can also expect higher levels of productivity and morale, and for employees to be more forthcoming with new ideas, improvements and suggestions on how they work.

Measuring impact

Evaluating levels of trust may be a highly individualized task, and one that can be very subjective, as the trust relationship exists primarily between two people. However, there is also a collective evaluation, as to whether a manager is considered trustworthy by his or her direct reports.

Managers can assess themselves as to whether the actions they are taking encourage a relationship of mutual trust. For example, they can assess whether they:

demonstrate they care through actions and not just words;

communicate often with their team members through informal as well as formal methods;

are honest and authentic in what and how they communicate;

- provide opportunities for employees to get involved;
- encourage risk taking and learning from experiences;
- are consistent in their application of people decisions and policies.

For an employee perspective on the levels of trust in their relationship with their manager, an engagement or opinion survey that specifically asks questions about trust and the relationship between employee and line manager can be a beneficial approach. Where this is not practical, consider using focus groups or representative groups (eg unions and staff councils) to gather feedback on what is or is not building trust.

Anti-bullying action

Introduction

A report published by ACAS in 2016 on workplace trends reported that in 2015 '20,000 calls were taken by the Acas (Arbitration and Conciliation Advisory Service in the UK) helpline on bullying and harassment with some people reporting truly horrifying incidents including humiliation, ostracism, verbal and physical abuse.' And whilst most organizations have policies in place to identify and address such issues, it is clear that in many instances they are not having the desired effect. Codes of conduct, whistleblowing policies, bullying and harassment policies and other anti-discrimination policies have an important part to play in the workplace, but how an organization prevents, or responds to, complaints made is critical.

Promoting wellbeing

Bullying, or inappropriate behaviours that fall short of the formal definition of bullying, can have a strong negative effect on the wellbeing of employees. At the very least, it could cause conflict in the workplace and lead to a loss of motivation and reduced team spirit. At its worst, it can have serious impacts on mental health, causing anxiety, stress and depression. You may see an increase in absence, or a loss of concentration and focus at work, leading to more mistakes. Victims can lose sleep, and may find that the issues at work cause them to have relationship issues at home as a result of the additional stresses they are under.

Prevention is of course the primary aim, to ensure that all employees can come to work confident that they will be treated fairly and reasonably. When actions or behaviours fall short of expectations and a complaint is made, the stress for the employee/complainant can be exacerbated, meaning the situation needs to be handled delicately and appropriately. Employees will want to know that their complaint is taken seriously, and that a thorough process will ensue, with appropriate action taken where it is deemed necessary. Support for a victim throughout the process will be essential.

Approach

There should be a proactive approach to anti-bullying strategies that go beyond the publication of relevant policies. Informing all employees about their own obligations, and the expectations of both employer and employee, is a positive step to ensure that everyone understands what is, and what isn't, acceptable behaviour in the workplace. Providing training and development to support those policies will also ensure that people know what to do and how to act. And finally, if those proactive actions fail to prevent issues arising, those issues must be swiftly and appropriately addressed.

Inform

Having established a whistleblowing and/or bullying and harassment policy in line with both the legal obligations and best practice, it is important to communicate them, not just publish them. As with many policies, many employees won't read them on issue, and will instead only use them as reference documents when needed. With these policies, it is much more important to ensure that managers and employees know and understand the contents of the policies, the rights they are afforded under them, and the expectations placed on them by the publication of the policy.

For a simple approach, it can be useful for leaders to talk through the policy documents, ensuring that all people managers know and understand their contents. In turn, as part of a normal communications approach, anyone managing a team should have the same talk during a team briefing, etc.

Train

Providing training to employees takes the communication a stage further. This training may include some of the following:

- basic employment law for people managers;
- handling grievance and disciplinary complaints and investigations;
- equality, diversity and inclusion training;
- mediation training to enable conflicts to be settled in house.

Act

When any issues are identified or reported, they must be addressed quickly and thoroughly. As a manager or leader, if you notice or hear any behaviours that you think could be inappropriate, you have a responsibility to act on it.

- Call it out: If you see or hear anything that you believe could represent bullying behaviour, you should tell the people involved in factual terms what you have witnessed, and be transparent that this could be considered to be bullying, depending on the situation and how the treatment was perceived by the receiver.

Check it: Ask the person to whom the behaviour was directed whether they are concerned about it. It can often be 'banter' that doesn't cause offence or concern, but checking with the person concerned that they are ok with it is important. And even if they say they are, make them aware that if at any time their perspective changes, they can discuss it with you in confidence.

Report it: If necessary, report the incident to a line manager or HR. Follow up to ensure that appropriate action is taken.

Investigate it: You may need to investigate the matter further, using your disciplinary or grievance policy as a guide for the approach you take. Ensure that you speak to all parties concerned, and anyone else who may have experienced or witnessed the incident, or similar incidents.

Manage it: If the reported behaviour is found to be bullying, take decisive action using your disciplinary process as your guide. If considered appropriate, and if in line with your procedure, you may need to issue a warning, but support this with information and training about acceptable standards of behaviour.

Review

As part of the action to address any issues, you should conduct a lessons-learnt review. Having received a complaint, anonymous or otherwise, investigated and acted you should consider whether:

the policy needs to be reviewed to address any issues that have come to light;

more or different communication or training are required to enable employees and managers to act appropriately, have clear expectations, etc;

training is required in the management of the complaint, investigations or the disciplinary/grievances processes;

any elements of your normal leadership or management development or training need re-focusing or specific emphasis on bullying matters.

By taking action as part of this review you can ensure that your policies and your people practice are fit for purpose in eliminating or managing bullying behaviours or other whistleblowing complaints.

Outcomes

Preventative measures should go some way to reducing the risk of bullying behaviours in the workplace, and can be quick and simple to implement. But whilst the risk is reduced, it can sometimes be the case that well-intended humour and camaraderie can tip over an acceptable boundary into harassment or bullying, without malicious intent, but with serious consequences. Information, education and training can reduce this risk, but for many issues, clear and decisive disciplinary action may be required to reinforce the importance of appropriate workplace and colleague behaviour.

Incidences of bullying should be reduced through a mix of preventative measures and decisive reactive responses to issues that arise, and in turn this should have an impact on employee wellbeing, reducing the risks of stress and anxiety at work.

Measuring impact

Organizations would do well to keep track of the number of issues raised under whistleblowing or grievance procedures, so that trends can be identified in the types of complaint being made, the areas in which the complainants and aggressors work (and who manages them) and how the issues are handled. Monitoring such numbers won't give a complete picture of the issues, as some may be managed informally and not recorded, but it will give an indication of the details and trends in more serious matters.

Reducing instances of bullying may also have an impact on productivity and teamwork (which can be negatively affected by bullying), although it may be hard to quantify. Similarly, there may be a reduction in stress-related absenteeism.

Giving back

Introduction

Setting up charitable activities and methods for charitable giving is a great way to get your employees behind a worthy cause. Many do so individually, with their own connections to charities and their own initiatives, from sports to bake sales. In 2015 in the UK £9.6 billion was donated to charities (a slight reduction on the previous year) according to a report by the Charities Aid Foundation (CAF, 2015). They also found that only 2 per cent of the population are donating to charity through payroll giving, although two-thirds of the population have donated in other ways, and that 13 per cent had volunteered for a charity in the 12 months prior to the survey.

Promoting wellbeing

Harnessing this enthusiasm in the workplace can also present great benefits. Whilst the primary concern is of course always the charity and their work, organizations might also see greater collaboration, improved engagement, creativity and innovation ... and, let's not forget, people having fun. Most of the major employee engagement surveys will also include some element of charitable activity or, more broadly, corporate social responsibility, as an indicator of engagement. But there is also evidence to suggest that charitable efforts and doing good can also be good for mental wellbeing and health.

A report by the Mental Health Foundation published in 2012 suggested that helping others can reduce stress, improve emotional wellbeing, benefit physical health, bring a sense of belonging and eliminate negative feelings. They report that helping others promotes positive physiological changes in the brain that are associated with happiness, and that these changes are often followed by periods of calm.

Charity work can also help us to maintain a realistic perspective – at times when things are stressful, we are able to connect with organizations or individuals who can make us realize we should be more positive and appreciative, and less stressed and worried.

Approach

Random acts of kindness

Promote the recognition of random acts of kindness in and around your workplace. Encourage employees to share stories or experiences of giving or receiving such random acts. Use your internal communications media to highlight and celebrate random acts, and encourage people to generate new ideas. The Random Acts of Kindness website (www.randomactsofkind-ness.org) has many ideas, including a section for workplace kindness – such as writing a letter of thanks, or buying someone a coffee – and resources you can use to promote your initiative. They refer to themselves as (and have trademarked) 'RAKtivists' ... maybe that could catch on in your organization!

Work-based events

Workplace charity activities are usually employee-led and manager-supported initiatives that encourage team members to decide on a charity, an activity and an event or programme, and run it themselves. This can range from a simple bake sale, to a static cycle challenge (ie completing a long distance on an exercise bike in relay with other team members), to dress-down or fancy-dress theme days at work. From an organization's perspective, the only real consideration here should be recognition of some lost productivity in the name of charity, and a check to ensure that customer service, or reputation, will not be damaged by the activities going ahead. Encouraging employees to tap into the resources of national UK programmes such as Comic Relief, Sport Relief, Red Nose Day, Macmillan Coffee Mornings, etc, can encourage great team spirit towards a common cause, and give a great deal to the charities involved.

Payroll giving

Payroll giving allows employees to make donations to charity from their gross pay (ie without paying tax on it) via their payroll on a regular (usually monthly) basis. Dependent on the agency providing the service, employees can select from a broad range of charities to donate to.

There are a number of agencies that have been established to provide payroll giving services – a list of such agencies can be found on the gov. uk website. These agencies may charge an administration fee, which can be deducted from the collated donations before they are sent on to the charities, or can be paid upfront by the employer, ensuring more of the donated funds reach the charity.

Nominated charity

A top-down approach to selecting a nominated charity for each business year (ie the organization selects its charity of the year and sticks to undraising for that one cause) can be more engaging for employees than working towards various charity events and targets. Selecting a charity that has significant meaning for your business, or one of your employees, will help to make the connection stronger, and may encourage greater participation. Asking employees for suggestions for nominations may also encourage fundraising for some lesser known charities that have meaning for some of the workforce.

Throughout the year, encourage employees to participate in events and activities for the nominated charity, and communicate regularly about progress and events.

Matched fundraising

Matching an employee's fundraising efforts is a simple and effective way for an organization to support charity work among the workforce. Setting out a company policy on how and when matching will be honoured will be important so that expectations are clear, but should not be too strict. You may want to limit the amount you will match (eg up to £500 or £1,000 per employee per year, less if you need to) and you will probably need to restrict the matching to charities registered with the Charities Commission (with a registered charity number). Other than those two factors, there should be no other need for constraints within your policy.

Matched giving is also tax-effective, as qualifying donations can be deducted from corporation tax.

Charity days

Allowing employees one or two days' additional leave to participate in charity events, or a few days each year for voluntary work, can be an effective way for employers to 'give something back'. Policy needs to be established to ensure that this is well managed; simply set out a number of days per employee per year, and that the charity work must be carried out on the day of leave (not as a day in lieu for charity work at weekends for example) and that it is carried out for a registered charity or a confirmed community or government initiative.

An alternative is to involve collective teams in charity days – for example instead of a teambuilding away day, consider taking the team for a beach clean-up or schools interviewing practice day. Ask your team for their suggestions and recommendations.

If you need to have the away day, bear in mind that some charities will work with you to support teambuilding too, using activities that build bikes, wheelchairs, etc, for charities, whilst helping you to learn about being more effective and communicating well as a team. A win-win!

Outcomes

The connections between giving something back and physical and mental health and wellbeing have been highlighted above. For those individuals who are regularly participating in charitable activities and worthy causes, the benefits are likely to include improvements in their own feelings of self-worth, a sense of balance and perspective, less stress, and feelings of happiness, confidence and positive community spirit.

Of course, there are benefits for the charities involved. Not all charitable work has to involve fundraising, many are keen to secure resources (donations), expertise (a finance expert, some social media or PR capabilities, for example), or just time. Mentoring, buddying and befriending charities are looking for individual who are willing to commit some time to talk to their client groups. If organizations are able to advocate, fund, support and provide resources and people, this will make a big difference to those the charities seek to serve.

And, in turn, there are organizational benefits too. Some of those charity requirements described above provide the opportunity for your employees to grow their skills and experiences as well as their confidence and happiness, and these can bring great value to an organization. In addition, the health benefits reaped by the individual will also benefit the organization, as stress may become less prevalent, absence may decline, and engagement and commitment to the organization are increased.

Measuring impact

As mentioned above, employee engagement or opinion surveys will often ask questions about charitable contribution and social responsibility as one indicator of the level of employee engagement. Watching the results in these categories specifically will provide some indication of the impacts of your 'giving back' initiatives in the workplace.

Setting up a charity committee will also enable you to champion and evaluate the impacts of any charitable or social responsibility initiatives undertaken.

You can measure the 'inputs' too – metrics about how many charity days or charity initiatives have been run will give a measure of the amount of activity. Aggregate the donations to charity, with operations for company onations through matched giving, employee money raised through activity, nd the number of employees using payroll giving. You might also measure he number of charitable days used by employees. These input measures re all extremely valuable for the charities involved, and whilst they may ot express a return on investment for the organization, the real purpose n establishing these initiatives is in the value seen by the charity and those hey serve.

44 Shared interest groups

Introduction

One way to balance the stressful and demanding nature of today's work is to offer employees the opportunity to combine work and their hobbies and interests. Whilst not all will want to blur this boundary, some will find that bringing some of their own interests into the workplace, and engaging with colleagues who participate in the same or similar activities, can provide some light relief. In addition, it can build connections across the organization, and develop a learning culture, as employees work together to build knowledge and experience in their specific interests. This appetite for learning may spill over into their professional capacity too.

Promoting wellbeing

In 2016 US-based learning company Udemy carried out a workplace boredom study in America, and found that 43 per cent of office workers were bored at work – for some this was because they didn't have enough to do, for others there was too much to do. Some felt unchallenged, and some felt that they were not given the opportunity to utilize their skills. You may recognize that boredom can be linked to addiction, anxiety and of course lower productivity and quality of output at work. The study also found that bored employees were twice as likely to leave the company than their colleagues – and soon. Half of them said they would leave within the next three months. Whilst we cannot make everyone's job interesting all the time, we can consider how to engage people in topics that interest them, and provide them the opportunity to learn, to challenge themselves and to connect with others in ways that are to their advantage, but bring business benefits too.

Approach

Promote the opportunity for people to start up shared interest groups in your organization. You might offer a range of topic areas as a prompt to garner interest, such as travel, photography, conservation, charitable causes, cooking, crafts, astronomy, comic books, ancestry, etc. If you know of people in your team with specific interests, encourage them to champion the initiative, gauging the appetite and encouraging other employees with an interest to support the group.

As a leader in the organization, show support for the initiative and for the different groups that emerge. Offer resources or time where practical to get the group started (eg using company systems to create and share information about the new groups, and allowing champions the time to engage with others to get participation and commitment).

Encourage the groups to meet out of office hours, but provide the facilities for them to use – and maybe even the refreshments.

Encourage groups to showcase their talents. This could be at lunchtime presentations, or stalls set up to display their products or artworks, for example. Also encourage them to share the benefits of the shared interest group – use your internal communications media to share stories about the successes of the groups, particularly about how colleagues have developed their skills and learnt new things from each other by becoming part of the group.

Outcomes

Given the research mentioned above on boredom and the propensity for bored employees, engaging them in an activity in which they are already interested, and in which they can heavily influence the activities and benefits derived, will clearly be an advantage and an opportunity to encourage improved retention. Alongside that, the specialist interest groups will be focused on sharing knowledge and experiences, and whilst this is not about a work topic, employees who are involved in learning activities outside of work do tend to become more interested in learning at work too. Signs of this increased appetite for learning should be optimized, and it will be beneficial for managers to seek opportunities to provide some professional development (on-the-job, learning from peers, continuous improvement projects, etc) where there is need and interest.

As well as the organizational benefits, the special interest groups may also give some of your employees a chance to shine. Whilst they may not have that opportunity professionally, it is possible that their hobby or interest is an area where they are both enjoying and delivering great things. The group will provide them with the opportunity to showcase their skills and strengths in the workplace – where they might otherwise not have been seen.

Connected to that, where there are successes or achievements in the special interest groups, there may also be recognition. That recognition of great things will no doubt come from within the group, but there could also be opportunities for leaders in the business, colleagues – and maybe even other stakeholders – to recognize and acknowledge those achievements, formally or informally. Recognition here is in the form of non-financial rewards – a thank-you letter, a note or a mention to communicate successes to broader teams, etc.

Measuring impact

Consider some of the following metrics:

- retention and turnover rates – reducing;
- absence and lateness – reducing;
- sign-up for learning and development opportunities – increasing;
- number of shared interest groups active in your organization;
- number of participants in shared interest groups in your organization.

You might also consider qualitative impact measures. These are more likely to be indirect benefits that you notice, rather than hard measures that you can track with metrics, but keeping an eye on some of the following behaviours:

- Cross-organization collaboration: Are people collaborating and communicating more freely across team, functional and geographical boundaries? As people across the business meet more informally, so relationships are created and developed.

- Creativity and innovation: Are you seeing more ideas generation, and follow up of those ideas, since the special interest groups came into being?

- Proactive problem solving: As people work more together across the organization, they have access to a group of people who may be able to help with work-based problems and challenges before they turn to colleagues or managers.

Netwalking

Introduction

Netwalking combines two activities that are beneficial for an employee's wellbeing – networking, which offers opportunities to meet fellow professionals and colleagues; and walking, which offers benefits of fresh air, exercise and time away from a formal office environment. Instead of offering the opportunity to meet others in the confined environment of an office or a function room, netwalking provides the opportunity to have similar interactions in the fresh air, whilst undertaking light physical exercise.

Promoting wellbeing

The benefits of walking are noted in Tool 11 about the manager–employee walk-and-talk approach (page 56): it mentions that benefits can include becoming healthier, losing excess weight, reducing risks of heart disease and high blood pressure, and improving the quality of sleep.

However, there are additional benefits in walking in a social group with others, as the community spirit of netwalking can also be an advantage to a person's wellbeing. The opportunity to engage in discussion with others can be a great support for those who might feel isolated in their role, or who value the opportunity to share concerns, opportunities or ideas. Research for the *British Journal of Sports Medicine* reported that social walkers were significantly less likely to become depressed (Hanson and Jones, 2015). In addition, walking in groups can help you to stick to your healthy goals, and provide support and motivation to keep you active.

Approach

There are a number of netwalking opportunities that you may want to consider:

Internal: The benefits of wider networking in a business are well documented. By encouraging employees at all levels and across all functions, departments or divisions to engage with each other you can reduce silos, improve communication, encourage learning about the organization, build collaboration, etc. The informality of netwalking, as well as its voluntary nature, encourages the breakdown of barriers across the organization.

- Local business: If your business is located close to other businesses – maybe on a retail or industrial park, or in a shared office block – it could be interesting to begin a netwalking group that spans across the local geography or premises. This grouping provides the opportunity for colleagues in different businesses to meet informally, to discuss common challenges, provide support to each other and spread ideas innovation and potential collaborations.

- External: The external netwalking group could be considered to be more community or geography based. The group is not limited to a tight geographical area or specific companies, as is the case for the local business netwalks, but instead offers the opportunity for a range of walkers from any type of business across a broad location base. Provided they are willing to travel to your walk, they could be welcomed. This diversity of participants can bring great value to the networking part of the walking group. Traditional benefits of networking will come to the fore – as well as those mentioned above, participants may build confidence, create wider business opportunities for each other, coach and support, and raise their profiles.

Plan your netwalking group

There are just a few simple steps to make netwalking a reality, but it needs perseverance on the part of an organizer or leader to make sure it continues and builds.

Consider whether you want to build an internal, external or local netwalking group and consider the frequency for your walks – weekly, monthly or quarterly?

When you have that scope clear, you can determine some potential routes, walk lengths, meeting points, etc. To ensure that your group is inclusive, think about accessibility of your meeting point and your route.

It may be beneficial to consider some conversation topics for each walk. Whilst this will be informal, providing a talking topic can help people to get conversation started. Consider what your target audience may want to be talking about that will benefit the wide range of participants you might engage.

Promote your netwalking group

Promote your netwalking group idea internally in your organization, inviting fellow employees from across the organization to attend, mix and build relationships. Use your internal communications methods (noticeboards, intranet, etc) and prepare fliers, a marketing stand in the canteen, etc.

Consider your target audience as you prepare to market your group. Create social media and intranet content, flyers, emails, posters, desk drops or letters; for external, groups could consider placing adverts in the local press, community newsletters, social media, etc.

Be clear about the purpose, who is welcome, fitness levels, what to wear, where and when to meet, duration/distance. Provide contact details so that people can register their interest.

Invite and welcome netwalkers. Provide joining details to those who want to participate. Include details about meeting points, the types of walks duration, physical exertion, etc), and who else they may meet. A few photographs to put names to faces can help to reduce the anxiety of meeting new people.

Make your netwalks happen

As the organizer, welcome walkers, outline some introductions and conversation topics and get the walk under way. Be the role model for how you want netwalking to happen – be open and interactive with all members of the group, and make introductions among participants. At the end, recognize the things that went well, and take some time to consider what you might do differently next time.

Keep going! Build on the success of your events and organize more. Grow the network by welcoming new participants. Change routes to keep it interesting, add challenge to the walk by increasing intensity, distance or duration, and encourage interesting discussion with topical and relevant conversation points.

Outcomes

As well as providing the opportunity to make new connections, to build opportunities for collaboration and team working, netwalking also has great health benefits. The physical activity alongside the networking process supports employee wellbeing, utilizing the benefits of clean, fresh air to refresh brain cells, and promotes improvement and maintenance of fitness levels.

Evaluating impact

With the various benefits that a netwalking initiative can bring about, it is worth considering a number of layers of potential impacts that it could have – at individual, organizational and external interaction levels.

Measuring individual impact

As a 'netwalker' you can various levels of impact – physical, mental and social. Physically, are you benefiting from the walk. Do you feel energized? Are you maintaining or improving your level of fitness? Mentally, does the walk afford you the opportunity to relive some of your work pressure, and free your mind a little? And socially, are you making new connections and meeting new people, collaborating more and able to offer support to others?

Measuring organizational impact

If the netwalking sessions are part of an organizational initiative, there are other factors that can be evaluated in addition to those individual impacts noted above. For example, you could consider the collaboration benefits by asking whether team or functional barriers have begun to breakdown as a result of their involvement in networking opportunities. Are people collaborating more to solve problems or create new ideas?

In addition, you could consider the wider organizational wellbeing impacts. Have you seen a reduction in absence or lateness? Are employees more energetic and engaged?

Measuring your group's effectiveness

To establish how effective the group itself is, consider whether the group is maintaining its size or growing in popularity. Is it attracting walkers who add value and/or new perspectives to the group discussion? What feedback are you receiving from your participants – either formally or anecdotally?

Netwalking in practice – a case study

At the beginning of each year, Julia Smith and Tracy Gilmour, MDs of Cre8 Sales Solutions, run a business planning session during which they plan their goals and vision for the coming year. At the start of 2016 they decided to don their walking boots and head off to the Clent Hills in Worcestershire to see if being out in the fresh air would provide them with the inspiration they needed to plan the year ahead. Whilst walking they talked about how much they would like to set up a networking group that was informal and where people could be comfortable – as big advocates of being yourself, the group had to be a place where the attendees could be just that. And, this is where netwalking was born. Netwalking events combine business networking, walking and talking in the great outdoors. It's not just about exchanging business cards, it's about building real relationships and helping each other. It's about work–life balance, combining work and life in a real way, so people are working whilst doing something they enjoy. People have the time to really get to know each other on a two-hour walk with a break for coffee at the top of a nice hill and it's noticeable how much more natural and relaxed people are when they're walking. Personally, Cre8's team have made some great friends from starting the group, and feel they really benefit mentally from the time outdoors after a busy week in front of a screen and on the telephone.

46 Fun at work

Introduction

Work doesn't have to be serious, and given that employees spend such a large proportion of their lives at work, it would be a shame if it were all serious. Of course, it's important to take the work seriously, and to ensure that performance, and customer satisfaction, remain as high priorities. Organizations and their leaders can take steps to encourage fun in the workplace, supporting, advocating and taking part in programmes, initiatives and schemes. One person's fun can be another person's nightmare, though, so it is important to have variety, and to involve as many people as possible on a voluntary basis, particularly through employee-led initiatives.

Promoting wellbeing

Research has identified several positive impacts of laughter on an individual's wellbeing, including:

- Openness to new relationships (Gray et al, 2015): This study found that through laughter people seemed more open, and were therefore more likely to forge new relationships. In a work environment, this can help to break down silos and improve collaboration and networking.

- Reducing your stress levels and improving memory: A study by the Federation of American Societies for Experimental Biology (FASEB, 2014) found that 'Humor reduces detrimental stress hormones like cortisol that decrease memory hippocampal neurons, lowers your blood pressure, and increases blood flow and your mood state. The act of laughter – or simply enjoying some humor – increases the release of endorphins and dopamine in the brain, which provides a sense of pleasure and reward.' Knowing that laughter can have this impact on stress as a physiological, not just psychological, reaction must surely be advantageous to organizations, and as such leaders should seek to contribute toward the management of stress levels at work by increasing the fun levels.

The conclusions from a study by Boehm and Lyubomirsky (2008) state that people who are happy will typically experience greater job satisfaction, perform better and are more likely to take on additional tasks and help their colleagues out when needed. They report that happy people tend to ave fewer absences, are more successful and are less likely to experience unemployment. And we are much more likely to laugh when we are in the company of others than we are when we are alone, so team or collective activities are likely to have a bigger impact on individuals.

Approach

Encouraging ideas and advocates

Leaders should take steps to enable employees to find, suggest and implement ideas and initiatives to encourage fun at work. Employees might feel concerned about raising suggestions that could be seen as distracting or disruptive to the working day, and that don't have a direct impact on business deliverables or objectives. By setting the example (ie doing some of this stuff yourself!), and encouraging ideas, you are more likely to generate enthusiasm and ideas from within your teams.

One idea is to set up a 'fun committee' – a group of volunteers to coordinate such activities. Be clear with them about budget and time constraints, and offer your guidance about inclusion and diversity, but empower them as much as possible.

Finding inspiration

Charities There are so many charity days each year that it can be difficult to choose how many or which ones to support, particularly if you want to have fun, and not wear people down with a charity event every week. Consider whether there are any charities that might be aligned or connected to your business, or of specific interest to an employee or team within your organization.

Many charities will provide fundraising kits to help make the most of your efforts, and ideas and offer inspiration on the kinds of activities that will get people involved and donating. There are a wide range of initiatives that these charities promote, and this might also be a deciding factor – a range of activities will encourage broader participation, rather than focusing on those that require physical fitness or creative capabilities.

Consider gathering a team of enthusiastic volunteers from across your business to get everyone involved, with a lead coordinator who can make sure that things stay safe, responsible and timely. You do have to run a business too, after all.

Information from charities can be found on their websites, but the list below includes some in the UK that are easy to get involved with, and/or will provide you with fundraising kits to support your efforts. The list is not exhaustive – involve your employees in finding and supporting similar activities:

- Comic Relief and Sports Relief;
- Children in Need;
- Red Nose Day;
- Macmillan Coffee Morning;
- BBQ for Heroes (fundraising for Help for Heroes);
- Jeans for Genes Day (raises money for children and families affected by genetic disorders);
- Wear it Pink (fundraising for breast cancer charities);
- Movember (for men's health);
- Christmas Jumper Day (Save the Children);
- Dressed by the Kids Day (Oxfam).

Sports   The sporting calendar is a great opportunity for some fun in the workplace. From sweepstakes to your own team games, there are lots of opportunities for people of all nationalities, ages and abilities to get involved. These kinds of activities can be great for teambuilding, breaking down silos and improving communication – and just having fun. Do make sure that they don't get too competitive though! Consider ideas such as:

- Your home country formula 1 grand prix: Bring in or hire a Scalextric or other driving-related games, organize some qualifying and team competitions and have your own winner's podium (probably without the champagne!).
- American Football Superbowl – a great opportunity to theme your office with stars and stripes for the day.
- For the Olympics or Commonwealth Games, why not host your own games (with everything from egg and spoon races to eating doughnuts without licking your lips) – have a daily competition for each day of the Olympics, a medal ceremony and lots of internal communication.
- A sweepstake is a great way to get involved in a variety of sports, from major horse racing events to the football World Cup. Make it more interesting by not only selecting your winner, but theming your workspace, desks or office with the team you picked.

The Tour de France can be matched with a 'relay' Tour de Office – set up an exercise bike, and involve employees as they cycle as little or as much as they can of the Tour de France mileage each day, before handing over to someone else to have a go!

Themes The calendar is full of theme days, from World Book Day to Dry January to Random Act of Kindness Day – most months will have a whole series of them that you can find online, or sometimes through social media trends.

Becoming familiar with some of these dates and themes, including those that might be relevant to your business, and many that really are just for fun could provide some inspiration for events, activities and initiatives that can get everyone involved at work. For example, consider some of the following:

- World Book Day (March): Promote a 'book swap', where people can lend their favourite or most inspirational book to a colleague who hasn't read it.

- National Vegetarian Week (May): Ask team members to bring an unusual-looking or home-grown vegetable to work – and have a fun competition at the end of the week to celebrate!

- National Quiet Day (September): Try a sponsored silence!

- National Poetry Day (October): Encourage your team members to write a poem or limerick about the team, the business, the customer etc. Ask them to keep it courteous, but make it hilarious. Post them on a board for everyone to read throughout the day.

Don't forget the national celebration days, eg St George's Day, St David's Day, American Independence Day etc.

Business-led Theme days connected to your business can build engagement and awareness of your progress or some of your challenges or opportunities. A few examples include:

- When you land a new client, celebrate with a theme day focused around that client, perhaps based around their location, or their type of business. For example, if your new client is based in France, have French breakfast, have a French language half-hour masterclass for beginners, wear traditional French clothing and promote typical French cultural aspects.

- When developing a new product or service, involve people in fun brainstorming activities that can help the development process. Encourage creative (and wild!) ideas for naming them too.

Be spontaneous   Come up with new ideas and be practical and spontaneous about how you do them. People may find it fun to suddenly take a few moments out of manning the phones or working through admin tasks to do something apparently non-work related with other people, that generates laughter. So why not:

- Search the internet for some very short-team build or ice breaking exercises. They may not be geared towards a spontaneous act, but you can adapt them. For example, there are many exercises you could find instructions for that involve teams building towers from just paper and paperclips, or creating a flying object and making it travel furthest, or creating a vehicle that allows you to drop an egg from a 2 metre height without breaking it. As well as a bit of fun, they are low cost, low effort and seemingly different to the normal daily work routine – but you can also add a few lessons at the end if you want to about teamwork, communication, innovation etc.

- Bring in a 'decorate your own...' kit, usually found in craft shops or supermarkets. You can decorate anything from your own mug to a gingerbread man or cupcake. Take out 10 minutes from the working day to try something like this, and gift your creations to each other!

Outcomes

Noted above are some of the well-researched health benefits of injecting a bit of fun into the workplace and encouraging laughter and good humour among employees. If that wasn't enough, perhaps common sense alone suggests that you are likely to see that people's moods will lift, that the ice can be broken between teams, functions or locations, and that communication is more frequent and more informal. Your employees are more likely to enjoy coming to work, knowing that there can be some fun in their day, as well as hard work, focus and achievement. Getting the balance right is important, but you – and your employees – will reap the benefits of an occasional time-out.

Measuring impact

Employee engagement surveys will often ask questions about whether people 'enjoy' working here, or have fun at work, and these can be a great measure of the impact of your 'fun-ness' initiatives. However, this can be a costly and time-consuming way to measure fun, and there are quicker and easier ways to assess whether individuals at work are enjoying their office time.

Pulse checks can be a much quicker way to gauge reactions and impacts of initiatives to evoke fun at work – asking a few short questions on an internal survey, intranet or via email can give you an indication. For example, ask people if they agree or disagree that 'it is fun to work here', 'we take time out occasionally to have fun' or 'I can/do laugh at work'. Use the responses to see whether your initiatives or programmes have landed well with your employees.

Ask for feedback. Getting feedback directly from employees on what they enjoy or have fun doing, or don't like so much, can help you to shape your fun-ness programme. Asking for ideas can ensure that there is shared responsibility.

Ultimately, leaders will want to know that having fun at work is supporting both employee wellbeing and their bottom line business results. Making a direct connection may be difficult, but again, you can just ask. Employees will tell you whether they feel that having fun is a distraction, or whether it acts as an energy booster and team builder for them at work. Acting on the information you receive to adjust your programmes accordingly can help you to focus on ideas that are mutually beneficial.

47 Pets at work

Introduction

As workplaces are becoming more relaxed, more open plan and more flexible in their accommodation, so there has been a rise in the trend for companies to encourage pet owners to bring their pets into work with them. Companies like Nestle, Mars Petcare, Google and the Blue Cross among others allow pets to be brought into work, and others participate in Bring Your Dog to Work Day on 24 June each year to get the benefits for employees and the company alike. An article in the Guardian reported that an estimated 8 per cent of employees are allowed to take their dog to work at present, but this is likely to grow in the future (Ferguson, 2016). It is important to separate out a 'pets at work' policy from the use of assistance or service animals (which could include guide dogs for the blind, hearing dogs, seizure alert dogs and mental health service dogs), which should be considered separately.

Promoting wellbeing

Research indicates that having pets in the workplace can have a number of wellbeing benefits for employees – workers tend to feel happier and experience less stress as a result of pets' presence, and just the act of enabling can encourage employees to feel a stronger sense of engagement with their employer. The Blue Cross for Pets report that 89 per cent of healthcare professionals agree that stroking a pet can lower blood pressure (Blue Cross for Pets, 2017). In addition, it can reduce the concerns that employees may have about leaving pets at home alone, connecting to their need for a better work–life balance that meets their conflicting priorities.

However, there are some potential risks – pets distracting employees from their tasks, allergies and people who are not fond of animals, for example – and these need to be carefully managed to ensure that the negatives do not outweigh any potential benefits.

Approach

Assess attitude

It is important to first gauge the attitude of the workforce towards having pets in the workplace. A simple survey or vote will indicate how many employees are in favour, and further work should be carried out to understand the concerns of those who are not. This won't necessarily mean that you should follow the preference of the objectors, but you do need to understand their concerns so that they can be proactively managed.

Test it out

Some organizations have tested the approach on Bring Your Dog to Work Day, using the national initiative as a testing ground for a future policy. Others have furthered this with some additional 'pet experience' days, allowing employees to bring their pets to the office on occasional set days as a pilot programme. This allows the company the opportunity to see how it works in practice, and to give those who are unsure about its practicality or their own level of comfort with it a chance to test it out.

Set your guidelines

Establishing clear guidelines for a pet policy will be key to the success and comfort of the programme for all concerned, including the pet. Your policy should include the following:

- Scope – location: Set out the office locations or zones within the office where pets are allowed, and be clear about those where they are not allowed.

- Scope – pets: Define what pets are included in the pets at work policy. Some organizations specify dogs only, but others extend the scope to include any animal or pet that has been house trained and is well behaved. Typically, young animals are not encouraged as they may not be fully trained, and some animals may be considered impractical or intimidating to others (eg mice, snakes, etc) and so could be excluded.

- Regularity: You may want to consider whether you invite employees to bring their pets to work every day if they wish to, or whether you set a guideline of welcoming a pet a couple of times a week. This may depend on the amount of space you have in the office to accommodate them, or on the number of employees that wish to bring their pets to work. Consider the capacity, distraction and objectors when deciding on reasonable frequency guidelines.

- Owner responsibilities: Detail what is expected of the owner, for example that they ensure cleanliness, good behaviour, responsible ownership, staying hygienic, walking and feeding their pet, etc.

- Assessing suitability: It may be beneficial to implement an assessment methodology to determine a pet's suitability for the workplace. This could include a health review by a vet, a behaviour assessment (for example with a dog trainer) and a probation period that allows the pet to visit the workplace and for their behaviour – and that of the owner – to be reviewed regularly.

• Pet-free zones: You will need to have some areas of the office environment where pets are not allowed to roam, particularly in rest or eating areas, so that all employees have a place to relax and/or focus, and so that there is no concern about hygiene issues. In addition, there may be areas such as production that could be a hazard, or laboratory areas where it may be impractical, dangerous or unhygienic to welcome pets.

Deal with the issues

Pet performance   The performance and behaviour of the pet at work does need to be monitored, and addressed if it becomes too distracting, disruptive or difficult to manage. In certain workplace situations (eg meetings or client events), owners may need to be asked not to bring their pets, and overall managers will need to take a proactive stance to ensure that the presence of pets remains a positive one for all concerned.

Objectors and allergies   If pets are to be allowed in the workplace, all employees have to be made to feel comfortable – otherwise the concept can no longer be considered as promoting wellbeing. If it is practical, offering separate areas for those who cannot or do not want to be in the same environment will be important. But where this is not possible, the implementation of a scheme may have to be reconsidered.

Have fun with it

Encouraging people to interact based around pets at work can bring some fun, informality and interaction into the workplace. Encouraging photographs of pets at work, social media posts, and activities such as team dog walks during the day, or 'best dressed pet of the month' competitions, can bring an additional fun element to the initiative that everyone can get involved with, pet owners or not.

Outcomes

If well implemented, a pets at work programme can have beneficial effects on morale, engagement and stress management in the workplace. In addition, the presence of pets at work can create a new energy, and encourage people to talk to each who maybe wouldn't normally have cause to do so – the pet connection breaks down barriers and can enable improved communication and collaboration.

Measuring impact

A regular review of your pets at work policy and guidelines will ensure that it continues to be practical and a welcome approach within your organization or office location. Using a simple survey or a focus group, managers should ask general questions about acceptability, tolerance, behaviour and impacts. This will provide feedback about:

- how practical the pets at work policy is;

- any changes or adaptations that need to be made to improve the scheme – eg facilities, office layout, policy changes, communication, etc;

- any concerns that need to be raised – eg behaviour of pets, allergies or fears, etc;

- any benefits that employees are experiencing – eg improved interactions between staff, higher morale, less stress, more work–life balance, good feelings about the employer.

48 Music at work

Introduction

Offices, factories and stores can often be heard playing music or broadcasting TV. This can have mixed reactions from both employees and customers, and if it is not carefully managed, a well-intentioned initiative can have negative impacts. However, there is evidence, both scientific and anecdotal, that suggests that it can also bring some great advantages.

Promoting wellbeing

In 1972, a landmark study identified a connection between playing music in factory environments and the efficiency of workers performing their roles, despite intrusive background noise of machinery etc (Fox and Embrey, 1972). Research has continued to investigate this connection, and in 2005 Le Roux reported that not only do people find music enjoyable, but it can also reduce boredom at work, and can result in increased productivity. He reports some evidence that it reduces errors, and can improve overall performance at work. Psychological wellbeing can be improved, and music can have positive effects on mental health and mood.

Lesiuk's research (2005) supports these assertions, too, with research carried out on information systems. Developers suggested that emotional expression and quality of work were at their lowest when there was no music was playing, though focus on task was better. However, participants in the study reported that music in the workplace had positive impacts on their mood. Lesiuk reports that music can reduce anxiety, demonstrated in a study in which participants completed a task without music, and with. In the latter grouping, both mental and physical changes were noted, including reducing feelings of anxiety, and suppressing increases in systolic blood pressure and heart rate.

Haake's study (2011) provided evidence of further benefits of 'individual listening' to music at work, including providing inspiration, improving concentration, stress relief and the management of their own personal space. However, there are suggestions from this study that the effects are improved if employees can select their own music, and that they should be encouraged to manage their own 'listening practices' so that colleagues are not disturbed and professionalism is not compromised.

PRS quote research that suggests that 88 per cent of participants in a study worked most accurately when listening to music, and 58 per cent worked faster when spell checking and entering data when listening to pop music (PRS, 2014). They report that 91 per cent of managers/business owners either agreed or agreed strongly that playing music makes customers and staff happier, and over half felt that turning off music permanently would have negative effects on the workforce.

Of course, it must be noted that not everyone at work will be keen to listen to music, and a compromise has to be reached that meets all employees needs in order to maintain positive workplace relationships and wellbeing for all.

Approach

There are two approaches that organizations can take to introducing music or TV into the workplace – individual listening, or collective listening.

Individual listening

Individual listening allows or encourages employees to bring their own music source to work, and to listen through headphones. Whilst some employees can find this beneficial, allowing them to focus and concentrate, others around them may find it less so. There can be concerns that the individual listener is detached from the team or group, and working too independently, though this may depend on the type of work being done. The volume of individual listeners' music must be considerate to others, and guidelines must be clear – for example, the listener is still able to respond to, and interact with, their colleagues and customers. Health and safety also needs to be considered – the employee must be able to hear and react to alarms and alerts.

Collective listening

Collective listening is playing music or music videos to an employee and or customer group, and is categorized as a public broadcast, and as such there are some legal issues to take into account, alongside the manager and employee concerns that may be raised.

Broadcast regulations

Before you consider broadcasting music in the workplace, you need to consider the legal licencing requirements, and any associated costs. Any music broadcast through speakers to your employees and/or your customers requires you to have permission, under the Copyright, Designs and Patents Act 1988. There are two organizations that govern this permission:

- The Performing Rights Society represents songwriters, composers and publishers of music and collects and pays them royalties for the use of their musical composition and lyrics.

- The Phonographic Performance Licence collects royalties on behalf of record companies and performers.

It is likely that you will need both to broadcast radio, videos or music in the workplace. Application can be completed online, and costs will vary according to the type and size of business and your broadcasting intentions. Failure to comply with the licensing requirements means that you are breaching copyright regulations. You may be subject to a fine or to a legal claim for damages.

It's worth noting that there is no requirement for such licences if you only allow employees to play their own music through headphones.

Managers as advocates

Rather than having managers who are disengaged from or, worse, actively disruptive of, the playing of music at work, encourage them to understand the benefits (perhaps share some of the research findings above), and to proactively manage and lead by example so that the use of music at work can realize its benefits. Encourage them to collaboratively set guidelines with their teams, and to reach consensus on what is played and when. They also need to be enabled to deal with issues that arise without escalation, either through senior support or clear policy and practice.

Ask employees

In considering introducing music at work, ask employees first. The benefits as mentioned above might be useful collateral, but primarily a majority preference by a group of employees sharing office space should be the main deciding factor. Ask them about their preference for music or not, and if they want music, what type of music. Ask employees to define some guidelines and boundaries (ie volumes, preferred radio stations or music styles, how to deal with dissatisfaction among themselves, when music will and will not be played, etc) such that they are both empowered and responsible for resolving matters quickly and maturely.

Trial and review

If there are any concerns about the acceptability of music at work, a trial period may help to resolve them. Agree a trial period with employees, and eek feedback from them (and customers where relevant or appropriate) to gauge the impact it has on individual and team morale, productivity, quality, effectiveness, collaboration and communication. Use a feedback to inform your decisions.

Outcomes

Research has suggested that playing music in the workplace can have some benefits, both for the organization and for the individual. Organizational outcomes can include improvements in productivity, greater quality, and overall effectiveness in the workplace. Individually, employees can experience improvements in mood, focus and relationships, which of course also have knock-on benefits for the organization, potentially creating a 'happier' workplace, greater collaboration and improved accuracy of work. However these benefits will be dependent on whether the team is listening 'collectively' or 'individually'. Individual listening is less likely to build relationships and teams, but can improve concentration and focus.

> The take-home message is that music is a very powerful management tool if you want to increase not only the efficiency of your workforce but also their mental state, their emotional state – they're going to become more positive about the work.
>
> (Dr David Lewis, neuropsychologist and chairman of Mindlab International)

Measuring impact

It can be difficult to directly connect the benefits of listening to music at work with productivity, quality or effectiveness metrics. As such, the key measure of the effectiveness of introducing music into the workplace will be to ask employees about the effects it is having on them, specifically about their mood, their wellbeing, their focus and concentration and their relationships at work.

It may also be appropriate to seek feedback from customers and other stakeholders about whether the music playing has had any impact on them.

Financial 05

49 Flexible benefits

Introduction

In recent years, employers have begun to offer more flexibility to employees in the provision of their total reward package (which includes salary and all employee benefits). In doing so, employees have greater choice about the way in which their reward is structured, and can therefore tailor their package to their own circumstances, needs and preferences. For organizations, there is a cost involved in providing and administering flexible benefit schemes, but for employees the opportunity to select the optimum package can be invaluable, and can help them to make their reward not only more relevant, but also more tax efficient.

Promoting wellbeing

The provision of flexible benefits allows employees to select benefits for themselves. Providing some level of control over the selection of benefits that make up a total reward package can be empowering for individuals, and can enable them to prioritize. This means that if they have stresses or pressures in their life outside of work, the flexibility of benefits may afford them an opportunity to release some of those concerns, for example by trading leave for extra cash, or by trading cash for extra leave or childcare vouchers for example.

Combining the opportunity for flexible benefits with some financial wellbeing support can help employees to ensure that they are making the most appropriate financial and benefit decisions for their individual situation.

Approach

Create a business case

A first step is to consider the business case for implementing flexible benefits. The business case should outline the objectives for such a scheme, and what benefit both the organization and the individuals will receive from it.

n addition, the business case should consider the set-up and administration
osts of a flexible benefits programme.

Assess your current package

Take a fresh look at your current benefits programme. Getting clarity on
your 'as-is' package will help you to assess and map out your current offer-
ng for employees. Consider all elements of the package (see our checklist
below for some reminders) and map the different availability and levels of
benefits for different grades or levels of employee.

You could consider the following as part of the current package:

- Compensation: Basic salary, overtime, bonus, commission, long-term
incentives, shares.

- Benefits: Discounts, staff offers, sick pay, pension, medical insurance, life
cover.

Recognition: Non-financial incentives (eg a family cinema gift voucher, a
box of chocolates or a dinner for two).

- Balance: Flexible working, retirement planning, annual leave, carer's
leave, emergency leave, maternity/paternity/adoption leave.

Development: Training budget per employee, further education allowances, study leave.

- Other: Company party budget per employee.

Consider flexibility potential

There is not necessarily a requirement to create a new benefits package in
order to offer some elements of flexibility. At the simple end of the flexibility spectrum, an organization could simply offer to buy and sell additional
annual leave, trading days off and cash.

However, you should review your assessment of the current package, and
determine which elements could be flexibly applied. Consider some of the
following challenges:

- Is there an advantage to the employee in being able to buy or sell each
benefit?

- Is there a tax liability or benefit – to the business and/or the employee?

- How easy/difficult is it to administer the potential change?

- What would the impact be if everyone opted to flex certain benefits (for example if all employees chose to buy annual leave?)? Are you able to offer this benefit with those constraints?

Consider external suppliers

It may be beneficial to use a third-party benefits supplier to administer your flexible benefits programme. Such organizations will be managing flexible benefits programmes for a range of businesses, and as such can provide subject matter expertise, platforms and processes and greater buying power with benefits providers, which might lead to more competitive pricing or greater discounts. An example of such an organization is Employee Benefits (www.employeebenefits.co.uk), who help you to find suppliers of flexible benefits programmes.

Communicate with employees

Whatever level of flexibility you are able to offer to employees, you will need to support the implementation of your plans with a clear communication plan. Explain the aims and objectives of the scheme, explain the process of selecting benefits, and provide some high-level guidance about where there may be tax implications. Remember that you are not able to provide specific advice or details, as the full picture of an individual's tax liabilities may not be known to you. However, you should be able to indicate whether there is or is not a potential tax implication to the benefit you offer.

Outcomes

Offering flexible benefits to your employees can offer you a number of advantages. In the context of employee wellbeing, the simple act of providing choice, empowerment and flexibility to your people is likely to have a positive impact on their employee experience. You may be providing opportunities to help them to address wellbeing issues in their work–life scenario, whether that be financial pressures, the need for greater balance between work and home, or just the opportunity to benefit from discounts or incentives.

In addition, flexible benefits can be seen as both an attraction and retention tool. By providing a great range of benefits, organizations are more likely to be considered as an 'employer of choice'.

Evaluating impact

An annual evaluation of your flexible benefits strategy will allow you the opportunity to consider whether it is effective, appropriate and well utilized by employees. Evaluate the scheme from a number of perspectives, considering the employee impact, organizational impact and, particularly, compared with the initial costs and benefits that were described in the business case. A regular review will also ensure that your benefits package remains legally compliant and can be updated to reflect any changes in tax or NI liabilities.

Consider the impact that flexible benefits have on your employees:

- How many employees have taken up some element of flexibility in their benefits package?
- Which benefits are well subscribed – and which ones aren't?
- What feedback do you hear about the flexible benefits scheme – anecdotally, or through employee focus groups/opinion surveys?

Consider what impact flexible benefits have on your business:

- the costs associated with providing and administering the scheme;
- candidate attraction;
- employee retention;
- the impacts of the benefits selected on your 'business as usual';
- the impacts on absence, morale, engagement, etc.

50 Pre-retirement planning

Introduction

According to the Office of National Statistics, the population of the UK is getting older, with 18 per cent aged 65 and over, and 2.4 per cent aged 85 and over (ONS, 2017b). The same trend can be seen in the USA, where the population of over 65s is expected to double over the next 40 years, according to the Population Reference Bureau (PRB, 2016). This is primarily due to an increase in life expectancy driven by improvements in healthcare, living standards and lifestyle choices.

In the UK, the Equality Act 2010 protects against discrimination and harassment on the grounds of a number of characteristics, and one of those is age. As a result, there is no longer a statutory retirement age, although some professions may be able to enforce an upper age limit if that can be justified – for example, if a role requires certain levels of physical fitness. However, in the main, as long as a job exists and they perform as required, employees can continue to work until they choose to retire.

For employees approaching retirement, the prospect can be exciting, or daunting, or a mix of both. The opportunity to have more leisure time, to focus on hobbies or domestic matters, or to volunteer or do different work, can be exciting. For others it can seem to be something of a black hole, lonely and uninspiring. Added to that, the loss of income, and for an estimated 1 in 7 retirees no pension pot to benefit from, can create stressful financial concerns (Kirton, 2016).

Whilst the employer does not have full responsibility for these aspects of retirement, there are actions that can be taken to reduce the anxiety in the period running up to an employee's retirement.

Promoting wellbeing

There are a number of health risk factors associated with retirement, from mental health, to loneliness, to the age-related physical health issues that are associated with later life. Whilst work-related stress reduces and ultimately disappears, new stress factors can arise that result in 22 per cent of men and 28 per cent of women aged 65 years and over experiencing depression, according to the Mental Health Foundation. Age Concern and the Mental Health Foundation reported in 2006 that there were five key factors that affected mental wellbeing in later life – discrimination, participation n meaningful activities, relationships, physical wellbeing and financial oncerns (Mental Health Foundation, 2006).

Providing pre-retirement planning and preparation support and advice to mployees can help to mitigate the risks of some of the mental health issues xperienced in later life. A programme that seeks to address all five of the actors mentioned above will be extremely beneficial.

Approach

Equality

Take some time to ensure that your policies, procedures and working practices provide equality of employment opportunity, security and dignity to older workers. Whilst a desk audit of paperwork may confirm that you are compliant, investigating genuine practice may uncover issues of indirect discrimination or harassment. Equality cases can be brought in scenarios where older workers are subject to so-called banter about age, nicknames related to age and, in some cases, lack of opportunity or access to promotion, training, new experiences, etc, because of age. A full review of documentation, attitudes and practice will ensure that discrimination is proactively addressed.

Flexible working

It can be valuable to consider flexible working arrangements as the employee transitions from full-time employment to full retirement.

Annual leave entitlement could be increased gradually in the two to five years prior to full retirement, perhaps by just a couple of days each year. In doing so, the employee gradually becomes accustomed to having more 'spare' time.

The employee could transition from full-time to part-time working over a period of time. Again, this allows them the opportunity to adjust their balance and priorities.

Mentoring

Encouraging pre-retirees to take on the role of mentor can add value to both the company and the employee – and of course the mentee. From a company perspective, the role of mentor can ensure that legacy knowledge and experience can be shared and transferred rather than just lost in retirement. The pre-retiree is likely to feel valued as a result of the mentoring role, and will likely feel committed and loyal to the organization as their exit draws near. The mentee will benefit from the years of experience, the pre-retiree's connections and knowledge.

Volunteering

Organizations can help employees to transition to retirement through volunteering. Initially, the company can support this by encouraging the connection between the employee and any company-supported charities. The company can also support transition by providing the employee with additional volunteer leave in the year leading to their retirement. By volunteering in this way, the employee can build an interest in charity work and gain experience that is transferable to other organizations, and may build a network of new social and professional connections. Charities can of course gain through the experience and time commitment offered by the pre-retiree.

Pre-retirement club

If your organization is big enough, establishing a network for those due to retire within a given timeframe can be beneficial for a couple of reasons. First, it provides the opportunity for people to make friendships and connections before they leave. Second, they can share their experiences, connections and learning so that they can benefit from each other's knowledge. The company should encourage the network to flourish inside the organization and outside (after retirement) – for example, by continuing to invite retirees to attend company network meetings and providing facilities and resources.

Pre-retirement workshops

Training courses and workshops run by external providers can be extremely beneficial for pre-retirees. Age charities and private organizations offer workshops that focus on managing and addressing the anticipated lifestyle changes as individuals transition from employment to retirement.

Pension visibility

Providing employees with early information about their company pension will create a few helpful opportunities for them. First, they can take advice from a financial advisor as to their personal financial situation on retirement. Second, they can make a decision as to whether they want to make any additional voluntary contributions to enhance their pensions. And third, it ensure that the employee is not surprised by the value of their pension pot when it is too late to do anything about it.

Outcomes

The above approaches are suggested with a view to proactively addressing the health risks noted above:

- Discrimination: By educating and advising your workforce about all aspects of discrimination, and the impacts of policy, process, attitudes and behaviours at work, the risks of age discrimination can be reduced, allowing for equal opportunity regardless of age. Sound policy and practice also means that if they arise, complaints can be quickly and effectively managed.

- Meaningful activities and contribution: Offering opportunities to continue to work flexibly, to mentor, and to get involved in volunteering before retirement ensure that the employee is able to continue to contribute meaningfully to the workplace and beyond

- Relationships: Creating a network of contacts inside the organization, and with pre-retirement courses encouraging retirees to consider their networks outside, employees can begin to consider and build new social networks for retirement.

- Financial concerns: Providing transparent information on company pensions, etc, will help to prepare employees for the financial adjustment to retirement, and pre-retirement courses can offer advice, information and support in this area too.

Measuring impact

Assessing the impact of your pre-retirement support will be difficult, as the real success or otherwise of a programme of activities can only be measured once the employee is in retirement. However, informal feedback should be sought on any or all the approaches mentioned above, so that their effectiveness can be evaluated, and adjusted accordingly to ensure that they remain relevant, fit for purpose and welcomed by the target audience.

Supporting information

Table 6.1 shows the typical cost of the 50 tools in the book, and the size of firm they are appropriate for.

Table 6.1 Quick view

		Cost			Company size	
	Tool	High	Medium	Low	Large	Small
1	Creating a wellbeing strategy		•	•		•
2	Workplace wellbeing assessments	•		•	•	•
3	Developing a wellbeing programme	•		•	•	•
4	Wellbeing committees			•	•	•
5	Championing wellbeing			•	•	•
6	Strengths-based people management			•	•	•
7	Peer coaching			•	•	•
8	Promoting learning			•	•	•
9	Finding purpose			•	•	
10	Communicating	•		•	•	•
11	A walk-and-talk			•	•	•
12	Enabling flow			•	•	•
13	Encouraging a growth mindset			•	•	•

(continued)

Table 6.1 (Continued)

	Tool	Cost High	Cost Medium	Cost Low	Company size Large	Company size Small
14	Mentoring			•	•	•
15	Giving great feedback			•	•	•
16	The check-in			•	•	•
17	Involvement			•	•	•
18	Engagement		•		•	•
19	Change		•	•	•	•
20	Return to work interviews			•	•	•
21	Managing employee illness			•	•	•
22	The fruit box		•		•	•
23	Exercise at work		•	•	•	•
24	Workplace massage		•	•	•	•
25	Travel health		•		•	•
26	Stress prevention and signalling			•	•	•
27	Managing 'overwhelm'			•	•	•
28	Employee assistance programmes		•	•	•	•
29	Emotional intelligence			•	•	•
30	Building resilience			•	•	•
31	Reframing			•	•	•
32	Mindfulness		•	•	•	•
33	Mediation		•	•	•	•
34	Switching off			•	•	•
35	Getting organized			•	•	•
36	Designing the work environment		•	•	•	•
37	Remote working		•		•	•
38	Flexible working			•	•	•

(continued)

Table 6.1 *(Continued)*

	Tool	Cost			Company size	
		High	Medium	Low	Large	Small
39	Motivation			•	•	•
40	Harmony initiatives			•	•	•
41	Building trust			•	•	•
42	Anti-bullying action			•	•	•
43	Giving back			•	•	•
44	Shared interest groups			•	•	•
45	Netwalking			•	•	•
46	Fun at work	•	•		•	•
47	Pets at work			•	•	•
48	Music at work			•	•	•
49	Flexible benefits	•	•		•	
50	Pre-retirement planning			•		•

While the tools work effectively on their own, there are connections between some of them that can enhance their effectiveness. Table 6.2 gives some ideas, but you may be able to make your own links.

Table 6.2　Supporting tools

	Tool	Consider also using:
1	Creating a wellbeing strategy	Developing a wellbeing programme
2	Workplace wellbeing assessments	Developing a wellbeing programme Creating a wellbeing strategy
3	Developing a wellbeing programme	
4	Wellbeing committees	Creating a wellbeing strategy
5	Championing wellbeing	Involvement
6	Strengths-based people management	The check-in
7	Peer coaching	Emotional intelligence
8	Promoting learning	Building resilience Great feedback Reframing
9	Finding purpose	Building resilience Change
10	Communicating	Building resilience Peer coaching Giving great feedback Change
11	A walk-and-talk	The check-in
12	Enabling flow	Involvement Change
13	Encouraging a growth mindset	The check-in
14	Mentoring	Pre-retirement planning
15	Giving great feedback	Reframing The check-in Emotional intelligence
16	The check-in	A walk–and-talk Giving great feedback Emotional intelligence

(continued)

Table 6.2   *(Continued)*

Tool	Consider also using:
17 Involvement	Championing wellbeing
18 Engagement	Finding purpose Involvement Communicating
19 Change	Building resilience
20 Return to work interviews	Managing employee illness
21 Managing employee illness	Return to work interviews
22 The fruit box	Designing the work environment
23 Exercise at work	
24 Workplace massage	
25 Travel Health	
26 Stress prevention and signalling	Employee assistance programmes Building resilience
27 Managing 'overwhelm'	Building resilience Employee assistance programmes Stress prevention and signalling
28 Employee assistance programmes	Building resilience Managing 'overwhelm' Managing employee illness
29 Emotional intelligence	Building resilience Reframing Giving great feedback The check-in
30 Building resilience	Mindfulness Employee assistance programmes
31 Reframing	Giving great feedback The check-in Building resilience
32 Mindfulness	Building resilience Managing 'overwhelm'
33 Mediation	Anti-bullying action
34 Switching off	Designing the work environment Remote working Flexible working

(continued)

Table 6.2 *(Continued)*

	Tool	Consider also using:
35	Getting organized	Designing the work environment
36	Designing the work environment	Music at work Pets at work
37	Remote working	Switching off The check-in
38	Flexible working	Switching off Remote working
39	Motivation	The check-in Giving great feedback Strengths-based people management
40	Harmony initiatives	Giving back Shared interest groups Anti-bullying action
41	Building trust	Communicating The check-in Giving great feedback
42	Anti-bullying action	Harmony initiatives Mediation Employee assistance programmes
43	Giving back	Fun at work Harmony initiatives
44	Shared interest groups	Fun at work
45	Netwalking	A walk-and-talk
46	Fun at work	Shared interest groups Giving back
47	Pets at work	Designing the work environment
48	Music at work	Designing the work environment
49	Flexible benefits	Workplace massage Employee assistance programmes The fruit box
50	Pre-retirement planning	Mentoring Flexible working Giving back Employee assistance programmes

Table 6.3 provides some references for further support on the topics covered by tools in this book – including websites, publications and organizations.

Table 6.3   Further support

Tool	Further support and information
Encouraging a growth mindset	Watch Carol Dweck's TED Talk – search for Dweck and choose her talk on the power of believing that you can improve. www.TED.com
Mentoring	Mitchell Palmer Ltd deliver mentoring training for newly appointed mentors. www.mitchellpalmer.co.uk
Involvement	The Mind website has lots of information about workplace mental health. www.mind.org.uk
Engagement	Emerge Development Ltd developed the EPIC tool and can talk to you about engagement and the EPIC approach. www.emergeuk.com
Change	Mitchell Palmer Ltd deliver change management training and change coaching for leaders and team members experiencing change. www.mitchellpalmer.co.uk
The fruit box	Jones Dairies deliver fruit boxes to businesses in and around London www.jonesdairies.co.uk
Exercise at work	Some useful websites include: www.parkrun.org.uk www.thisgirlcan.co.uk www.sportengland.org www.efds.co.uk (English Federation of Disability Sport) www.ageuk.org.uk
Workplace massage	Jemma Giles, Clinical Massage Therapist, provides workplace massage in and around the Winchester area. www.massagetherapywinchester.co.uk

(continued)

Table 6.3   *(Continued)*

Tool	Further support and information
Travel health	The NHS and the UK Government websites offer advice and information about overseas travel health and safety. www.fitfortravel.nhs.uk www.gov.uk/foreign-travel-advice
Emotional intelligence	JCA Global, leaders in emotional intelligence in business, provide an emotional intelligence profiling tool that can support the awareness and development of emotional intelligence at work. www.jcaglobal.com info@jcaglobal.com 01242 282900 @jcaglobal LinkedIn: JCA Global
Mindfulness	Incendo Development offer mindfulness development programmes as part of their learning and development portfolio. www.incendo-uk.com
Mediation	Sharon Crooks is an accredited civil and commercial mediator and trainer in mediation skills. She has resolved conflicts in a variety of contexts including charities, multinationals, education and communities as well as teaching restorative justice in prisons. www.jadehrsolutions.co.uk
Harmony initiatives	We would like to thank the Australian Government Department of Social Services for the content provided in the tool about harmony initiatives. For more information about Harmony Day please go to www.harmony.gov.au
Anti-bullying action	The Acas website offers guidance to employers and employees about bullying at work, and has some really user-friendly guides that can be downloaded. www.acas.org.uk
Giving back	The Random Acts of Kindness Foundation offer inspiration and the opportunity to become a RAKctivist. www.randomactsofkindness.org

(continued)

Table 6.3 *(Continued)*

Tool	Further support and information
Netwalking	Cre8salessolutions set up a netwalking event, so they can offer advice about how to go about it, or you can join in their event in the West Midlands. https://cre8salessolutions.co.uk/netwalking Liebfrog coaching have also set up a netwalk in the London area. www.liebfrog.co.uk/netwalk
Pets at work	Purina provide an online toolkit to help you to consider how you will test and implement a pets at work scheme. It has literally everything you might need. www.purina.co.uk/pins/pets-at-work
Music at work	Both PPL and PRS may require you to have a licence to play music at work. Information you need is on their respective websites. www.prsformusic.com/licences http://www.ppluk.com/
Flexible benefits	Employee Benefits help you to find suppliers of flexible benefits schemes. https://www.employeebenefits.co.uk/
Pre-retirement planning	www.ageuk.org.uk

REFERENCES

70:20:10 Forum (2017) The 70:20:10 framework [Online] https://www. 702010forum.com/about-702010-framework [Last accessed 25.10.17]

Acas (2012) *Health, Work and Wellbeing* [Online] www.acas.org.uk/media/pdf/8/n/ Health-work-and-wellbeing-accessible-version.pdf [Last accessed 25.10.17]

Acas (2015) *Flexible Working and Work–Life Balance* [Online] www.acas.org.uk/ media/pdf/3/1/Flexible_working_and_work_life_balance_Nov.pdf [Last accessed 25.10.17]

Acas (2016) *Acas Workplace Trends 2016* [Online] www.acas.org.uk/media/pdf/ l/4/Workplace_trends_of_2016.pdf [Last accessed 25.10.17]

Acas (2017a) Wellbeing and workplace performance [Online] www.acas.org.uk/ index.aspx?articleid=5031 [Last accessed 25.10.17]

Acas (2017b) Mental ill-health in the workplace is costing UK employers billions [Online] m.acas.org.uk/index.aspx?articleid=3915 [Last accessed 25.10.17]

Action Coach (2012) Industry statistics [Online] exec.actioncoach.com/industry-statistics.php [Last accessed 25.10.17]

Bamberger, SG, Vinding, AL, Larsen, A, et al (2012) Impact of organisational change on mental health: A systematic review, *Occup Environ Med*, 69, pp 592–98

Barker, RT, Knisely, JS, Barker, SB, Cobb, RK and Schubert, CM (2012) Preliminary investigation of employee's dog presence on stress and organizational perceptions, *International Journal of Workplace Health Management*, 5(1), pp15–30

Barton, T (2017) Buyer's guide to employee assistance programmes, Employee Benefits [Online] https://www.employeebenefits.co.uk/issues/january-2016-2/ buyers-guide-to-employee-assistance-programmes-8/ [Last accessed 25.10.17]

Blue Cross for Pets (2017) Pets at work [Online] https://www.bluecross.org.uk/ pets-work [Last accessed 25.10.17]

Bodkin, H (2017) Just one in four adults eating their five a day, NHS reveals, *Telegraph* [Online] www.telegraph.co.uk/news/2017/03/30/just-one-four-adults-eating-five-day-nhs-reveals/ [Last accessed 25.10.17]

Boehm, JK and Lyubomirsky, S (2008) Does happiness promote career success? *Journal of Career Assessment*, 16(1), pp.101–16

Bridges, W (1991) *Managing Transitions*, Addison-Wesley, London

Brook, J and Brewerton, P (2016) *Optimize Your Strengths: Use your leadership strengths to get the best out of you and your team*, Wiley, London

Brower, HH, Lester, SW and Korsgaard, MA (2017) Want your employees to trust you? Show you trust them, *Harvard Business Review* [Online] https://hbr.org/ 2017/07/want-your-employees-to-trust-you-show-you-trust-them

CAF (2015) A look at how individuals give to charity in the UK [Online] https://www.cafonline.org/about-us/publications/2016-publications/uk-giving-report-2015 [Last accessed 25.10.17]

Carmeli, A, Yitzhak-Halevy, M and Weisberg, J (2009) The relationship between emotional intelligence and psychological wellbeing, *Journal of Managerial Psychology*, 24(1), pp.66–78

Cascade (2017) *Workplace Conflict Resolution* [Online] https://www.cascadehr.co.uk/app/uploads/2017/06/Workplace-Conflict-Resolution-1.pdf [Last accessed 25.10.17]

Chamorro-Premuzic, T (2015) The health risks of business travel [Online] https://hbr.org/2015/11/the-health-risks-of-business-travel [Last accessed 25.10.17]

Cho, J (2016) 6 scientifically proven benefits of mindfulness and meditation, Forbes [Online] https://www.forbes.com/sites/jeenacho/2016/07/14/10-scientifically-proven-benefits-of-mindfulness-and-meditation/#2a4703a263ce [Last accessed 25.10.17]

CIPD (2015) *Conflict Management: A shift in direction?* [Online] https://www.cipd.co.uk/knowledge/fundamentals/relations/disputes/conflict-management-report [Last accessed 25.10.17]

CIPD (2016a) Employee communication, factsheet [Online] www.cipd.co.uk/knowledge/fundamentals/relations/communication/factsheet [Last accessed 25.10.17]

CIPD (2016b) *Growing the Health and Wellbeing Agenda: From first steps to full potential*, CIPD, London [Online] https://www.cipd.co.uk/Images/health-well-being-agenda_2016-first-steps-full-potential_tcm18-10453.pdf [Last accessed 25.10.17]

Corporate Leadership Council (2005) Improving talent management outcomes

Csikszentmihalyi, M (1990) *Flow: The psychology of optimal experience*, Harper and Row, New York

Davidson, L (2016) This is the kind of music you should listen to at work [Online] www.telegraph.co.uk/business/2016/06/02/this-is-the-kind-of-music-you-should-listen-to-at-work/ [Last accessed 25.10.17]

Deakin Prime (2012) Demystifying 70:20:10, White Paper [Online] deakinprime.com/media/47821/002978_dpw_70-20-10wp_v01_fa.pdf [Last accessed 25.10.17]

Dweck, C (2014) The power of believing that you can improve [Online] https://www.ted.com/talks/carol_dweck_the_power_of_believing_that_you_can_improve [Last accessed 25.10.17]

EAPA (2008) [Online] www.eapa.org.uk [Last accessed 25.10.17]

EAPA (2013) EAP market watch report published [Online] www.eapa.org.uk/eap-market-watch-report-published/ [Last accessed 25.10.17]

Engen, JE et al (2012) Feasibility and effect of chair massage offered to nurses during working hours on stress related symptoms: A pilot study, *Complementary Therapies in Clinical Practice*, 18(4), pp 221–22

FASEB (2014) Fight memory loss with a smile (or chuckle) [Online] https://www.sciencedaily.com/releases/2014/04/140427185149.htm [Last accessed 25.10.17]

Ferguson, D (2016) Paws for thought: Why allowing dogs in the office is a good idea, *Guardian* [Online] https://www.theguardian.com/money/2016/may/18/dogs-in-office-canine-colleagues-staff-wellbeing [Last accessed 25.10.17]

Fox, JG and Embrey, ED (1972) Music: an aid to productivity,. *Applied Ergonomics*, 3(4), pp 202–05

Friedman, R (2014) What you eat affects your productivity [Online] https://hbr.org/2014/10/what-you-eat-affects-your-productivity [Last accessed 25.10.17]

Grant, AM (2008) The significance of task significance: Job performance effects, relational mechanisms and boundary conditions, *Journal of Applied Psychology*, 93(1), pp 198–24

Gray, AW, Parkinson, B and Dunbar, RI (2015) Laughter's influence on the intimacy of self-disclosure, *Human Nature*, 26(1), pp 28–43

Great Place to Work (2016) *Wellbeing and the Importance of Workplace Culture* [Online] www.greatplacetowork.co.uk/storage/Publications/wellbeing_and_culture_final_011216.pdf [Last accessed 25.10.17]

Guardian (2014) Strengths based job interviews: What are they and how do they work? [Online] https://jobs.theguardian.com/article/strengths-based-job-interviews-what-are-they-and-how-do-they-work-/ [Last accessed 25.10.17]

Haake, AB (2011) Individual music listening in workplace settings: An exploratory survey of offices in the UK, *Musicae Scientiae*, 15(1), pp107–29

Hanson, S and Jones, A (2015) Is there evidence that walking groups have health benefits? A systematic review and meta-analysis, *British Journal of Sports Medicine*, doi: 10.1136/bjsports-2014-094157

HSE (2016) Work-related stress, depression or anxiety statistics in Great Britain 2017 [Online] www.hse.gov.uk/statistics/causdis/stress/stress.pdf?pdf=stress [Last accessed 25.10.17]

HSE (2017) Work-related stress, depression or anxiety [Online] www.hse.gov.uk/statistics/causdis/stress/ [Last accessed 25.10.17]

Jones, A (2006) *Rising to the challenge of diversity: A discussion of the business case*, The Work Foundation

Kirton, H (2016) This is how many people there are retiring this year who have no pension savings... [Online] www.cityam.com/239730/this-is-how-many-people-there-are-retiring-this-year-who-have-no-pension-savings [Last accessed 25.10.17]

Le Roux, GM (2005) 'Whistle while you work': A historical account of some associations among music, work, and health, *American Journal of Public Health*, 95(7), pp 1106–09

Leary-Joyce, J (2004) *Becoming an Employer of Choice: Making your organization a place where people want to work*, Chartered Institute of Personnel and Development, London

Lesiuk, T (2005) The effect of music listening on work performance, *Psychology of Music*, 33(2), pp173–91

Long, CS (2017) The relationship between work–life balance (WLB) and firm performance, in *Handbook of Research on Organizational Culture and Diversity in the Modern Workforce*, pp 402–11, IGI Global

MacLeod, D and Clarke, N (2009) *Engaging for Success: Enhancing performance through employee engagement. A report to government*, Department for Business, Innovation and Skills. London

Maddocks, J. (2014) *Emotional Intelligence at Work: How to make change stick*, Spa House Publishing

Mann, A and Harter, J (2016) The worldwide employee engagement crisis, Gallup [Online]news.gallup.com/businessjournal/188033/worldwide-employee-engagement-crisis.aspx [Last accessed 25.10.17]

McKenna, J and Coulson, J (2005) How does exercising at work influence work productivity? A randomised cross-over trial, *Medicine & Science in Sports & Exercise*

Megginson, D and Clutterbuck, D (2007) *Mentoring Executives and Directors*, Routledge, Abingdon

Mental Health Foundation (2006) Mental health statistics: Older people [Online] https://www.mentalhealth.org.uk/statistics/mental-health-statistics-older-people [Last accessed 25.10.17]

Mental Health Foundation (2012) Doing good does you good [Online] https://www.mentalhealth.org.uk/publications/doing-good-does-you-good [Last accessed 25.10.17]

Mental Health Foundation (2017a) Mental health statistics: Mental health at work [Online] https://www.mentalhealth.org.uk/statistics/mental-health-statistics-mental-health-work [Last accessed 25.10.17]

Mercer (2017) Employees in overstressed, inactive and unproductive industries lose 27 days of productive time each year [Online] https://www.uk.mercer.com/newsroom/stressed-employees-lose-productive-time.html [Last accessed 25.10.17]

Milligan, B (2015) Workplace bullying on the rise in UK, says Acas [Online] www.bbc.co.uk/news/business-34833261 [Last accessed 25.10.17]

Mitchell, D (2017) *50 Top Tools for Employee Engagement: A complete toolkit for improving motivation and productivity*, Kogan Page, London

NHS Choices (2017a) Get active for mental wellbeing [Online] www.nhs.uk/Conditions/stress-anxiety-depression/Pages/mental-benefits-of-exercise.aspx [Last accessed 25.10.17]

NHS Choices (2017b) Obesity [Online] www.nhs.uk/conditions/Obesity/Pages/Introduction.aspx [Last accessed 25.10.17]

NICE (2009) Mental wellbeing at work [Online] https://www.nice.org.uk/guidance/ph22/resources/mental-wellbeing-at-work-1996233648325 [Last accessed 25.10.17]

ONS (2016) Sickness absence in the labour market: 2016 [Online] https://www.ons.gov.uk/employmentandlabourmarket/peopleinwork/labourproductivity/articles/sicknessabsenceinthelabourmarket/2016 [Last accessed 25.10.17]

ONS (2017a) Labour Force Survey [Online] https://www.ons.gov.uk/ employmentandlabourmarket/peopleinwork/employmentandemployeetypes/ methodologies/labourforcesurveyuserguidance [Last accessed 25.10.17]

ONS (2017b) Overview of the UK population [Online] https://www.ons.gov.uk/ peoplepopulationandcommunity/populationandmigration/populationestimates/ articles/overviewoftheukpopulation/july2017 [Last accessed 25.10.17]

Pescud, M, Waterworth, P, Shilton, T, Teal, R, Slevin, T, Ledger, M, Lester, L and Rosenberg, M (2016) A healthier workplace? Implementation of fruit boxes in the workplace, *Health Education Journal*, 75(7), pp 843–54

PRB (2016) Fact sheet: Ageing in the United States [Online] www.prb.org/ Publications/Media-Guides/2016/aging-unitedstates-fact-sheet.aspx [Last accessed 25.10.17]

PRS (2014) New research shows music hits the right notes for business success [Online] https://www.prsformusic.com/press/2014/new-research-shows-music-hits-the-right-notes-for-business-success [Last accessed 25.10.17]

Quartz Media (2017) The complete guide to listening to music at work [Online] https://qz.com/185337/the-complete-guide-to-listening-to-music-at-work/ [Last accessed 25.10.17]

Rock, D (2008) SCARF: A brain-based model for collaborating with and influencing others, *Neuroleadership*, 1

Schwartz, T and Porath, C (2014) Why you hate work, *NY Times* [Online] https:// www.nytimes.com/2014/06/01/opinion/sunday/why-you-hate-work.html?_r=1 [Last accessed 25.10.17]

Shriar, J (2016) Employee engagement: Seeing the bigger picture [Online] https:// www.officevibe.com/employee-engagement-solution/guide [Last accessed 25.10.17]

Staples (2011) There's no place like a home office: Staples survey shows telecommuters are happier and healthier, with 25% less stress when working from home [Online] investor.staples.com/phoenix.zhtml?c=96244&p=irol-newsArticle_print& ID=1586360&highlight [Last accessed 25.10.17]

State of Obesity (2017) Obesity rates and trends [Online] https://stateofobesity.org/ rates/ [Last accessed 25.10.17]

Steelcase (2017) Five key findings [Online] https://info.steelcase.com/global-employee-engagement-workplace-comparison#compare-about-the-report [Last accessed 25.10.17]

Telegraph (2015) Dealing with conflict in the workplace [Online] https://jobs. telegraph.co.uk/article/dealing-with-conflict-in-the-workplace/ [Last accessed 25.10.17]

Telegraph (2017) Eat 10 fruit and veg a day for a longer life, not five [Online] www.telegraph.co.uk/news/2017/02/23/five-a-day-fruit-veg-must-double-10-major-study-finds/ [Last accessed 25.10.17]

TUC (2014) *Hazards at Work: Organizing for safe and healthy workplaces*, TUC, London.

Udemy (2016) Boredom at work report [Online] https://business.udemy.com/resources/boredom-work-report/ [Last accessed 25.10.17]

Vitality Britain's Healthiest Workplace (2016) Key findings [Online] https://www.vitality.co.uk/business/healthiest-workplace/findings/ [Last accessed 25.10.17]

Walking for Health (2017) [Online] https://www.walkingforhealth.org.uk/

Wise, A (2017) Why fresh air is so good for you [Online] www.huffingtonpost.co.uk/entry/tk-ways-fresh-air-impacts_0_n_5648164 [Last accessed 25.10.17]

Woollaston, V (2015) How often do you check your phone? Average user picks up their device 85 times a day – twice as often as they realise, *Daily Mail* [Online] www.dailymail.co.uk/sciencetech/article-3294994/How-check-phone-Average-user-picks-device-85-times-DAY-twice-realise.html [Last accessed 25.10.17]

Workplace Wellbeing Charter [Online] wellbeingcharter.org.uk [Last accessed 25.10.17]

World Health Organization (2016) Investing in treatment for depression and anxiety leads to fourfold return [Online] www.who.int/mediacentre/news/releases/2016/depression-anxiety-treatment/en/ [Last accessed 25.10.17]

YouGov (2015) A seven hour working day is 'most productive' [Online] https://yougov.co.uk/news/2015/10/14/british-people-say-7-hour-work-day-most-productive/ [Last accessed 25.10.17]

INDEX